THE

OXFORD BOOK OF

DREAMS

STEVEN BROOK was born in London, and after a career in publishing became a full-time writer in 1982, specializing in travel, wine, and anthologies. His books include *New York Days, New York Nights, The Double Eagle,* and *LA Lore*. In addition he has written three books on the wines of Bordeaux, and two on the wines of California.

THE
OXFORD BOOK OF
DREAMS

CHOSEN BY
STEPHEN BROOK

OXFORD
UNIVERSITY PRESS

OXFORD
UNIVERSITY PRESS

Great Clarendon Street, Oxford OX2 6DP

Oxford University Press is a department of the University of Oxford.
It furthers the University's objective of excellence in research, scholarship,
and education by publishing worldwide in

Oxford New York

Auckland Bangkok Buenos Aires Cape Town Chennai
Dar es Salaam Delhi Hong Kong Istanbul Karachi Kolkata
Kuala Lumpur Madrid Melbourne Mexico City Mumbai Nairobi
São Paulo Shanghai Singapore Taipei Tokyo Toronto

with an associated company in Berlin

Oxford is a registered trade mark of Oxford University Press
in the UK and in certain other countries

Published in the United States
by Oxford University Press Inc., New York

First published 1983 by Oxford University Press
First issued as an Oxford University Press paperback 1987
Reissued 2002

British Library Cataloguing in Publication Data

Data available

Library of Congress Cataloging in Publication Data
Main entry under title:
The Oxford book of dreams.
Includes index.
1. Dreams—Literary collection.
I. Brook, Stephen.
PN6071.D6709 1983 808.8'.8'0353 81–24601

ISBN 0–19–280385–9

1 3 5 7 9 10 8 6 4 2

Printed in Great Britain by
Clays Ltd., St Ives plc

For
Simon Stuart

Contents

✤

Introduction

✄

BECAUSE dreaming is a ubiquitous activity, dreams have always been ascribed the greatest significance. Dreams, the cryptic underside of our conscious waking existence, fleetingly revealed while our critical faculties and our grip on reality are numbed, are seen to contain messages of various kinds, whether portents or warnings or allegories. From earliest times dreams have been transcribed and interpreted, and numerous examples can be found in such very different works as the *Epic of Gilgamesh*, the *Iliad*, and the Bible. Side by side with these early accounts of dreams we find volumes of dream interpretation. Artemidorus, from whose *Oneirocriticon* (*The Interpretation of Dreams*) I quote in the selections that follow, compiled his comprehensive guide in the 2nd century AD and in the course of his book he refers to a number of earlier books of the same kind, thus making it clear that his own volume was merely the latest in a long tradition of dream interpretation.

This tradition is still alive, and ranges from the scientific studies of Maury, Freud, and Jung to the tawdry interpretations offered by *Napoleon's Book of Fate* and other such compilations of varying degrees of spuriousness. The power and subtlety of Freud's theory must command respect, however much we may wish to take issue with it, whereas the often anonymous volumes alleging to offer dream interpretations may confidently be tossed aside, though they may be of value as repositories of folklore. Most such books offer a principle of interpretation based on a system of correspondences; this is not only simplistic but alien to the actual experience of dreaming.

Although this anthology does contain examples of dream interpretation, most of the dreams in this book are instances of the literary exploitation of the dream experience. Of course the distinction is in many respects a false one, if only because the dream as a literary device is bound up with the use its creator chooses to make of it. The invention of a dream is in itself an act of interpretation, bearing burdens that the dreamer may either carry or reject but can hardly ever ignore. They enlighten or perplex but are rarely neutral or without purpose. Dreams, because they are regarded as beyond our conscious control, are often made in literature to convey information or desires that, if overt, might be regarded as preposterous, psychologically inadmissible, or in some other way subversive of our sense of normality. Unpinned even by rudimentary notions of time and space, they float or flash by, leaving in their wake trails of unease, hopes, fears, and anxieties. It is scarcely surprising that these uncontrollable companions of our sleeping hours offer a rich resource to the poet or novelist, for the very absence of rules that characterizes dreams means there is no limit to the possibilities of invention and signification at the writer's disposal.

In medieval literature dreams often function as the form as well as the content, and there is no more famous example of this than *The Divine Comedy*. This structural use of the dream device is one that necessarily eludes the anthologizer, as do dreams, even short ones, that operate as a form of subtext and thus resist being taken out of context. For obvious reasons it is impossible to include entire literary works that employ a dream structure. Casualties of this kind are such splendid pieces as Dostoevsky's *The Dream of a Ridiculous Man*, the 'Dream Fugue' from De Quincey's *The English Mail Coach*, Addison's somewhat ponderous offerings in *The Spectator*, and a large number of complete short stories. Fortunately it was possible to dissect Charles Kingsley's extraordinary 'Dreamland' chapter in *Alton Locke*, and I hope the results, however mutilated, are reasonably satisfactory.

Even after making these excisions, a vast corpus still remained and the greatest problem, not surprisingly, has been to decide not what to include, but what to omit. As I began work, scouring the literatures of the world for good dreams, I tried to devise definitions and criteria, but I soon abandoned them. For instance, how exactly does one distinguish, even in literature, between dream, daydream, hallucination, and reverie? I rapidly gave up trying, if only because most of the dreams I was looking at were, after all, inventions, and their precise generic labelling seemed, finally, irrelevant. The net was cast even wider so as to permit the inclusion not only of invented dreams from poetry and fiction, but of dreams recorded by diarists and letter-writers and biographers. On the other hand it seemed sensible to leave out dreams cited for purposes of clinical or theoretical interpretation both in the great psychoanalytic textbooks and in more exclusively medical investigations of the act of dreaming. This has not prevented the quotation of some of the actual dreams recorded by Freud, and by Jung in his autobiography. Similarly, some remarkable dreams were transcribed by other prolific writers on dreams and dreaming, such as Havelock Ellis, and it seemed wise to include some of them on the grounds that they read as well as the dreams recorded by more obviously 'literary' writers.

Again, no hard and fast rules have been made regarding geographical criteria. Most of the material comes from the literatures of Europe and North America, but there are also examples in this book of dreams composed in other literatures, from South America to the Far East. If there are conspicuous gaps in national or cultural representation, this is because no attempt has been made to present a comprehensive or balanced picture, if only because there can be no such thing. For the most part the dreams have been taken from literary traditions that are easily accessible to the reader of this anthology. One category of dreams that has been ruthlessly, though regretfully, excluded is that of dreams recorded in so-called primitive cultures. Anthropological studies are full of accounts of dreams from, for instance, American-Indian and Aboriginal cultures. To have given a representative selection of such dreams might have added considerably to the interest and range of the anthology, but it would also have added immeasurably to its length. Moreover, many of these dreams require some kind of elucidation or placing in a broad cultural context, which is a task far beyond my competence.

Dream literature is so varied it mocks any kind of rigid classification. Nevertheless some kind of order had to be imposed on the unruly material, and this anthology has been divided into three principal sections. This impression of harmony and order is to some extent misleading, but dreams do sometimes focus on distinct themes – such as childhood or death or erotic desire – and so it has been possible to group much of the material in thematic categories of this kind. Rarely, however, do dreams fall squarely into one category alone. A dream about a horse may also have undertones of violence and sexuality. Choices, then, have been made which could have been made differently. Other dreams defy any kind of thematic labelling and entries of this kind have often been grouped under categories that are labelled according to the overriding 'feel' or sensation of the dream.

Part I contains dreams that dwell on the great inescapable experiences that are common to us all: childhood, love and sex, and finally death. Dreams disturb because they often flout taboos, and there can be few of us who have no hidden or barely acknowledged preoccupations, fears, and desires to be seized upon by our dreams and flaunted while we sleep and our defences are down. Sex and death are the obvious examples. Dreams constantly remind us of longings and fears and griefs we would sooner forget.

The dreams gathered in the second section are, by and large, more earthbound than those in the other two principal sections. Whatever the motivation or feeling that prompts the dreams in Part II, their ostensible subject-matter is not so much the grand themes of living and dying as the more tangible features of the world around us.

Part III tries to come to terms with the very peculiarity of the dream experience. It suggests its relation to the processes of sleeping and waking, and categorizes dreams mostly by the sensations or oddities that characterize them, whether these be the frustration we feel when dreams refuse to proceed logically, or that constantly shifting ground that is common to dreams I label 'Transformations'. I have also included a few examples of dream interpretation, and for good measure some instances of anti-interpretation.

Within each section there has been no attempt to force any predetermined order on the contents. A purely chronological organization would be as random as any other, and the sole organizing principle throughout has been readability. Thus there is a deliberate juxtaposition (and occasional linking) of long and short, poem and prose, old and new. This book has been devised as entertainment, not as thesis or instruction, and in the diversity and unpredictability of dreams, their power to heighten, distort, confuse, and even illuminate our often tenuous sense of reality, lies their fascination and mystery.

STEPHEN BROOK

Prologue

❧

Traveller repose and dream among my leaves.

WILLIAM BLAKE

—

>   Friend,
> many and many a dream is mere confusion,
> a cobweb of no consequence at all.
> Two gates for ghostly dreams there are: one gateway
> of honest horn, and one of ivory.
> Issuing by the ivory gates are dreams
> of glimmering illusion, fantasies,
> but those that come through solid polished horn
> may be borne out, if mortals only know them.

HOMER (*c*.9th century BC), *The Odyssey*, Book XIX

Our dreams are a second life. I have never been able to penetrate without a shudder those ivory or horned gates which separate us from the invisible world. The first moments of sleep are an image of death; a hazy torpor grips our thoughts and it becomes impossible for us to determine the exact instant when the 'I', under another form, continues the task of existence. Little by little a vague underground cavern grows lighter and the pale gravely immobile shapes that live in limbo detach themselves from the shadows and the night. Then the picture takes form, a new brightness illumines these strange apparitions and gives them movement. The spirit world opens before us.

GÉRARD DE NERVAL, *Aurélia*, 1855

A dream is a theatre in which the dreamer is himself the scene, the player, the prompter, the producer, the author, the public, and the critic.

C. G. JUNG, 'General Aspects of Dream Psychology', 1948

Human dreams do not easily forget old grudges.

VLADIMIR NABOKOV, 'Perfection', 1974

> Our life is two-fold: Sleep hath its own world,
> A boundary between the things misnamed
> Death and existence: Sleep hath its own world,
> And a wide realm of wild reality.
> And dreams in their development have breath,
> And tears, and tortures, and the touch of joy;
> They leave a weight upon our waking thoughts,
> They take a weight from off our waking toils,
> They do divide our being; they become
> A portion of ourselves as of our time,
> And look like heralds of eternity;
> They pass like spirits of the past, – they speak
> Like Sybils of the future: they have power –
> The tyranny of pleasure and of pain;
> They make us what we were not – what they will,
> And shake us with the vision that's gone by,
> The dread of vanish'd shadows – Are they so?
> Is not the past all shadow? – What are they?
> Creations of the mind? The mind can make
> Substance, and people planets of its own
> With beings brighter than have been, and give
> A breath to forms which can outlive all flesh.

LORD BYRON, from 'The Dream', 1816

What seems incontrovertible in the case of dreams is, that they are most apt to take place when the body is most affected. They seem to turn most upon us when the suspension of the will has been reduced to its most helpless state by indulgence. The door of the fancy is left without its keeper, and forth issue, pell-mell, the whole rout of ideas or images, which had been stored within the brain, and kept to their respective duties.

LEIGH HUNT, 'Of Dreams', 1820

One can write, think and pray exclusively of others; dreams are all egocentric.

EVELYN WAUGH, *Diaries*, autumn 1962

Dreams! My dreams are always disagreeable – mere confusions – losing my clothes and the like, nothing beautiful. The same dreams go on night after night for a long time. I am a *worse* man in my dreams than when awake – do cowardly acts, dream of being tried for a crime. I long ago came to the conclusion that my dreams are of no importance to me whatever.

THOMAS CARLYLE, quoted in William Allingham's *Diary*, 7 February 1868

There is no law to judge of the lawless, or canon by which a dream may be criticised.

CHARLES LAMB, 'Witches, and Other Night Fears', 1823

God forbid that my worst enemy should ever have the nights and the sleeps that I have had, night after night – surprised by sleep, while I struggled to remain awake, starting up to bless my own loud screams that had awakened me – yea, dear friend! till my repeated night-yells had made me a nuisance in my own house. As I live and am a man, this is an unexaggerated tale – *my dreams become the substances of my life*.

S. T. COLERIDGE, 1803

I

FROM BIRTH TO DEATH

Children and Parents

❧

My Lady Seymour dreamed that she saw a nest, with nine finches in it. And so many children she had by the Earl of Winchelsey, whose name is Finch.

JOHN AUBREY, *Miscellanies Upon Various Subjects*, 1696

[*Gunnhildr dreams before the birth of her son King Sverrir.*]

She thought she was in a fine house and that she was delivered of the child she was carrying. Her serving-woman sat before her and was to receive the child as soon as it was born. And when it seemed to her [Gunnhildr] that the child was born, a great fear seized upon the woman who was with her, and she called aloud to her and said: 'Dear Gunnhildr, you have given birth to an extraordinary infant, awe-inspiring to look upon.' Three times she called out the same words. When Gunnhildr heard the woman saying the same thing so often with trembling voice, she was curious as to what sort of infant she had been delivered of. It seemed to her that it was a rather large stone, snow-white in colour; it shone so that sparks flew in all directions, as with glowing iron, when the hearth is blown up sharply with the bellows. She spoke thus to her serving-woman: 'Let us look after this infant carefully, and let no one know of it, because most people who saw it would think it strange.' After that she thought they took the stone and laid it on a chair and covered it with a fine cloth. When they had attended to the stone as they wished, the sparks flew, nevertheless, in all directions through the cloth, and all about inside the house. They grew very frightened, being filled with awe. After that she woke out of the dream.

Sverris Saga, c.AD 900

. . . Last night, in sleep,
Walking through April fields I heard the far-off bleat of sheep
And from the trees about the farm, not very high,
A flight of pigeons fluttered up into an early evening mackerel sky;
      Someone stood by and it was you:
      About us both a great wind blew.
      My breast was bared

But sheltered by my hair
I found you, suddenly, lying there,
Tugging with tiny fingers at my heart, no more afraid:
The weakest thing, the most divine
That ever yet was mine,
Something that I had strangely made,
So then it seemed –
The child for which I had not looked or ever cared,
Of whom, before, I had never dreamed.

CHARLOTTE MEW, from 'Ne Me Tangito', 1929

'. . . I am just as fond of children as ever, and have a strange yearning at my heart whenever I see a mother with her baby in her arms. Nay, my dear' (and by a sudden blaze which sprang up from a fall of the unstirred coals, I saw that her eyes were full of tears – gazing intently on some vision of what might have been), 'do you know I dream sometimes that I have a little child – always the same – a little girl of about two years old; she never grows older, though I have dreamt about her for many years. I don't think I ever dream of any words or sound she makes; she is very noiseless and still, but she comes to me when she is very sorry or very glad, and I have wakened with the clasp of her dear little arms round my neck. Only last night – perhaps because I had gone to sleep thinking of this ball for Phoebe – my little darling came in my dream, and put up her mouth to be kissed, just as I have seen real babies do to real mothers before going to bed. But all this is nonsense, dear! only don't be frightened by Miss Pole from being married. I can fancy it may be a very happy state, and a little credulity helps one on through life very smoothly – better than always doubting and doubting and seeing difficulties and dis-agreeables in everything.'

ELIZABETH GASKELL, *Cranford*, 1853

I had a dream of nourishment
Against a breast
My infant face was presst
Ah me the *suffisance* I drew therefrom
What strength, what glory from that fattening fluid,
The fattening most
Was to my infant taste
For oh the sun of strength beat in my veins

And swelled me full, I lay in brightest sun
All ready to put forth, all bursting, all delight.

But in my dream the breast withdrew
In darkness I lay then
And thin,
Thin as a sheeted ghost
And I was famished . . .
Hankered for a dish
I thought, of blood, as in some classicist's
Old tale
To give me hue and substance, make me hale.

Oh breast, oh Best
That I held fast
Oh fattening draught
Timely repast
Quaffed, presst
And lost.

The breast was withdrawn violently
And oh the famishment for me.

STEVIE SMITH, 'A Dream of Nourishment', 1966

Mother,
strange goddess face
above my milk home,
that delicate asylum,
I ate you up.
All my need took
you down like a meal.

What you gave
I remember in a dream:
the freckled arms binding me,
the laugh somewhere over my woolly hat,
the blood fingers tying my shoe,
the breasts hanging like two bats
and then darting at me,
bending me down.

The breasts I knew at midnight
beat like the sea in me now.
Mother, I put bees in my mouth
to keep from eating
yet it did you no good.
In the end they cut off your breasts
and milk poured from them
into the surgeon's hand
and he embraced them.
I took them from him
and planted them.

I have put a padlock
on you, Mother, dear dead human,
so that your great bells,
those dear white ponies,
can go galloping, galloping,
wherever you are.

ANNE SEXTON, 'Dreaming the Breasts', 1972

When Arch Bishop Abbot's mother (a poor clothworker's wife in Guilford) was with child of him, she did long for a Jack, and she dreamt that if she should eat a Jack, her son in her belly should be a great man. She arose early the next morning and went with her pail to the river-side (which runneth by the house, now an ale-house, the sign of the three mariners) to take up some water, and in the water in the pail she found a good Jack, which she dressed, and eat it all, or very near. Several of the best inhabitants of Guilford were invited (or invited themselves) to the christening of the child; it was bred up a scholar in the town, and by degrees, came to be Arch Bishop of Canterbury.

JOHN AUBREY, *Miscellanies Upon Various Subjects*, 1696

Having fallen asleep last night while in a state of great perplexity about the care and education of my daughter, I dreamt as follows.

I was walking with the child along the border of a high cliff, at the foot of which was the sea. The path was exceedingly narrow, and on the inner side was flanked by a line of rocks and stones. The outer side was so close to the edge of the cliff that she was compelled to walk either before or behind me, or else on the stones. And, as it was unsafe to let go her hand, it was on the stones that she had to walk, much to her distress. I was in male attire, and carried a staff in my hand. She wore skirts and had no staff; and every moment she stumbled or her dress caught and was torn by some jutting crag or bramble. In this way our progress was being continually interrupted and rendered almost impossible, when suddenly we came upon a sharp declivity leading to a steep path which wound down the side of the precipice to the beach below. Looking down, I saw on the shore beneath the cliff a collection of fishermen's huts, and groups of men and women on the shingle, mending nets, hauling up boats, and sorting fish of various kinds. In the midst of the little village stood a great crucifix of lead, so cast in a mould as to allow me from the elevated position I occupied behind it, to see that though in front it looked solid, it was in reality hollow. As I was noting this, a voice of some one close at hand suddenly addressed me; and on turning my head I found standing before me a man in the garb of a fisherman, who evidently had just scaled the steep path leading from the beach. He stretched out his hand to take the child, saying he had come to fetch her, for that in the path I was following there was room only for one. 'Let her come to us,' he added; 'she will do very well as a fisherman's daughter.' Being reluctant to part with her, and not perceiving then the significance of his garb and vocation, I objected that the calling was a dirty and unsavoury one, and would soil her hands and dress. Whereupon the man became severe, and seemed to insist with a kind of authority upon my acceptance of his proposition. The child, too, was taken with him, and was moreover anxious to leave the rough and dangerous path; and she accordingly went to him of her own will and, placing her hand in his, left me without any sign of regret, and I went on my way alone.

ANNA KINGSFORD, *Dreams and Dream-Stories*, 1888

Dream that my little baby came to life again; that it had only been cold, and that we rubbed it before the fire, and it lived. Awake and find no baby. I think about the little thing all day. Not in good spirits.

MARY SHELLEY, *Journal*, 19 March 1815

All that I try to save him from
Is what he dreams about:
Abandonment, abandonment.
I watch his face

Each night emerging clearer,
Stern son who reads my dreams:
The dreams I had,
And those my brother had
And which my parents learned from theirs,
Moving behind mauve lids
That seal his eyes.

He dreams I want to leave him,
Roams through night-forests, desolate.
And I dream I've abandoned him,
Feel waxy pleasure of that sin,
Its subsequent atonement.
Next morning both our faces
Mark the change:
Mine with the guilty look of those
Who knowingly succumb to dreams,
And his the speculative gaze
Of someone learning.

RUTH FAINLIGHT, 'Sleep-Learning', 1968

[In dreams] if you are governing children, expect a coming danger.
ASTRAMPSYCHUS, *The Oneirocriticon*, c.AD 350

My early childhood was often haunted by a dream, which at first I took for a reality – a transcendent dream of some interest and importance to mankind, as the patient reader will admit in time. But many years of my life passed away before I was able to explain and account for it.

I had but to turn my face to the wall, and soon I found myself in company with a lady who had white hair and a young face – a very beautiful young face.

Sometimes I walked with her, hand in hand – I being quite a small child – and together we fed innumerable pigeons who lived in a tower by a winding stream that ended in a water-mill. It was too lovely, and I would wake.

Sometimes we went into a dark place, where there was a fiery furnace with many holes, and many people working and moving about – among them a man with white hair and a young face, like the lady, and beautiful red heels to his shoes. And under his guidance I would contrive to make in the furnace a charming little cocked hat of coloured glass – a treasure! And the sheer joy thereof would wake me.

Sometimes the white-haired lady and I would sit together at a square box from which she made lovely music, and she would sing my favourite song – a song that I adored. But I always woke before this song came to an end, on account of the too insupportably intense bliss I felt on hearing it; and all I could remember when awake were the words 'triste – comment – sale.'

The air, which I knew so well in my dream, I could not recall.

It seemed as though some innermost core of my being, some childish holy of holies, secreted a source of supersubtle reminiscence, which, under some stimulus that now and again became active during sleep, exhaled itself in this singular dream – shadowy and slight, but invariably accompanied by a sense of felicity so measureless and so penetrating that I would always wake in a mystic flutter of ecstasy, the bare remembrance of which was enough to bless and make happy many a succeeding hour.

GEORGE DU MAURIER, *Peter Ibbetson*, Part I, 1891

I had the earliest dream I can remember, a dream which was to preoccupy me all my life. I was then between three and four years old.

The vicarage stood quite alone near Laufen castle, and there was a big meadow stretching back from the sexton's farm. In the dream I was in this meadow. Suddenly I discovered a dark, rectangular, stone-lined hole in the ground. I had never seen it before. I ran forward curiously and peered down into it. Then I saw a stone stairway leading down. Hesitantly and fearfully, I descended. At the bottom was a doorway with a round arch, closed off by a green curtain. It was a big, heavy curtain of worked stuff like brocade, and it looked very sumptuous. Curious to see what might be hidden behind, I pushed it aside. I saw before me in the dim light a rectangular chamber about thirty feet long. The ceiling was arched and of hewn stone. The floor was laid with flagstones, and in the centre a red carpet ran from the entrance to a low platform. On this platform stood a wonderfully rich golden throne . . . Something was standing on it which I thought at first was a tree trunk twelve to fifteen feet high and about one and a half to two feet thick. It was a huge thing, reaching almost to the ceiling. But it was of a curious composition: it was made of skin and naked flesh, and on top there was something like a rounded head with no face and no hair. On the very top of the head was a single eye, gazing motionlessly upwards.

It was fairly light in the room, although there were no windows and no apparent source of light. Above the head, however, was an aura of brightness. The thing did not move, yet I had the feeling that it might at any moment crawl off the throne like a worm and creep towards me. I was paralysed with terror. At that moment I heard from outside and above me my mother's voice. She called out, 'Yes, just look at him. That is the man-eater!' That intensified my terror still more, and I awoke sweating and scared to death. For many nights afterwards I was afraid to go to sleep, because I feared I might have another dream like that.

C. G. JUNG, *Memories, Dreams, Reflections*, 1963

He was from a child an ardent and uncomfortable dreamer. When he had a touch of fever at night, and the room swelled and shrank, and his clothes, hanging on a nail, now loomed up instant to the bigness of a church, and now drew away into a horror of infinite distance and infinite littleness, the poor soul was very well aware of what must follow, and struggled hard against the approaches of that slumber which was the beginning of sorrows. But his struggles were in vain; sooner or later the night-hag would have him by the throat, and pluck him, strangling and screaming, from his sleep. His dreams were at times commonplace enough, at times very strange, at times they were almost formless: he would be haunted, for instance, by nothing more definite than a certain hue of brown, which he did not mind in the least while he was awake, but feared and loathed while he was dreaming; at times, again, they took on every detail of circumstance, as when once he supposed he must swallow the populous world, and awoke screaming with the horror of the thought. The two chief troubles of his very narrow existence – the practical and everyday trouble of school tasks and the ultimate and airy one of hell and judgment – were often confounded together into one appalling nightmare. He seemed to himself to stand before the Great White Throne; he was called on, poor little devil, to recite some form of words, on which his destiny depended; his tongue stuck, his memory was blank, hell gaped for him; and he would awake, clinging to the curtain rod with his knee to his chin.

R. L. STEVENSON, 'A Chapter on Dreams', 1892

She must have been dreaming. She was standing in someone else's house, the furniture less pretentious, the real table and chairs chosen by those who lead 'normal' lives.

She was waiting in a passage for some explanation of why she was there, when she heard a voice calling to her from a nearby room. She went in. There was nothing to make her immediately aware of the room's function, except that a closeness, a warmth, a benign light converging on the centre of the carpet suggested an intangible cocoon. There was a young woman, her face softened by the light to a blur in which her features were lost, just as the details of the room were lost in a timeless blur. Everything about the young woman was familiar, but the dreamer could not identify her. She was kneeling on the fleecy carpet, bathing a recently born child. As the mother (so the dreamer sensed) squeezed the sponge, the child lay propped partly against the scuttle back of the enamel bath, partly by the mother's other solicitous hand.

The child was the rosiest, the most enviable the dream-walker had ever encountered. She dropped to her knees beside the bath, to join in the simple game of bathing this most radiant of all children. The mother seemed to have invited collaboration, but as their hands met over soap or sponge, resentment set in: the dreamer became an invader. She was warned back, at first not overtly, but by implication, till finally the fleece on which both were kneeling turned to grit, stones, road-metal. Dishwater, sewage, putrid blood were gushing out of the faceless mother from the level at which her mouth should have been. The intruder was desolated by a rejection she should have expected.

Eadith awoke. It was about lunchtime by the normal rule. She continued snoozing, protecting her arms and shoulders from the dangers to which they had been exposed. In spite of them, she would have chosen to return to her dream for the sake of the radiant child. She must recall every feature, every pore, every contour of wrists and ankles, and the little blond comma neatly placed between the thighs.

PATRICK WHITE, *The Twyborn Affair*, 1979

A man dreamt that he flayed his own child and made a wineskin out of him. On the following day, his little child fell into the river and was drowned. For a wineskin is made from dead bodies and is capable of receiving liquids.

ARTEMIDORUS, *The Interpretation of Dreams*, Book 5, c.AD 150

1. *The Crib*

You sleeping I bend to cover.
Your eyelids work. I see
your dream, cloudy as a negative,
swimming underneath.
You blurt a cry. Your eyes
spring open, still filmed in dream.
Wider, they fix me –
– death's head, sphinx, medusa?
You scream.
Tears lick my cheeks, my knees
droop at your fear.
Mother I no more am,
but woman, and nightmare.

2. *Her Waking*

Tonight I jerk astart in a dark
hourless as Hiroshima,
almost hearing you breathe
in a cot three doors away.

You still breathe, yes –
and my dream with its gift of knives,
its murderous hider and seeker,
ebbs away, recoils
back into the egg of dreams,
the vanishing point of mind.
All gone.

But you and I –
swaddled in a dumb dark
old as sickheartedness,
modern as pure annihilation –

we drift in ignorance.
If I could hear you now
mutter some gentle animal sound!
If milk flowed from my breast again. . . .

ADRIENNE RICH, 'Night-Pieces: For a Child', 1964

A morning later, Nancy described her first dream, the first remembered dream of her life. She and Judy Thorne were on a screened porch, catching ladybugs. Judy caught one with one spot on its back and showed it to Nancy. Nancy caught one with two spots and showed it to Judy. Then Judy caught one with three spots, and Nancy one with four. Because (the child explained) the dots showed how old the ladybugs were!

She had told this dream to her mother, who had her repeat it to her father at breakfast. Piet was moved, beholding his daughter launched into another dimension of life, like school. He was touched by her tiny stock of imagery – the screened porch (neither they nor the Thornes had one; who?), the ladybugs (with turtles the most toylike of creatures), the mysterious power of numbers, that generates space and time. Piet saw down a long amplifying corridor of her dreams, and wanted to hear her tell them, to grow older with her, to shelter her forever.

JOHN UPDIKE, *Couples*, 1968

The children are playing in the snow again. In their midst, with her back to me, is the hooded figure of the girl. At moments, as I struggle towards her, she is obliterated from sight behind the curtain of falling snow. My feet sink so deep that I can barely lift them. Each step takes an age. This is the worst it has snowed in all the dreams.

As I labour towards them the children leave off their play to look at me. They turn their grave shining faces on me, their white breath drifting from them in puffs. I try to smile and touch them as I pass on my way to the girl, but my features are frozen, the smile will not come, there seems to be a sheet of ice covering my mouth. I raise a hand to tear it off: the hand, I find, is thickly gloved, the fingers are frozen inside the glove, when I touch the glove to my face I feel nothing. With ponderous movements I push my way past the children.

Now I begin to see what the girl is doing. She is building a fort of snow, a walled town which I recognize in every detail: the battlements with the four watchtowers, the gate with the porter's hut beside it, the streets and houses, the great square with the barracks compound in one corner. And here is the very spot where I stand! But the square is empty, the whole town is white and mute and empty. I point to the middle of the square. 'You must put people there!' I want to say. No sound comes from my mouth, in which my tongue lies frozen like a fish. Yet she responds. She sits up on her knees and turns her face towards me. I fear, at this last instant, that she will be a disappointment, that the face she will present to me will be obtuse, slick, like an internal organ not meant to live in the light. But no, she is herself, herself as I have never seen her, a smiling child, the light sparkling on her teeth and glancing from her jet-black eyes. 'So this is what it i see!' I say to myself. I want to speak to her through my clumsy frozen muzzle. 'How do you do all that fine work with your hands in mittens?' I want to say. She smiles kindly on my mumbling. Then she turns back to her fort in the snow.

I emerge from the dream cold and stiff. It is an hour yet to first light, the fire is dead, my scalp feels numb with cold. The girl beside me sleeps huddled in a ball. . . .

The dream has taken root. Night after night I return to the waste of the snowswept square, trudging towards the figure at its centre, reconfirming each time that the town she is building is empty of life.

J. M. COETZEE, *Waiting for the Barbarians*, 1980

The night before [the parents of Alexander the Great] lay in wedded bed, the bride dreamed, that lightning fell into her belly, and that withal, there was a great light fire that dispersed itself all about into divers flames. King Philip her husband also, shortly after he was married, dreamed that he did seal his wife's belly, and that the seal wherewith he sealed, left behind the print of a lion. Certain wizards and soothsayers, told Philip that this dream gave him warning to look straightly to his wife. But Aristander Telmesian answered again, that it signified his wife was conceived with child, for that they do not seal a vessel that hath nothing in it: and that she was with child with a boy, which should have a lion's heart.

PLUTARCH, 'The Life of Alexander the Great', *c*.AD 100

I discovered that King Fernando el Catholico was my father, to my inexpressible grief, and told my mother, that of all human beings there was scarcely one whom I regarded with more horror and hatred, and that I would submit to any torments which could purge his blood out of my veins.

ROBERT SOUTHEY, 10 February 1805, *Correspondence of Robert Southey with Caroline Bowles*, 1881

A dream about my father: There was a small audience ... before which my father was making public for the first time a scheme of his for social reform. He was anxious to have this select audience, an especially select one in his opinion, undertake to make propaganda for his scheme. On the surface he expressed this much more modestly, merely requesting the audience, after they should have heard his views, to let him have the address of interested people who might be invited to a large public meeting soon to take place. My father had never yet had any dealings with these people, consequently took them much too seriously, had even put on a black frock coat, and described his scheme with that extreme solicitude which is the mark of the amateur. The company, in spite of the fact that they weren't at all prepared for a lecture, recognized at once that he was offering them, with all the pride of originality, what was nothing more than an old, outworn idea that had been thoroughly debated long ago. They let my father feel this. He had anticipated the objection, however, and, with magnificent conviction of its futility (though it often appeared to tempt even him), with a faint bitter smile, put his case even more emphatically. When he had finished, one could perceive from the general murmur of annoyance that he had convinced them neither of the originality nor the practicability of his scheme. Not many were interested in it. Still, here and there someone was to be found who, out of kindness, and perhaps because he knew me, offered him a few addresses. My father, completely unruffled by the general mood, had cleared away his lecture notes and picked up the piles of white slips that he had ready for writing down the few addresses. I could hear only the name of a certain Privy Councillor Strizanowski, or something similar.

Later I saw my father sitting on the floor, his back against the sofa, as he sits when he plays with Felix. Alarmed, I asked him what he was doing. He was pondering his scheme.

FRANZ KAFKA, *Diaries*, 21 September 1917

I found myself one of a family of children travelling with my father and mother in a caravan through some eastern country – I think Hungary. I remember a flat landscape with a village at the end of a long straight road. We had to be continually showing passports to the local police, whose language (presumably Hungarian) we did not know. At the point where the dream becomes clear to me, my father and other members of the family had gone far on ahead leaving my mother and me beside the caravan, when a policeman came up. My father had the passports, and I shouted to him, but couldn't make him hear. At last, however, I saw him turn, and noticed with satisfaction that he too was a policeman, a burly London policeman, who I thought would inspire respect in his local colleagues. I spoke of him to my mother as 'Papalov', thinking that this was the Hungarian word for father, to which we had become accustomed. The dream ended before we came close to him, so I don't know what his face was like, but am sure it bore no relation whatever to the face of my real father.

WILLIAM ARCHER, *On Dreams*, 20–21 February 1920

[*The Chorus discusses the dreams of Clytemnestra, who has murdered her husband Agamemnon.*]

Chorus . . . It was dreams, night-walking terrors,
  That frightened the godless woman and made her send these gifts.

Orestes. Did you ask what the dream was? Can you describe it clearly?

Chorus. She told us herself. She dreamt that she gave birth to a snake.

Orestes. What followed? Or was that all? Tell me the point of it.

Chorus. She wrapped it in shawls and lulled it to rest like a little child.

Orestes. Surely this new-born monster needed food – what food?

Chorus. She herself, in her dream, gave it her breast to suck.

Orestes. Her nipple surely was wounded by its loathsome fang?

Chorus. Yes; with her milk the creature drew forth clots of blood.

Orestes. This dream was sent. It came from her husband, Agamemnon.

Chorus. She screamed out in her sleep, and woke in a fit of trembling;
  And through the palace many lamps, that the dark had dimmed,
  Flared up to reassure her. Immediately she sends
  Libations, hoping to purge this poison at its source.

Orestes. I pray, then, to this earth that holds my father's bones,
  That the dream's meaning may be thus fulfilled in me.
  As I interpret, point by point it fits. Listen:
  First, if this snake came forth from the same place as I,
  And, as though human, was then wrapped in infant-clothes,
  Its gaping mouth clutching the breast that once fed me;
  If it then mingled the sweet milk with curds of blood,
  And made her shriek with terror – why, it means she

Who nursed this obscene beast must die by violence;
I must transmute my nature, be viperous in heart and act!
The dream commands it: I am her destined murderer.

AESCHYLUS, The Choephori, c.460 BC

An athlete dreamt that he was pregnant and that he gave birth to two
black baby girls. He went blind and the pupils of his eyes protruded
and turned black.

ARTEMIDORUS, The Interpretation of Dreams, Book 5, c.AD 150

Many of her dreams were recurrent and are common enough to
childhood. One constantly repeated vision, she tells us, brought to
her her dearly loved father. She would dream that, gazing into his
face, the countenance would change and be, not his face, but
another's. With this change would come an agony of misery, and she
would desperately tear off the false face, only to be confronted by
another and yet another, but never his own, until in mercy she awoke
and knew that the terrible mutations were as unreal as they were
terrifying.

M. H. SPIELMANN and G. S. LAYARD, Kate Greenaway, 1905

I dreamed I was going along a narrow, ill-paved street of an
old-fashioned town, between stone houses of many storeys, with
pointed roofs. I was looking for my father, who was not dead, but,
for some reason or other, hiding away from us, and living in one of
these very houses. And so I entered a low, dark gateway, crossed a
long courtyard, lumbered up with planks and beams, and made my
way at last into a little room with two round windows. In the middle
of the room stood my father in a dressing-gown, smoking a pipe. He
was not in the least like my real father; he was tall and thin, with
black hair, a hook nose, with sullen and piercing eyes; he looked
about forty. He was displeased at my having found him; and I too
was far from being delighted at our meeting, and stood still in
perplexity. He turned a little way, began muttering something, and
walking up and down with short steps. . . . Then he gradually got
farther away, never ceasing his muttering, and continually looking
back over his shoulder; the room grew larger and was lost in fog. . . .
I felt all at once horrified at the idea that I was losing my father again,

and rushed after him, but I could no longer see him, I could only hear his angry muttering, like a bear growling. . . . My heart sank with dread; I woke up and could not for a long while get to sleep again. . . . All the following day I pondered on this dream, and naturally could make nothing of it.

IVAN TURGENEV, *Dream Tales*, 1883

I dreamed once more that my house had a large wing which I had never visited. I resolved to look at it, and finally entered. I came to a big double door. When I opened it, I found myself in a room set up as a laboratory. In front of the window stood a table covered with many glass vessels and all the paraphernalia of a zoological laboratory. This was my father's workroom. However, he was not there. On shelves along the walls stood hundreds of bottles containing every imaginable sort of fish. I was astonished: so now my father was going in for ichthyology.

As I stood there and looked round I noticed a curtain which bellied out from time to time, as though a strong wind were blowing. Suddenly Hans, a young man from the country, appeared. I told him to look and see whether a window were open in the room behind the curtain. He went, and was gone for some time. When he returned, I saw an expression of terror on his face. He said only, 'Yes, there is something. It's haunted in there!'

Then I myself went, and found a door which led to my mother's room. There was no one in it. The atmosphere was uncanny. The room was very large, and suspended from the ceiling were two rows of five chests each, hanging about two feet above the floor. They looked like small garden pavilions, each about six feet in area, and each containing two beds. I knew that this was the room where my mother, who in reality had long been dead, was visited, and that she had set up these beds for visiting spirits to sleep. They were spirits who came in pairs, ghostly married couples, so to speak, who spent the night or even the day there.

*   *   *

Equally important to me were the dream-experiences I had before my mother's death. News of her death came to me while I was staying in the Tessin. I was deeply shaken, for it had come with unexpected suddenness. The night before her death I had a frightening dream. I was in a dense, gloomy forest; fantastic, gigantic boulders lay about among huge jungle-like trees. It was a heroic, primeval landscape. Suddenly I heard a piercing whistle that seemed to resound through the whole universe. My knees shook. Then there were crashings in the underbrush, and a gigantic wolfhound with a fearful, gaping maw burst forth. At the sight of it, the blood froze in my veins. It tore past me, and I suddenly knew: the Wild Huntsman had commanded it to carry away a human soul. I awoke in deadly terror, and the next morning I received the news of my mother's passing.

* * *

Six weeks after his death my father appeared to me in a dream. Suddenly he stood before me and said that he was coming back from his holiday. He had made a good recovery and was now coming home. I thought he would be annoyed with me for having moved into his room. But not a bit of it! Nevertheless, I felt ashamed because I had imagined he was dead. Two days later the dream was repeated. My father had recovered and was coming home, and again I reproached myself because I had thought he was dead. Later I kept asking myself: 'What does it mean that my father returns in dreams and that he seems so real?' It was an unforgettable experience, and it forced me for the first time to think about life after death.

c. g. jung, Memories, Dreams, Reflections, 1963

[My father] arrived at Exeter about six o'clock – and was pressed to take a bed there by the Harts – but he refused – and to avoid their intreaties he told them – that he had never been superstitious – but that the night before he had had a dream which had made a deep impression. He dreamt that Death had appeared to him, as he is commonly painted, and touched him with his dart. Well he returned home – and all his family, I excepted, were up. He told my mother his dream –; but he was in high health and good spirits – and there was a bowl of punch made – and my father gave a long and particular account of his travel, and that he had placed Frank under a religious captain etc. – / At length, he went to bed, very well, and in high spirits. – A short time after he had lain down he complained of a pain in his bowels, which he was subject to, from the wind – my mother got him some peppermint water – and after a pause, he said – 'I am much better now, my dear!' – and lay down again. In a minute my mother heard a noise in his throat – and spoke to him – but he did not answer – and she spoke repeatedly in vain. Her shriek awaked me – and I said, 'Papa is dead.' – I did not know [of] my father's return, but I knew that he was expected. How I came to think of his death, I cannot tell; but so it was. – Dead he was – some said it was the gout in the heart – probably, it was a fit of apoplexy.

S. T. COLERIDGE, letter to Thomas Poole, 1797

Love and Sex

✁

Forwearied with my sportes, I did alight
From loftie steed, and downe to sleepe me layd;
The verdant gras my couch did goodly dight,
And pillow was my helmett fayre displayd;
Whiles every sence the humour sweet embayd,
And slombring soft my hart did steale away,
Me seemed, by my side a royall Mayd
Her daintie limbes full softly down did lay:
So fayre a creature yet saw never sunny day.

Most goodly glee and lovely blandishment
She to me made, and badd me love her deare;
For dearely sure her love was to me bent,
As, when just time expired, should appeare.
But whether dreames delude, or true it were,
Was never hart so ravisht with delight,
Ne living man like wordes did ever heare,
As she to me delivered all that night;
And at her parting said, She Queene of Faeries hight.

When I awoke, and found her place devoyd,
And nought but pressed gras where she had lyen,
I sorrowed all so much as earst I joyd,
And washed all her place with watry eyen.
From that day forth I lov'd that face divyne;
From that day forth I cast in carefull mynd,
To seek her out with labor and long tyne,
And never vowd to rest till her I fynd:
Nyne monethes I seek in vain, yet ni'll that vow unbynd.

EDMUND SPENSER, *The Faerie Queene*, Book I, Canto IX, 1589

The last summer, on the day of St. John the Baptist, 1694, I accidentally was walking in the pasture behind Montague house, it was 12 o'clock. I saw there about two or three and twenty young women, most of them well habited, on their knees very busy, as if they had been weeding. I could not presently learn what the matter was; at last a young man told me, that they were looking for a coal under the root of a plantain, to put under their head that night, and they should dream who would be their husbands: It was to be sought for that day and hour.

The women have several magical secrets handed down to them by tradition, for this purpose, as, on St. *Agnes'* night, 21st day of January, take a row of pins, and pull out every one, one after another, saying a *Pater Noster*, or (Our Father) sticking a pin in your sleeve, and you will dream of him, or her, you shall marry. Ben Jonson in one of his Masques makes some mention of this.

> And on sweet Saint *Agnes* night
> Please you with the promis'd sight,
> Some of husbands, some of lovers,
> Which an empty dream discovers.

Another. *To know whom one shall marry*.

You must lie in another county, and knit the left garter about the right legged stocking (let the other garter and stocking alone) and as you rehearse these following verses, at every comma, knit a knot.

> This knot I knit,
> To know the thing, I know not yet,
> That I may see,
> The man (woman) that shall my husband (wife) be,
> How he goes, and what he wears,
> And what he does, all days, and years.

Accordingly in your dream you will see him: if a musician, with a lute or other instrument; if a scholar, with a book or papers.

JOHN AUBREY, Miscellanies Upon Various Subjects, 1696

The scene was an Oriental one; and there also it was Easter Sunday, and very early in the morning. And at a vast distance were visible, as a stain upon the horizon, the domes and cupolas of a great city – an image or faint abstraction, caught perhaps in childhood from some picture of Jerusalem. And not a bow-shoot from me, upon a stone, and shaded by Judean palms, there sat a woman; and I looked; and it was – Ann! She fixed her eyes upon me earnestly; and I said to her at length: 'So then I have found you at last.' I waited: but she answered me not a word. Her face was the same as when I saw it last, and yet again how different! Seventeen years ago, when the lamp-light fell upon her face, as for the last time I kissed her lips (lips, Ann, that to me were not polluted), her eyes were streaming with tears: the t〈 were now wiped away; she seemed more beautiful than she wa〉 a〈 that time, but in all other points the same, and not older. Her looks were tranquil, but with unusual solemnity of expression: and I now gazed upon her with some awe, but suddenly her countenance grew dim, and, turning to the mountains, I perceived vapours rolling between us; in a moment, all had vanished; thick darkness came on; and, in the twinkling of an eye, I was far away from mountains, and by lamp-light in Oxford-street, walking again with Ann – just as we walked seventeen years before, when we were both children.

THOMAS DE QUINCEY, *Confessions of an English Opium-Eater*, 1822

I fell in love at my first evening party.
You were tall and fair, just seventeen perhaps,
Talking to my two sisters. I kept silent
And never since have loved a tall fair girl,
Until last night in the small windy hours
When, floating up an unfamiliar staircase
And into someone's bedroom, there I found her
Posted beside the window in half-light
Wearing that same white dress with lacy sleeves.
She beckoned. I came closer. We embraced
Inseparably until the dream faded.
Her eyes shone clear and blue . . .

Who was it, though, impersonated you?

ROBERT GRAVES, 'A Dream of Frances Speedwell', 1971

Voss was dozing and waking. The grey light upon which he floated was marvellously soft, and flaking like ashes, with the consequence that he was most grateful to all concerned, and looked up once in an effort to convey his appreciation, when the old man, or woman, bent over him. For in the grey light, it transpired that the figure was that of a woman, whose breasts hung like bags of empty skin above the white man's face.

Realizing his mistake, the prisoner mumbled an apology as the ashy figure resumed its vigil. It was unnecessary, however, for their understanding of each other had begun to grow. While the woman sat looking down at her knees, the greyish skin was slowly revived, until her full, white, immaculate body became the shining source of all light.

By its radiance, he did finally recognize her face, and would have gone to her, if it had been possible, but it was not; his body was worn out.

Instead, she came to him, and at once he was flooded with light and memory. As she lay beside him, his boyhood slipped from him in a rustling of water and a rough towel. A steady summer had possessed them. Leaves were in her lips, that he bit off, and from her breasts the full, silky, milky buds. They were holding each other's heads and looking into them, as remorselessly as children looking at secrets, and seeing all too clearly. But, unlike children, they were comforted to recognize their own faults.

So they were growing together, and loving. No sore was so scrofulous on his body that she would not touch it with her kindness. He would kiss her wounds, even the deepest ones, that he had inflicted himself and left to suppurate.

Given time, the man and woman might have healed each other. That time is not given was their one sadness. But time itself is a wound that will not heal up.

'What is this, Laura?' he asked, touching the roots of her hair, at the temples. 'The blood is still running.'

But her reply was slipping from him.

And he fell back into the morning.

PATRICK WHITE, Voss, 1957

Cleopatra. I dreamt there was an Emperor Antony.
  O such another sleep, that I might see
  But such another man! . . .
  His face was as the heavens, and therein stuck
  A sun and moon, which kept their course, and lighted
  The little O, the earth.
Dolabella.   Most sovereign creature, —
Cleopatra. His legs bestrid the ocean, his rear'd arm
  Crested the world: his voice was propertied
  As all the tuned spheres, and that to friends:
  But when he meant to quail, and shake the orb,
  He was as rattling thunder. For his bounty,
  There was no winter in't: an autumn 'twas

That grew the more by reaping: his delights
Were dolphin-like, they show'd his back above
The element they lived in: in his livery
Walk'd crowns and crownets: realms and islands were
As plates dropp'd from his pocket.

Dolabella.   Cleopatra!

Cleopatra. Think you there was, or might be such a man
As this I dreamt of?

Dolabella.   Gentle madam, no.

Cleopatra. You lie up to the hearing of the gods.
But if there be, or ever were one such,
It's past the size of dreaming: nature wants stuff
To vie strange forms with fancy, yet to imagine
An Antony were nature's piece, 'gainst fancy,
Condemning shadows quite.

WILLIAM SHAKESPEARE, *Antony and Cleopatra,* c.1607

Lock up, fair lids, the treasures of my heart:
Preserve those beams, this age's only light:
To her sweet sense, sweet sleep, some ease impart,
Her sense too weak to bear her spirit's might.

And while o sleep thou closest up her sight,
(Her sight where love did forge his fairest dart)
O harbour all her parts in easeful plight:
Let no strange dream make her fair body start.

But yet o dream, if thou wilt not separte
In this rare subject from thy common right:
But wilt thy self in such a seat delight,

Then take my shape, and play a lover's part:
Kiss her from me, and say unto her sprite,
Till her eyes shine, I live in darkest night.

PHILIP SIDNEY, from *Arcadia,* 1590

When most I wink, then do mine eyes best see,
For all the day they view things unrespected;
But when I sleep, in dreams they look on thee,
And darkly bright are bright in dark directed:

Then thou whose shadow shadows doth make bright,
How would thy shadow's form form happy show
To the clear day with thy much clearer light,
When to unseeing eyes thy shade shines so!
How would, I say, mine eyes be blessèd made
By looking on thee in the living day,
When in dead night thy fair imperfect shade
Through heavy sleep on sightless eyes doth stay!
 All days are nights to see till I see thee,
 And nights bright days when dreams do show thee me.

WILLIAM SHAKESPEARE, Sonnet 43, c.1595

It occurred when I was on the eve of marriage, a season when, if lovers sleep sparingly, they dream profusely. A brief slumber sufficed to carry me in the night coach to Bognor. It had been concerted between Honoria and myself that we should pass the honeymoon at some place along the coast.

The purpose of my solitary journey was to procure an appropriate dwelling, which, we had agreed upon, should be a little pleasant house, with an indispensable lookout upon the sea. I chose one accordingly, a pretty villa, with bow-windows, and a prospect delightfully marine. The ocean murmur sounded incessantly upon the beach. A decent elderly body, in decayed sables, undertook on her part, to promote the comfort of the occupants by every suitable attention and, as she assured me, at a very reasonable rate. So far the nocturnal faculty had served me truly. A day-dream could not have proceeded more orderly. But, alas! Just here, when the dwelling was selected, the sea view was secured, the rent agreed upon, when everything was plausible, consistent and rational, the incoherent fancy crept in and confounded all — by marrying me to the old woman of the house!

THOMAS HOOD, _Whims and Oddities_, 1826

O what a tormenting night have my dreams led me abt. You Eliza — Mrs. Draper a Widow! — with a hand at Liberty to give! — and gave it to another! — She told me — I must acquiesce — it could not be otherwise. Acquiesce! cried I, waking in agonies — God be prais'd cried I — tis a dream — fell asleep after . . .

LAURENCE STERNE, _The Journal to Eliza_, 1767

I dreamt that I dwelt in marble halls,
With vassals and serfs at my side,
And of all who assembled within these walls
That I was the hope and the pride.

I had riches too great to count —
Could boast of a high ancestral name;
But I also dreamt, which pleas'd me most,
That you lov'd me still the same.

I dreamt that suitors sought my hand,
That knights upon bended knee,
And with vows no maiden heart could withstand
They pledg'd their faith to me.

And I dreamt that one of that noble host
Came forth my hand to claim;
But I also dreamt, which charm'd me most,
That you lov'd me still the same.

ALFRED BUNN, *The Bohemian Girl*, 1843

I dreamt I dwelt in marble halls,
And each damp thing that creeps and crawls
Went wobble-wobble on the walls.

LEWIS CARROLL, from 'The Palace of Humbug', 1855

. . . I'll dreamt that I'll dwealth mid warblers' walls when throstles
and choughs to my sigh hiehied . . .

JAMES JOYCE, *Finnegans Wake*, 1939

'And then I fell asleep. Ah, can I tell
The enchantment that afterwards befell?
Yet it was but a dream — yet such a dream
That never tongue, although it overteem
With mellow utterance like a cavern spring,
Could figure out and to conception bring

All I beheld and felt. Methought I lay
Watching the zenith, where the milky way
Among the stars in virgin splendour pours . . .
And lo! from opening clouds, I saw emerge
The loveliest moon, that ever silvered o'er
A shell for Neptune's goblet. She did soar
So passionately bright, my dazzled soul
Commingling with her argent spheres did roll
Through clear and cloudy, even when she went
At last into a dark and vapoury tent –
Whereat, methought, the lidless-eyèd train
Of planets all were in the blue again.
To commune with those orbs, once more I raised
My sight right upward; but it was quite dazed
By a bright something, sailing down apace,
Making me quickly veil my eyes and face.
Again I looked, and, O ye deities
Who from Olympus watch our destinies!
Whence that completed form of all completeness?
Whence came that high perfection of all sweetness?
Speak, stubborn earth, and tell me where, oh where,
Hast thou a symbol of her golden hair?
Not oat-sheaves drooping in the western sun;
Not – thy soft hand, fair sister, let me shun
Such follying before thee! Yet she had,
Indeed, locks bright enough to make me mad;
And they were simply gordianed up and braided,
Leaving, in naked comeliness, unshaded,
Her pearl-round ears, white neck, and orbèd brow;
The which were blended in, I know not how,
With such a paradise of lips and eyes,
Blush-tinted cheeks, half smiles, and faintest sighs,
That, when I think thereon, my spirit clings
And plays about its fancy, till the stings
Of human neighbourhood envenom all.
Unto what awful power shall I call?
To what high fane? Ah, see her hovering feet,
More bluely veined, more soft, more whitely sweet
Than those of sea-born Venus, when she rose
From out her cradle shell. The wind out-blows
Her scarf into a fluttering pavilion;
'Tis blue, and over-spangled with a million

Of little eyes, as though thou wert to shed,
Over the darkest, lushest blue-bell bed
Handfuls of daisies.' 'Endymion, how strange!
Dream within dream!' 'She took an airy range,
And then, towards me, like a very maid,
Came blushing, waning, willing, and afraid,
And pressed me by the hand. Ah, 'twas too much! . . .
           Madly did I kiss
The wooing arms which held me, and did give
My eyes at once to death – but 'twas to live,
To take in draughts of life from the gold fount
Of kind and passionate looks, to count and count
The moments, by some greedy help that seemed
A second self, that each might be redeemed
And plundered of its load of blessedness.
Ah, desperate mortal! I e'en dared to press
Her very cheek against my crownèd lip,
And, at that moment, felt my body dip
Into a warmer air – a moment more,
Our feet were soft in flowers. There was store
Of newest joys upon that alp. Sometimes
A scent of violets and blossoming limes
Loitered around us; then of honey cells,
Made delicate from all white-flower bells;
And once, above the edges of our nest,
An arch face peeped – an Oread as I guessed.

  'Why did I dream that sleep o'er-powered me
In midst of all this heaven? Why not see,
Far off, the shadows of his pinions dark,
And stare them from me? But no, like a spark
That needs must die, although its little beam
Reflects upon a diamond, my sweet dream
Fell into nothing – into stupid sleep.
And so it was, until a gentle creep,
A careful moving, caught my waking ears,
And up I started. . . .'

                JOHN KEATS, *Endymion*, I, 1817

Methought I saw my late espousèd Saint
  Brought to me like Alcestis from the grave,
  Whom Jove's great son to her glad husband gave,

Rescued from death by force, though pale and faint.
Mine, as whom washt from spot of child-bed taint
	Purification in the old Law did save,
	And such, as yet once more I trust to have
	Full sight of her in Heaven without restraint,
Came vested all in white, pure as her mind.
	Her face was veiled; yet to my fancied sight
	Love, sweetness, goodness, in her person shined
So clear, as in no face with more delight.
	But O as to embrace me she inclined,
	I waked, she fled, and day brought back my night.

JOHN MILTON, 'On his Deceased Wife', c.1655

I had an odd dream about you the other night. The man I dreamt of
was someone I had never seen and who stood nearly all the time with
his back to me and yet it could have been no one but you and I knew
it in my bones. In the dream I had great difficulties in getting to you,
running through the snow so that I was too much out of breath to
speak to you when at last I caught up with you. Then you turned
round and I just saw your face – like a blend and transfiguration of
all the faces you have presented me with, young and old, and really
like a vision of your *true* face – before I walked straight into your
arms. This was the first and only dream I have had about you and it
was happy and beautiful.

ANTONIA WHITE, *The Hound and the Falcon*, 1965

I never dream of the face of any one I am particularly attached to. I
have thought almost to agony of the same person for years, nearly
without ceasing, so as to have her face always before me, and to be
haunted by a perpetual consciousness of disappointed passion, and
yet I never in all that time dreamt of this person more than once or
twice, and then not vividly. I conceive, therefore, that this
perseverance of the imagination in a fruitless track must have been
owing to mortified pride, to an intense desire and hope of good in the
abstract, more than to love, which I consider as an individual and
involuntary passion, and which therefore, when it is strong, must
predominate over the fancy in sleep. I think myself into love, and
dream myself out of it.

WILLIAM HAZLITT, 'On Dreams', 1826

I knew that in many cases it is a mistake to pay too much attention to the appearance of the people one saw in one's dream, who may perhaps have been disguised or have exchanged faces, like those mutilated saints in cathedrals which ignorant archaeologists have restored, fitting the head of one to the body of another and jumbling all their attributes and names. Those that people bear in a dream are apt to mislead us. The person whom we love is to be recognised only by the intensity of the pain that we suffer.

MARCEL PROUST, *Within a Budding Grove*, 1918

I dream of you, to wake: would that I might
   Dream of you and not wake but slumber on;
    Nor find with dreams the dear companion gone,
As, summer ended, summer birds take flight.
In happy dreams I hold you full in sight,
   I blush again who waking look so wan;
    Brighter than sunniest day that ever shone,
In happy dreams your smile makes day of night.
Thus only in a dream we are at one,
   Thus only in a dream we give and take
    The faith that maketh rich who take or give;
   If thus to sleep is sweeter than to wake,
    To die were surely sweeter than to live,
Though there be nothing new beneath the sun.

CHRISTINA ROSSETTI, 'Monna Innominata' 3, 1882

I dream'd we both were in a bed
Of roses, almost smotherèd:
The warmth and sweetness had me there
Made lovingly familiar;
But that I heard thy sweet breath say,
Faults done by night, will blush by day:
I kissed thee (panting), and I call
Night to the record! that was all.
But ah! if empty dreams so please,
Love, give me more such nights as these.

ROBERT HERRICK, 'The Vision of Electra', 1648

All dreams of the soul
End in a beautiful man's or woman's body.

w. b. YEATS, from 'The Phases of the Moon', 1919

As his temperature rose, untruths took their place quite naturally among these recollections. One of the earliest was that they were lying together on the floor of some room in each other's arms. He could feel her lips pressed against his, but he could not feel the rest of her. He could not feel her with his body at all. He hugged her harder, rolling desperately against her, but it was all nothing, he could not feel her at all. Everything was confined to the mouth and he would wake up with burning lips.

This became a root dream, into which numbers of others would change. Time and again different climaxes of different dreams would end in this. One of the most vivid was in a sort of cottage where they had been for some time: it was near the sea and had a long overgrown garden full of weeds and raspberry canes. They sprawled together on the couch and John was filled with a lassitude so great that it alarmed him, it seemed a kind of treachery. They had lived there so long together that their love had worn thin like a coat; it was shabby with wearing. He looked at the young girl he held, at her perfect, composed face so near to his, and was frightened at his own indifference. His mood was easily definable: it was simply the boredom of no longer loving. Yet he covered it up, frantically, with layer after layer of dishonest thoughts, and kissed her neck, just below the ear. She wrinkled her nose slightly, but made no comment. He got up and crossed to the window with his hands in his pockets, staring moodily up the garden that was hung with trees. And there he saw Christopher, moving about half-way up the garden, poking about the bushes for something. An unreasoning terror seized him: he knew that Christopher must not see Jill or he would come in and take her away, and though he did not care much for her now, he was determined to stop this at all costs. He began talking to her very fast and insincerely, trying to occupy her attention, but to his horror she got up, wanting to go to the window. He gripped her, to hold her back, and as a last resort turned his grip into an embrace, hoping to cloud her mind with sensuality, pressing his face against hers, though knowing all the time that she looked over her shoulder out through the window, that Christopher had seen her and was coming towards the house. On this vertiginous note of expectancy the dream began curdling and slurring into the first one, and they were lying on the floor again together.

PHILIP LARKIN, *Jill*, 1946

Dear love, for nothing less then thee
Would I have broke this happy dream,
          It was a theme
For reason, much too strong for fantasy,
Therefore thou wakd'st me wisely; yet
My dream thou brok'st not, but continued'st it,
Thou art so truth, that thoughts of thee suffice,
To make dreams truths; and fables histories;
Enter these arms, for since thou thoughtst it best,
Not to dream all my dream, let's act the rest.

As lightning, or a taper's light,
Thine eyes, and not thy noise wak'd me;
          Yet I thought thee
(For thou lovest truth) an angel, at first sight,
But when I saw thou sawest my heart,
And knew'st my thoughts, beyond an angel's art,
When thou knew'st what I dreamt, when thou knew'st when
Excess of joy, would wake me, and cam'st then,
I must confess, it could not choose but be
Profane, to think thee any thing but thee.

Coming and staying show'd thee, thee,
But rising makes me doubt, that now,
          Thou art not thou.
That love is weak, where fear's as strong as he;
'Tis not all spirit, pure, and brave,
If mixture it of fear, shame, honour, have.
Perchance as torches which must ready be,
Men light and put out, so thou deal'st with me,
Thou cam'st to kindle, goest to come; then I
Will dream that hope again, but else would die.

JOHN DONNE, 'The Dream', *c.*1600

Here is a dream.
It is my dream –
I dreamt it.
I dreamt that my hair was kemp,
Then I dreamt that my true love unkempt it.

OGDEN NASH, 'My My: 1. My Dream', 1961

He awoke, heated and unrefreshed. During his sleep his inflamed imagination had presented him with none but the most voluptuous objects. Matilda stood before him in his dreams, and his eyes again dwelt upon her naked breast. She repeated her protestations of eternal love, threw her arms round his neck, and loaded him with kisses: He returned them; He clasped her passionately to his bosom, and . . . the vision was dissolved. Sometimes his dreams presented the image of his favourite Madonna, and He fancied that He was kneeling before her: As He offered up his vows to her, the eyes of the Figure seemed to beam on him with inexpressible sweetness. He pressed his lips to hers, and found them warm: The animated form started from the Canvas, embraced him affectionately, and his senses were unable to support delight so exquisite. Such were the scenes, on which his thoughts were employed while sleeping: His unsatisfied Desires placed before him the most lustful and provoking Images, and he rioted in joys till then unknown to him.

MATTHEW LEWIS, *The Monk*, 1796

A vision on his sleep
There came, a dream of hopes that never yet
Had flushed his cheek. He dreamed a veilèd maid
Sate near him, talking in low solemn tones. . . .
Soon the solemn mood
Of her pure mind kindled through all her frame
A permeating fire: wild numbers then
She raised, with voice stifled in tremulous sobs
Subdued by its own pathos: her fair hands
Were bare alone, sweeping from some strange harp
Strange symphony, and in their branching veins
The eloquent blood told an ineffable tale.
The beating of her heart was heard to fill
The pauses of her music, and her breath
Tumultuously accorded with those fits
Of intermitted song. Sudden she rose,

As if her heart impatiently endured
Its bursting burthen: at the sound he turned,
And saw by the warm light of their own life
Her glowing limbs beneath the sinuous veil
Of woven wind, her outspread arms now bare,
Her dark locks floating in the breath of night,
Her beamy bending eyes, her parted lips
Outstretched, and pale, and quivering eagerly.
His strong heart sunk and sickened with excess
Of love. He reared his shuddering limbs and quelled
His gasping breath, and spread his arms to meet
Her panting bosom: . . . she drew back a while,
Then, yielding to the irresistible joy,
With frantic gesture and short breathless cry
Folded his frame in her dissolving arms.
Now blackness veiled his dizzy eyes, and night
Involved and swallowed up the vision; sleep,
Like a dark flood suspended in its course,
Rolled back its impulse on his vacant brain.

  Roused by the shock he started from his trance . . .
The spirit of sweet human love has sent
A vision to the sleep of him who spurned
Her choicest gifts. He eagerly pursues
Beyond the realms of dream that fleeting shade;
He overleaps the bounds. Alas! Alas!
Were limbs, and breath, and being intertwined
Thus treacherously? Lost, lost, for ever lost,
In the wide pathless desert of dim sleep,
That beautiful shape!

PERCY BYSSHE SHELLEY, from 'Alastor', 1816

I saw her in a dream which was like a vision. She stood at some
distance from me, looking at me squarely. She was in her prime,
perhaps about thirty, and wearing the dress which had been made
for her many years before by my cousin the medium. It was perhaps
the most beautiful thing she had ever worn. Her expression was
neither joyful nor sad, but, rather, objectively wise and understanding, without the slightest emotional reaction, as though she were
beyond the mist of affects. I knew that it was not she, but a portrait
she had made or commissioned for me. It contained the beginning of
our relationship, the events of fifty-three years of marriage, and the

end of her life also. Face to face with such wholeness one remains speechless, for it can scarcely be comprehended.

C. G. JUNG, *Memories, Dreams, Reflections*, 1963

Restless and not good night, with the most unusual form of unpleasant nightmare. I had engaged myself (and with pleasure to the acceptants, evident, and to all their relations) to three delightful young ladies in the same day, and could neither decide which to keep, nor how to disengage the other two.

JOHN RUSKIN, *Diaries*, 29 December 1875

It was near last century's ending,
    And, though not much to rate
In a world of getting and spending,
    To her it was great.

The scene was a London suburb
    On a night of summer weather,
And the villas had back gardens
    Running together.

Her neighbours behind were dancing
    Under a marquee;
Two violoncellos played there,
    And violins three.

She had not been invited,
    Although her lover was;
She lay beside her husband,
    Perplexed at the cause.

Sweet after sweet quadrille rang:
    Absence made her weep;
The tears dried on her eyelids
    As she fell asleep.

She dreamt she was whirling with him
    In this dance upon the green
To which she was not invited
    Though her lover had been.

All night she danced as he clasped her –
    That is, in the happy dream
The music kept her dreaming
    Till the first daybeam.

'O damn those noisy fiddles!'
    Her husband said as he turned:
'Close to a neighbour's bedroom:
    I'd like them burned!'

At intervals thus all night-long
    Her husband swore. But she
Slept on, and danced in the loved arms,
    Under the marquee.

Next day she found that her lover,
    Though asked, had gone elsewhere,
And that she had possessed him in absence
    More than if there.

THOMAS HARDY, 'In the Marquee', 1928

The evening after the party I was at home sitting in a chair, exhausted. An image kept coming into my mind: it was like a shot from a film, then it was as if I was seeing a sequence from a film. A man and a woman, on a roof-top above a busy city, but the noise and the movement of the city are far beneath them. They wander aimlessly on the roof-top, sometimes embracing, but almost experimentally, as if they are thinking: How does this taste? – then they separate again and aimlessly move about the roof. Then the man goes to the woman and says: I love you. And she says, in terror: What do you mean? He says: I love you. So she embraces him, and he moves away, with nervous haste, and she says: Why did you say you loved me? And he says: I wanted to hear how it would sound. And she says: But I love you, I love you, I love you – and he goes off to the very edge of the roof and stands there, ready to jump – he will jump if she says even once again: I love you.

When I slept I dreamed this film sequence – in colour. Now it was not on a roof-top, but in a thin tinted mist or fog, an exquisitely-coloured fog swirled and a man and a woman wandered in it. She was trying to find him, but when she bumped into him, or found him, he nervously moved away from her; looking back at her, then away, and away again.

DORIS LESSING, *The Golden Notebook*, 1962

After this (B) haunted me for three days so that I could feel her presence in my room.

  Then I dreamt about her, thus. (I was lying in a bed, B came to me in her Puck's costume from the play. She was married to me. She said of me: 'Behold, the man who brewed me,' gave me her foot to kiss. She had no breasts, absolutely none!)

AUGUST STRINDBERG, *From an Occult Diary*, 15 November 1900

Me thought I saw (as I did dream in bed)
A crawling vine about Anacreon's head:
Flusht was his face; his hairs with oil did shine;
And as he spake, his mouth ran o'er with wine.
Tippled he was; and tippling lispt withal;
And lisping reeled, and reeling like to fall.
A young enchantress close by him did stand
Tapping his plump thighs with a myrtle wand:
She smil'd; he kist; and kissing, cull'd her too;
And being cup-shot, more he could not do.
For which (me thought) in pretty anger she
Snatcht off his crown, and gave the wreath to me:
Since when (me thinks) my brains about do swim,
And I am wild and wanton like to him.

ROBERT HERRICK, 'The Vision', 1648

I took too much wine. Dreamed of walk with Joan and Connie, in which I took all the short-cuts over the fields, and sent them round by the road, and then came back with them jumping up and down banks of earth, which I saw at last were washed away below by a stream. Then of showing Joanna a beautiful snake, which I told her was an innocent one; it had a slender neck and a green ring round it, and I made her feel its scales. Then she made me feel it, and it became a fat thing, like a leech, and adhered to my hand, so that I could hardly pull it off — and so I woke.

JOHN RUSKIN, *Diaries*, 9 March 1868

Iago. . . . I lay with Cassio lately,
  And being troubled with a raging tooth,
  I could not sleep.
  There are a kind of men so loose of soul
  That in their sleeps will mutter their affairs.
  One of this kind is Cassio.
  In sleep I heard him say, 'Sweet Desdemona,
  Let us be wary, let us hide our loves!'
  And then, sir, would he gripe and wring my hand,
  Cry 'O sweet creature!' Then kiss me hard,
  As if he plucked up kisses by the roots
  That grew upon my lips; laid his leg o'er my thigh,
  And sigh, and kiss, and then cry, 'Cursèd fate
  That gave thee to the Moor!'

Othello. O monstrous! monstrous!

Iago.   Nay, this was but his dream.

Othello. But this denoted a foregone conclusion,
  'Tis a shrewd doubt, though it be but a dream.

                    WILLIAM SHAKESPEARE, *Othello*, *c.*1604

When I dream that you love me, you'll surely forgive;
  Extend not your anger to sleep;
For in visions alone your affection can live, –
  I rise, and it leaves me to weep.

Then, Morpheus! envelope my faculties fast,
  Shed o'er me your languor benign;
Should the dream of to-night but resemble the last,
  What rapture celestial is mine!

They tell us that slumber, the sister of death,
  Mortality's emblem is given;
To fate how I long to resign my frail breath
  If this be a foretaste of heaven!

Ah! frown not, sweet lady, unbend your soft brow,
  Nor deem me too happy in this;
If I sin in my dream, I atone for it now,
  Thus doom'd but to gaze upon bliss.

Though in visions, sweet lady, perhaps you may smile,
  Oh! think not my penance deficient!
When dreams of your presence my slumbers beguile,
  To awake will be torture sufficient.

LORD BYRON, 'To M. S. G.' 1807

Sleep insensibly stole over him, and the tranquil solemnity of his mind when awake, for a while continued to influence his slumbers.

He still fancied himself to be in the Church of the Capuchins; but it was no longer dark and solitary. Multitudes of silver Lamps shed splendour from the vaulted Roof; Accompanied by the captivating chaunt of distant choristers, the Organ's melody swelled through the Church; The Altar seemed decorated as for some distinguished feast; It was surrounded by a brilliant Company; and near it stood Antonia arrayed in bridal white, and blushing with all the charms of Virgin Modesty.

Half hoping, half fearing, Lorenzo gazed upon the scene before him. Sudden the door leading to the Abbey unclosed, and He saw, attended by a long train of Monks, the Preacher advance to whom He had just listened with so much admiration. He drew near Antonia.

'And where is the Bridegroom?' said the imaginary Friar.

Antonia seemed to look round the Church with anxiety. Involuntarily the Youth advanced a few steps from his concealment. She saw him; The blush of pleasure glowed upon her cheek; With a graceful motion of her hand She beckoned to him to advance. He disobeyed not the command; He flew towards her, and threw himself at her feet.

She retreated for a moment; Then gazing upon him with unutterable delight; – 'Yes!' She exclaimed, 'My Bridegroom! My destined Bridegroom!'

She said, and hastened to throw herself into his arms; But before He had time to receive her, an Unknown rushed between them. His form was gigantic; His complexion was swarthy, His eyes fierce and terrible; his Mouth breathed out volumes of fire; and on his forehead was written in legible characters – 'Pride! Lust! Inhumanity!'

Antonia shrieked. The Monster clasped her in his arms, and springing with her upon the Altar, tortured her with his odious caresses. She endeavoured in vain to escape from his embrace. Lorenzo flew to her succour, but ere He had time to reach her, a loud burst of thunder was heard. Instantly the Cathedral seemed crumbling into pieces; The Monks betook themselves to flight, shrieking fearfully; The Lamps were extinguished, the Altar sank down, and in its place appeared an abyss vomiting forth clouds of flame. Uttering a loud and terrible cry the Monster plunged into the Gulph, and in his fall attempted to drag Antonia with him. He strove in vain. Animated by supernatural powers She disengaged herself from his embrace; But her white Robe was left in his possession. Instantly a wing of brilliant splendour spread itself from either of Antonia's arms. She darted upwards, and while ascending cried to Lorenzo,

'Friend! we shall meet above!'

At the same moment the Roof of the Cathedral opened; Harmonious voices pealed along the Vaults; and the glory into which Antonia was received, was composed of rays of such dazzling brightness, that Lorenzo was unable to sustain the gaze. His sight failed, and He sank upon the ground.

When He woke, He found himself extended upon the pavement of the Church.

MATTHEW LEWIS, *The Monk*, 1796

[*Anna Karenina has betrayed her marriage to Alexey Alexandrovich Karenin by her passion for Vronsky.*]

In her dreams, when she had no control over her thoughts, her position appeared to her in all its shocking nakedness. One dream she had almost every night. She dreamt that both at once were her husbands, and lavished their caresses on her. Alexey Alexandrovich wept, kissing her hands, saying: 'How beautiful it is now!' and Alexey Vronsky was there too, and he also was her husband. And she was surprised that formerly this had seemed impossible to her, and laughingly explained to them how much simpler it really was, and that they were both now contented and happy. But this dream weighed on her like a nightmare, and she woke from it filled with horror.

LEO TOLSTOY, *Anna Karenina*, 1876

[*Humbert Humbert is lodging with Mrs Charlotte Haze and her daughter Lolita.*]

I have turned on the light to take down a dream. It had an evident antecedent. Haze at dinner had benevolently proclaimed that since the weather bureau promised a sunny weekend we would go to the lake Sunday after church. As I lay in bed, erotically musing before trying to go to sleep, I thought of a final scheme how to profit by the picnic to come. I was aware that mother Haze hated my darling for her being sweet on me. So I planned my lake day with a view to satisfying the mother. To her alone would I talk; but at some appropriate moment I would say I had left my wrist watch or my sunglasses in that glade yonder – and plunge with my nymphet into the wood. Reality at this juncture withdrew, and the Quest for the Glasses turned into a quiet little orgy with a singularly knowing, cheerful, corrupt and compliant Lolita behaving as reason knew she could not possibly behave. At 3 a.m. I swallowed a sleeping pill, and presently, a dream that was not a sequel but a parody revealed to me, with a kind of meaningful clarity, the lake I had never yet visited: it was glazed over with a sheet of emerald ice, and a pockmarked Eskimo was trying in vain to break it with a pickaxe, although imported mimosas and oleanders flowered on its gravelly banks. I am sure Dr Blanche Schwarzmann would have paid me a sack of schillings for adding such a libidream to her files. Unfortunately, the rest of it was frankly eclectic. Big Haze and little Haze rode on horseback around the lake, and I rode too, dutifully bobbing up and down, bowlegs astraddle although there was no horse between them, only elastic air – one of those little omissions due to the absent-mindedness of the dream agent.

VLADIMIR NABOKOV, Lolita, 1955

I dreamt we slept in a moss in Donegal
On turf banks under blankets, with our faces
Exposed all night in a wetting drizzle,
Pallid as the dripping sapling birches.
Lorenzo and Jessica in a cold climate.
Diarmuid and Grainne waiting to be found.
Darkly asperged and censed, we were laid out
Like breathing effigies on a raised ground.
And in that dream I dreamt – how like you this? –
Our first night years ago in that hotel
When you came with your deliberate kiss
To raise us towards the lovely and painful
Covenants of flesh; our separateness;
The respite in our dewy dreaming faces.

SEAMUS HEANEY, 'Glanmore Sonnet X', 1979

[*Uncertain of the fate of her husband, the poet Osip Mandelstam, Nadezhda Mandelstam wrote him a final letter in October 1938. In January 1939 she learned that he was dead.*]

You came to me every night in my sleep, and I kept asking what had happened, but you did not reply.

In my last dream I was buying food for you in a filthy hotel restaurant. The people with me were total strangers. When I had bought it, I realized I did not know where to take it, because I do not know where you are.

When I woke up, I said to Shura: 'Osia is dead.' I do not know whether you are still alive, but from the time of that dream, I have lost track of you. I do not know where you are. Will you hear me? Do you know how much I love you? I could never tell you how much I love you. I cannot tell you even now. I speak only to you, only to you. You are with me always, and I who was such a wild and angry one and never learned to weep simple tears – now I weep and weep and weep.

It's me: Nadia. Where are you?

NADEZHDA MANDELSTAM, *Hope Abandoned*, 1972

Old Age and Illness

I dreamt a dream! what can it mean?
And that I was a maiden queen,
Guarded by an angel mild:
Witless woe was ne'er beguil'd!

And I wept both night and day,
And he wip'd my tears away,
And I wept both day and night,
And hid from him my heart's delight.

So he took his wings and fled;
Then the morn blush'd rosy red;
I dried my tears, and arm'd my fears
With ten thousand shields and spears.

Soon my angel came again:
I was arm'd, he came in vain;
For the time of youth was fled,
And grey hairs were on my head.

WILLIAM BLAKE, 'The Angel', 1793

Mr. Wesley related a dream which he had recently had. He thought he was walking down one of the streets of Bristol when he saw a man he knew well, and went across to accost him; but, on making the attempt to shake hands, found his own were gone. The interpretation put upon the dream was that his work on earth was nearly done, and his intercourse with mortals was about to cease.

JOHN WESLEY, *Journal*, pub. 1909–16, referring to a sermon of 1790

I am worn out with dreams;
A weather-worn, marble triton
Among the streams;
And all day long I look
Upon this lady's beauty
As though I had found in a book

A pictured beauty,
Pleased to have filled the eyes
Or the discerning ears,
Delighted to be but wise,
For men improve with the years;
And yet, and yet,
Is this my dream, or the truth?
O would that we had met
When I had my burning youth!
But I grow old among dreams,
A weather-worn, marble triton
Among the streams.

W. B. YEATS, 'Men Improve With the Years', 1919

Some person took me to call upon Mr. Spence, near Lewes, the humourist, who built Pigmy Hall. And there I saw three old ladies, whose ages were one, one hundred and thirty-five; one, one hundred and twenty-five; and one, one hundred and two. The youngest was the only one whose faculties were unimpaired. But the odd part of the dream was, that all their chins had grown to a great length, being prolonged eight or ten inches in a curve, and covered with a thick, black, bushy beard. I thought that this curious growth was akin to the production of the ligneous fungus which grows upon old wood, as if Nature were thus whimsically disposing of materials for which it had no better use.

ROBERT SOUTHEY, 7 July 1821

A dream of mine flew over the mead
   To the halls where my old Love reigns;
And it drew me on to follow its lead:
   And I stood at her window-panes;

And I saw but a thing of flesh and bone
   Speeding on to its cleft in the clay;
And my dream was scared, and expired on a moan,
   And I whitely hastened away.

THOMAS HARDY, 'The Dream-Follower', 1901

If you seem to be an old man, you will attain to honour.

ASTRAMPSYCHUS, *The Oneirocriticon*, c.AD 350

And seeing dreams are caused by the distemper of some of the inward parts of the body, divers distempers must needs cause different dreams. And hence it is that lying cold breedeth dreams of fear, and raiseth the thought and image of some fearful object, the motion from the brain to the inner parts and from the inner parts to the brain being reciprocal; and that as anger causeth heat in some parts of the body when we are awake, so when we sleep the overheating of the same parts causeth anger, and raiseth up in the brain the imagination of an enemy. In the same manner, as natural kindness, when we are awake, causeth desire, and desire makes heat in certain other parts of the body; so also too much heat in those parts, while we sleep, raiseth in the brain an imagination of some kindness shown. In sum, our dreams are the reverse of our waking imaginations; the motion when we are awake beginning at one end, and when we dream at another.

THOMAS HOBBES, *Leviathan*, 1651

He was in the hospital from the middle of Lent till after Easter. When he was better, he remembered the dreams he had had while he was feverish and delirious. He dreamt that the whole world was condemned to a terrible new strange plague that had come to Europe from the depths of Asia. All were to be destroyed except a very few chosen. Some new sorts of microbes were attacking the bodies of men, but these microbes were endowed with intelligence and will. Men attacked by them became at once mad and furious. But never had men considered themselves so intellectual and so completely in possession of the truth as these sufferers, never had they considered their decisions, their scientific conclusions, their moral convictions so infallible. Whole villages, whole towns and peoples went mad from the infection. All were excited and did not understand one another. Each thought that he alone had the truth and was wretched looking at the others, beat himself on the breast, wept, and wrung his hands. They did not know how to judge and could not agree what to consider evil and what good; they did not know whom to blame, whom to justify. Men killed each other in a sort of senseless spite. They gathered together in armies against one another, but even on the march the armies would begin attacking each other, the ranks would be broken and the soldiers would fall on each other, stabbing and cutting, biting and devouring each other. The alarm bell was ringing all day long in the towns; men rushed together, but why they were summoned and who was summoning them no one knew. The most ordinary trades were abandoned, because everyone proposed his own ideas, his own improvements, and they could not agree. The land too was abandoned. Men met in groups, agreed on something, swore to keep together, but at once began on something quite different from what they had proposed. They accused one another, fought and killed each other. There were conflagrations and famine. All men and all things were involved in destruction. The plague spread and moved further and further. Only a few men could be saved in the whole world. They were a pure chosen people, destined to found a new race and a new life, to renew and purify the earth, but no one had seen these men, no one had heard their words and their voices.

FYODOR DOSTOEVSKY, *Crime and Punishment*, 1866

I dreamed that I had great pain of the stone in making water, and that once I looked upon my yard in making water at the steps before my door, and there I took hold of the end of the thing and pulled it out, and it was a turd; and it came into my mind that I was in the same condition with my aunt Pepys, my uncle Robert's wife. And by and by, on the like occasion, I pulled out something and flung on the ground – it looked like slime or snot, and presently it swelled and turned into a grey kind of bird, and I would have taken it in my hand and it run from me to the corner of the door, going into the garden in the entry by Sir J. Mennes's; and so I waked.

SAMUEL PEPYS, *Diary*, 29 June 1667

When Sir Christopher Wren was at Paris, about 1671, he was ill and feverish, made but little water, and had a pain in his reins [kidneys]. He sent for a physician, who advised him to be let blood, thinking he had a plurisy: but bleeding much disagreeing with his constitution, he would defer it a day longer: that night he dreamt, that he was in a place where palm-trees grew, (suppose Egypt) and that a woman in a romantic habit, reached him dates. The next day he sent for dates, which cured him of the pain of his reins.

JOHN AUBREY, *Miscellanies Upon Various Subjects*, 1696

I passed a very bad night, in the course of which I had this dream. I thought that papa and I were travelling, and were sleeping in adjoining rooms. We were in some hot country, and I had just come

to the end of a night spent in great pain. Toward the morning I slept
fairly, and when I woke the sun was shining hot upon my darkened
room. For some reason or other papa had left his room, and I was
alone. As I rose a horrid sense of impending evil oppressed me. I
could hardly stand, and in great weakness I tottered to a chair that
stood before a tall looking-glass. There I saw myself a hideous sight.
My skin was leprous white, like parchment, and all shrivelled. From
every pore burst a river of perspiration, and ran to my feet. My feet
were cramped and blanched, and cockled up with pain. But the face
was the most awful sight. It was all white – the lips white and
parched – the eyes pale, and presenting a perfectly flat surface. They
were dilated, and shone with a cold blue eerie light. I heard a noise in
papa's room, and knocked. He said, 'Come in' in his usual tone, and
I crept up to him. He was shaving and did not see me, till I roused him
by touching him and saying slowly, 'Papa.' Then he turned round
and looked intently at me and inquiringly. I shrieked, 'Papa, don't
you know me?' but even while I cried the vision of my own distorted
features came across me, and filled me with my utter loneliness. At
last he cried, 'My son,' and, burying his face in his hands, he added,
'All in one night.' In an ecstasy of deliverance I clasped his neck, and
felt that now I need not go back into that twilight room with its bed
and the mystery behind its curtains. But he went on in a hesitating
voice, 'My poor boy! what fiend – or demon?' I stopped the question
with a yell. Something seemed to tear me, and I awoke struggling.
Such was my dream – more horrible than it seems, for the terror of
dreams bears no relation to the hideousness of their incidents, but to
some hidden emotion.

JOHN ADDINGTON SYMONDS, 3 July 1861

To wear a purple robe threatens a long disease.

ASTRAMPSYCHUS, *The Oneirocriticon*, c.AD 350

In my dream, I was deaf.
He touched my ear in friendship
but when he felt my deafness,

the ball of wax blocking my hearing,
he turned sadly away
leaving me alone in the dark foreign room.

This morning I listen to music
and recall the muffled dream,
his soundless footsteps on the paved floor.

I wonder what deafness lurks in me,
what handicap waits for my acknowledgement?
What wisdom have I closed my ears to?

What thoughts dishevelled between the old
and the new moon, what dishfuls of fear,
what enemy actions did he perceive, touching my ear?

I am unable to forget the dream's broken message,
have no splints to mend it.
I will not deprive myself of its warning.
All day I listen for the inauguration of my deafness.

The haze of dream is only the beginning.
Unless I travel to the right bondage,
I may never hear the word the dream wants to say,
never hear the word that will reshape my life.

And all the nights of dream to come
will be reproach, mouths uttering and no sound coming,
questions asked and answers given and I unable
to interpret any of these riches.

As I write
I feel again that touch of a hand against my ear,
a secret and strong act.
I believe the touch that discovered my deafness

also cured the blemish,
that my hindrances are temporary:
I believe that the gesture of warning is also a blessing.

I was locked into a silence of my own manufacture
but am now emerging free,
clear of the boundaries, out amid the bivouacs of cold,
listening hard to all weathers.

PENELOPE SHUTTLE, 'The Dream', 1980

I dreamt that I was lying on the sofa in my study; somebody came in with Lillan and held her out to me to fondle. I took her little face between my hands, wanting to look at her, but I could not open my eyes; it was dark, I was blind. Thereupon I woke up and wept a great deal. Felt sure that Lillan was ill. Dreamt about her time after time.

AUGUST STRINDBERG, *From an Occult Diary*, 21 August 1903

It was on that Sunday night that Olwen Phillips of Croeswen dreamed her wonderful dream. She was a girl of sixteen, the daughter of small farming people, and for many months she had been doomed to certain death. Consumption, which flourishes in that damp, warm climate, had laid hold of her; not only her lungs but her whole system was a mass of tuberculosis. As is common enough, she had enjoyed many fallacious brief recoveries in the early stages of the disease, but all hope had long been over, and now for the last few weeks she had seemed to rush vehemently to death. . . .

The girl slept in an inner room communicating with the room occupied by her father and mother. The door between was kept open, so that Mrs. Phillips could hear her daughter if she called to her in the night. And Olwen called to her mother that night, just as the dawn was breaking. It was no faint summons from a dying bed that came to the mother's ears, but a loud cry that rang through the house, a cry of great gladness. Mrs. Phillips started up from sleep in wild amazement, wondering what could have happened. And then she saw Olwen, who had not been able to rise from her bed for many weeks past, standing in the doorway in the faint light of the growing day. The girl called to her mother: 'Mam! mam! It is all over. I am quite well again.'

Mrs. Phillips roused her husband, and they sat up in bed staring, not knowing on earth, as they said afterwards, what had been done with the world. Here was their poor girl wasted to a shadow, lying on her death-bed, and the life sighing from her with every breath, and her voice, when she last uttered it, so weak that one had to put one's ear to her mouth. And here in a few hours she stood up before them; and even in that faint light they could see that she was changed almost beyond knowing . . . Olwen called out again, so the mother lit a candle and got up and went tottering across the room, and there was Olwen all gay and plump again, smiling with shining eyes. Her mother led her into her own room, and set down the candle there, and felt her daughter's flesh, and burst into prayers and tears of wonder and delight, and thanksgivings, and held the girl again to be sure that she was not deceived. And then Olwen told her dream, though she thought it was not a dream.

She said she woke up in the deep darkness, and she knew the life was fast going from her. She could not move so much as a finger, she tried to cry out, but no sound came from her lips. She felt that in another instant the whole world would fall from her – her heart was full of agony. And as the last breath was passing her lips, she heard a very faint, sweet sound, like the tinkling of a silver bell. It came from far away, from over by Ty-newydd. She forgot her agony and listened, and even then, she says, she felt the swirl of the world as it came back to her. And the sound of the bell swelled and grew louder, and it thrilled all through her body, and the life was in it. And as the bell rang and trembled in her ears, a faint light touched the wall of her room and reddened, till the whole room was full of rosy fire. And then she saw standing before her bed three men in blood-coloured robes with shining faces. And one man held a golden bell in his hand. And the second man held up something shaped like the top of a table. It was like a great jewel, and it was of a blue colour, and there were rivers of silver and gold running through it and flowing as quick streams flow, and there were pools in it as if violets had been poured out into water, and then it was green as the sea near the shore, and then it was the sky at night with all the stars shining, and then the sun and the moon came down and washed in it. And the third man held up high above this a cup that was like a rose on fire; 'there was a great burning in it, and a dropping of blood in it, and a red cloud above it, and I saw a great secret. And I heard a voice that sang nine times: "Glory and praise to the Conqueror of Death, to the Fountain of Life immortal." Then the red light went from the wall, and it was all darkness, and the bell rang faint again by Capel Teilo, and then I got up and called to you.'

ARTHUR MACHEN, 'The Great Return', 1915

I dreamt he drove me back to the asylum
Straight after lunch; we stood then at one end,
A sort of cafeteria behind, my friend
Behind me, nuts in groups about the room;
A dumbwaiter with five shelves was waiting (some-
thing's missing here) to take me up – I bend
And lift a quart of milk to hide and tend,
Take with me. Everybody is watching, dumb.

I try to put it first among some worm-
shot volumes of the N.E.D. I had
On the top shelf – then somewhere else . . . slowly
Lise comes up in a matron's uniform
And with a look (I saw once) infinitely sad
In her grey eyes takes it away from me.

JOHN BERRYMAN, 'Sonnet 79', 1967

I had been thinking intently for a long time before I slept of the
anxieties of a friend who was engaged in a difficult task of nursing. A
sudden spell of cold brought on some slight rheumatic pain during
the night, of which I had not been conscious before I went to sleep.
The pain came into my dream but was transferred to my friend. In it
she became the patient – I was helping to nurse her, and my mind was
concentrated on the problems and practical difficulties that she and I
had lately discussed; the pain, which was really my own, being one of
the symptoms of the illness that she was suffering from in the dream.

MARY ARNOLD-FORSTER, *Studies in Dreams*, 1921

To drink muddy water foretells disease of the body.

ASTRAMPSYCHUS, *The Oneirocriticon*, c.AD 350

I dreamed that I was troubled with the scurvy; and that on the
sudden all my teeth became loose; that one of them especially in the
lower jaw, I could scarce hold in with my finger, till I called out for
help.

WILLIAM LAUD, *Diary*, 9 February 1627

Dreamed a quite formidably clear dream of taking a large front tooth
out, with part of the jaw, and looking to see how much disfigured I
was, in the glass, saying at the same time, 'Well, for once *this* is no
dream.'

JOHN RUSKIN, *Diaries*, 21 January 1877

I dreamt last night that I had a disease of the heart that would kill me
in 6 months. Leonard, after some persuasion, told me. My instincts
were all such as I should have, in order, & some very strong: quite

unexpected, I mean voluntary, as they are in dreams, & thus have an authenticity which makes an immense, & pervading impression. First, relief – well I've done with life anyhow (I was lying in bed) then horror; then desire to live; then fear of insanity; then (no this came earlier) regret about my writing, & leaving this book unfinished; then a luxurious dwelling upon my friends sorrow; then a sense of death & being done with at my age; then telling Leonard that he must marry again; seeing our life together; & facing the conviction of going, when other people went on living.

VIRGINIA WOOLF, *Diary*, 2 November 1929

Death

❧

Dionysius was absurdly tyrannical to kill a man for dreaming that he had killed him, and really to take away his life who had but fantastically taken away his. Lamia was ridiculously unjust to sue a young man for a reward, who had confessed that pleasure from her in a dream, which she had denied unto his awaking senses, conceiving that she had merited somewhat from his fantastical fruition and shadow of herself. If there be such debts, we owe deeply unto sympathies, but the common spirit of the world must be judge in such arreareges.

If some have swounded they may have also died in dreams, since death is but a confirmed swounding. Whether Plato died in a dream, as some deliver, he must rise again to inform us. That some have never dreamed is as improbable as that some have never laughed. That children dream not the first half year, that men dream not in some countries, with many more, are unto me sick men's dreams, dreams out of the ivory gate, and visions before midnight.

SIR THOMAS BROWNE, 'On Dreams', c.1650

'I'm dying,' he thought. 'This is the end.' Nevertheless, he did manage to drag himself home where he lay gasping. He must have dozed off because he imagined that he was in his home town, Tishvitz. He had a sore throat and his mother was busy wrapping a stocking stuffed with hot salt around his neck. He could hear talk going on in the house; something about a candle and about how a frog had bitten him. He wanted to go out into the street but they wouldn't let him because a Catholic procession was passing by. Men in long robes, holding double edged axes in their hands, were intoning in Latin as they sprinkled holy water. Crosses gleamed; sacred pictures waved in the air. There was an odor of incense and corpses. Suddenly the sky turned a burning red and the whole world started to burn. Bells were ringing; people rushed madly about. Flocks of birds flew overhead, screeching. Dr. Fischelson awoke with a start. His body was covered with sweat and his throat was now actually sore. He tried to meditate about his extraordinary dream, to find its rational connection with what was happening to him and to comprehend it *sub specie eternitatis*, but none of it made sense. 'Alas, the brain is a receptacle for nonsense,' Dr. Fischelson thought. 'This earth belongs to the mad.'

And once more he closed his eyes; once more he dozed; once more he dreamed.

I. B. SINGER, 'The Spinoza of Market Street', 1961

The overwhelming power of names, and the resulting approach of martyrdom, had begun to prey heavily on Shaheed's mind; in his dreams, he began to see his death, which took the form of a bright pomegranate, and floated in mid-air behind him, following him everywhere, biding its time.

SALMAN RUSHDIE, *Midnight's Children*, 1981

A woman dreamt that stalks of wheat sprouted from her breast and that they bent back and went down into her vagina. Through some mishap, she unwittingly had sexual relations with her own child. Afterwards she committed suicide and died a wretched death. For the stalks of wheat signified her son. The descent into the vagina indicated sexual intercourse. The seeds that sprung forth from her body signified that death awaited her, since seeds spring forth from the earth, not from living bodies.

Someone dreamt that the sky was destroyed. He died.

Someone dreamt that he had an iron penis. He fathered a son who killed him. For iron is consumed by the rust that it produces from itself.

A man dreamt that he slipped out of his flesh just as a snake sheds its old skin. He died on the following day. For his soul, which was about to depart from his body, provided him with these images.

ARTEMIDORUS, *The Interpretation of Dreams*, c.AD 150

Brakenbury. Why looks your grace so heavily today?
Clarence. O, I have pass'd a miserable night,
  So full of fearful dreams, of ugly sights,
  That, as I am a Christian faithful man,
  I would not spend another such a night

Though 'twere to buy a world of happy days, —
So full of dismal terror was the time!

Brakenbury. What was your dream, my lord? I pray you, tell me.

Clarence. Methought that I had broken from the Tower,
   And was embark'd to cross to Burgundy;
   And, in my company, my brother Gloster;
   Who from my cabin tempted me to walk
   Upon the hatches: thence we look'd towards England,
   And cited up a thousand heavy times,
   During the wars of York and Lancaster,
   That had befall'n us. As we pac'd along
   Upon the giddy footing of the hatches,
   Methought that Gloster stumbled; and, in falling,
   Struck me, that thought to stay him, overboard
   Into the tumbling billows of the main.
   O Lord! methought what pain it was to drown!
   What dreadful noise of water in mine ears!
   What sights of ugly death within mine eyes!
   Methought I saw a thousand fearful wrecks;
   A thousand men that fishes gnaw'd upon;
   Wedges of gold, great anchors, heaps of pearl,
   Inestimable stones, unvalu'd jewels,
   All scatter'd in the bottom of the sea:
   Some lay in dead men's skulls; and in those holes
   Where eyes did once inhabit there were crept, —
   As 'twere in scorn of eyes, — reflecting gems,
   That woo'd the slimy bottom of the deep,
   And mock'd the dead bones that lay scatter'd by.

Brakenbury. Had you such leisure in the time of death
   To gaze upon the secrets of the deep?

Clarence. Methought I had; and often did I strive
   To yield the ghost: but still the envious flood
   Stopp'd in my soul, and would not let it forth
   To find the empty, vast, and wandering air;
   But smother'd it within my panting bulk,
   Which almost burst to belch it in the sea.

Brakenbury. Awak'd you not with this sore agony?

Clarence. No, no, my dream was lengthen'd after life;
   O, then began the tempest to my soul!
   I pass'd, methought, the melancholy flood
   With that grim ferryman which poets write of,

Unto the kingdom of perpetual night.
The first that there did greet my stranger soul
Was my great father-in-law, renowned Warwick;
Who cried aloud, 'What scourge for perjury
Can this dark monarchy afford false Clarence?'
And so he vanish'd: then came wandering by
A shadow like an Angel, with bright hair
Dabbled in blood; and he shriek'd out aloud,
'Clarence is come, – false, fleeting, perjur'd Clarence,
That stabb'd me in the field by Tewkesbury;
Seize on him, Furies, take him to your torments!'
With that, methought, a legion of foul fiends
Environ'd me, and howled in mine ears
Such hideous cries that, with the very noise,
I trembling wak'd, and for a season after
Could not believe but that I was in hell, –
Such terrible impression made my dream.

WILLIAM SHAKESPEARE, Richard III, c.1594

To be dead [in dreams] announces freedom from anxiety.

ASTRAMPSYCHUS, The Oneirocriticon, c.AD 350

'. . . I am going to die; I have had a dream.'

'A dream?' Vronsky instantly remembered the peasant of his dream.

'Yes, a dream,' she said. 'I dreamed it a long time ago. I thought I had run into my bedroom, that I had to fetch or find out something there: you know how it happens in dreams,' and her eyes dilated with horror. 'And in the bedroom there was something standing in the corner.'

'Oh, what nonsense! How can one believe? . . .'

But she would not allow him to stop her. What she was saying was of too much importance to her.

'And that something turned round, and I saw it was a peasant with a rough beard, small and dreadful. I wanted to run away, but he stooped over a sack and was fumbling about in it. . . .'

She showed how he fumbled in the sack. Her face was full of horror. And Vronsky, remembering his dream, felt the same horror filling his soul.

'He fumbles about and mutters French words, so quickly, so

quickly, and with a burr, you know: "*Il faut le battre, le fer: le broyer, le pétrir. . . .*" And in my horror I tried to wake, but I woke still in a dream and began asking myself what it could mean; and Korney says to me: "You will die in childbed, in childbed, ma'am. . . ." Then I woke.'

'What nonsense, what nonsense!' said Vronsky, but he felt that there was no conviction in his voice.

LEO TOLSTOY, Anna Karenina, 1875–7

Woke at one, and lay melancholy till three or four – then sleeping, only to dream of finding a dead body of a child in a box, a little girl whom I had put living into it and forgotten.

JOHN RUSKIN, Diaries, 24 February 1885

He sank into drowsiness. Perhaps the cold, or the dampness, or the dark, or the wind that howled under the window and tossed the trees roused a sort of persistent craving for the fantastic. He kept dwelling on images of flowers, he fancied a charming flower garden, a bright, warm, almost hot day, a holiday – Trinity day. A fine, sumptuous country cottage in the English taste overgrown with fragrant flowers, with flower beds going round the house; the porch, wreathed in climbers, was surrounded with beds of roses. . . . He went up the stairs and came into a large, high drawing-room and again everywhere – at the windows, the doors on to the balcony, and on the balcony itself – were flowers. . . . In the middle of the room, on a table covered with a white satin shroud, stood a coffin. The coffin was covered with white silk and edged with a thick white frill; wreaths of flowers surrounded it on all sides. Among the flowers lay a girl in a white muslin dress, with her arms crossed and pressed on her bosom, as though carved out of marble. But her loose fair hair was wet; there was a wreath of roses on her head. The stern and already rigid profile of her face looked as though chiselled of marble too, and the smile on her pale lips was full of an immense unchildish misery and sorrowful appeal. Svidrigailov knew that girl; there was no holy image, no burning candle beside the coffin; no sound of prayers: the girl had drowned herself. She was only fourteen, but her heart was broken. And she had destroyed herself, crushed by an insult that had appalled and amazed that childish soul, had smirched that angel purity with unmerited disgrace and torn from her a last scream of despair, unheeded and brutally disregarded, on a dark night in the cold and wet while the wind howled. . . .

Svidrigailov came to himself, got up from the bed and went to the window.

FYODOR DOSTOEVSKY, *Crime and Punishment*, 1866

The sight of the dead indicates the ruin of affairs.

ASTRAMPSYCHUS, *The Oneirocriticon*, c.AD 350

Saturday night I dreamed that I was dead, and afterwards my bowels were taken out and I walked and talked with diverse, and among other with the Lord Treasurer who was come to my house to burn my books when I was dead, and thought he looked sourly on me.

JOHN DEE, *Diary*, 24 November 1582

I was in Germany, and because some German friend was going to poison himself, agreed to poison myself to keep him company. Accordingly, in a large party I first drank to him 'to our next meeting,' then let him put the poison into my next glass, unperceived by anyone. It was a brown powder which by no means improved the wine. Presently we were both seized with violent pains in the stomach, and both fell; I suppose by the pain which I actually felt that I must have been plagued with flatulence at the time. We were each laid upon a bed to die there, and not one of the company, though they now knew what had happened, went for any assistance; it seemed to be a matter of etiquette to let us die if we chose it. Now for my part, though I was perfectly well satisfied to go upon a voyage of discovery to the next world, yet it certainly would not have displeased me to have had the physician sent for. My pain, however, abated and got into the abdomen. I went to my friend and told him this, and that I suspected the dose would not do its work. He said he was in the last agonies, and so should I be presently; but, however, it all went off.

ROBERT SOUTHEY, 23 January 1806

I dreamed that I had died (though, somehow, I was not myself, but had become more or less identified with an ugly old woman), and was being autopsied. Then very gradually I became faintly and peacefully conscious of what was going on, though I remained motionless, and all the time believed that I was dead, and that my faint consciousness was merely a part of death. Preparations for the funeral were meanwhile being made, and I was about to be nailed down in my coffin. At this point I became horribly aware that these proceedings would cause suffocation, and, with great effort, I succeeded in moving my arms and speaking incoherently. There-upon the funeral arrangements were discontinued, and very slowly I seemed to regain speech and the power of movement. But I felt that I must be extremely careful in making any movements, on account of the post-mortem wounds; especially I felt pain in my neck, and realised that it was necessary not to move my head, or the result might be instant death.

HAVELOCK ELLIS, *The World of Dreams*, 1911

> Shivering in fever, weak, and parched to sand,
> My ears, those entrances of word-dressed thoughts,
> My pictured eyes, and my assuring touch,
> Fell from me, and my body turned me forth
> From its beloved abode: then I was dead,
> And in my grave beside my corpse I sat,
> In vain attempting to return: meantime
> There came the untimely spectres of two babes,
> And played in my abandoned body's ruins;
> They went away; and, one by one, by snakes
> My limbs were swallowed; and, at last, I sat
> With only one, blue-eyed, curled round my ribs,
> Eating the last remainder of my heart,
> And hissing to himself. O sleep, thou fiend!
> Thou blackness of the night! how sad and frightful
> Are these thy dreams!

THOMAS LOVELL BEDDOES, 'Dream of Dying', 1823-5

'I have been sent a dream . . .' he said slowly, at last.

'What did you say?' my mother interrupted.

'A dream,' he repeated. 'I have the gift of seeing things in dreams, you know!'

'You?'

'Yes, I. Didn't you know?' Kharlov sighed. 'Well, then, . . . I was having a nap, ma'am, a week ago and more, right on the eve of St.

Peter's fast; I lay down after dinner for a little rest, and I fell asleep; and I dreamed that a black foal came running into my room. And this same foal began kicking up its heels and showing its teeth. A foal as black as a beetle.'

Kharlov stopped speaking.

'Well?' said my mother.

'And all of a sudden this foal turned round and gave me a kick on the left elbow, right on the point! I woke up: and I really couldn't move my arm, or my left leg either. Well, I thought it was paralysis; but I massaged it a bit, and then I could move it again; but I had pins and needles in my joints for a long time, and I still have them. When I open my hand they begin again.'

'Why, Martyn Petrovich, you must have been lying on your arm somehow.'

'No, ma'am, you are mistaken! It was a warning to me. . . . Of my death, I mean.'

IVAN TURGENEV, A Lear of the Steppes, 1870

> Then, ere that last weird battle in the west,
> There came on Arthur sleeping, Gawain killed
> In Lancelot's war, the ghost of Gawain blown
> Along a wandering wind, and past his ear
> Went shrilling, 'Hollow, hollow all delight!
> Hail, King! tomorrow thou shalt pass away.
> Farewell! there is an isle of rest for thee.
> And I am blown along a wandering wind,
> And hollow, hollow, hollow all delight.'
> And fainter onward, like wild birds that change
> Their season in the night and wail their way
> From cloud to cloud, down the long wind the dream
> Shrilled; but in going mingled with dim cries
> Far in the moonlit haze among the hills,
> As of some lonely city sacked by night,
> When all is lost, and wife and child with wail
> Pass to new lords; and Arthur woke and called,
> 'Who spake? A dream. O light upon the wind,
> Thine, Gawain, was the voice — are these dim cries
> Thine? or doth all that haunts the waste and wild
> Mourn, knowing it will go along with me?'

ALFRED, LORD TENNYSON, Idylls of the King: The Passing of Arthur, 1869

One evening, at about midnight, I was returning to the quarter where I lived, when I happened to raise my eyes and notice the number on a house, lit by a street-lamp. The number was that of my own age. As I looked down I saw in front of me a woman with hollow eyes, whose features seemed to me like Aurélia's. I said to myself: 'I am being warned of either her death or mine.' For some reason I decided on the latter of the two ideas, and had the impression that it would come about at the same time on the following day.

That night I had a dream which confirmed me in my belief.

I was wandering about a vast building composed of several rooms, some of which were given up to study, others to conversation or philosophical discussion. Rather interested I remained in one of the first of these, and thought I recognized my old instructors and fellow-students. The lessons on Greek and Latin authors went on in that steady hum which sounds like a prayer to the goddess Mnemosyne. I passed on into another room where the philosophical discussions were taking place. I took part in one for a while, then went to look for my own room in a sort of inn with gigantic staircases crowded with hurrying travellers.

I got lost several times in the long corridors and then, as I was going through one of the central galleries, I was struck by a strange sight. A creature of enormous proportions – man or woman I do not know – was fluttering painfully through the air and seemed to be struggling with heavy clouds. At last, out of breath and at the end of its strength, it collapsed into the middle of the dark courtyard, catching and crumpling its wings on the roofs and balustrades. For a moment I was able to observe it closely. It was colored with ruddy hues and its wings glittered with a myriad changing reflections. Clad in a long gown of antique folds, it looked like Dürer's *Angel of Melancholy*. I could not keep myself from crying out in terror and this woke me up with a start.

The next day I hurried to see all my friends. Mentally I said farewell to them and, telling them nothing of what was in my mind, I talked warmly on mystical matters. I surprised them by being particularly eloquent. It seemed to me as if I knew everything and that in those last moments of mine the mysteries of the world were being revealed to me.

GÉRARD DE NERVAL, *Aurélia*, 1855

I dreamed that my wife's bed was a deep pit with stone walls. It was a grave, and somehow had a suggestion of classical antiquity about it. Then I heard a deep sigh, as if someone were giving up the ghost. A figure that resembled my wife sat up in the pit and floated upwards. It wore a white gown into which curious black symbols were woven. I awoke, roused my wife, and checked the time. It was three o'clock in the morning. The dream was so curious that I thought at once that it might signify a death. At seven o'clock came the news that a cousin of my wife had died at three o'clock in the morning.

c. g. jung, *Memories, Dreams, Reflections,* 1963

My bed took it upon itself to continue the train of thought that night. It carried me away, like the enchanted carpet, to a distant place (though still in England), and there, alighting from a stage-coach at another Inn in the snow, as I had actually done some years before, I repeated in my sleep a curious experience I had really had here. More than a year before I made the journey in the course of which I put up at that Inn, I had lost a very near and dear friend by death. Every night since, at home or away from home, I had dreamed of that friend; sometimes as still living; sometimes as returning from the world of shadows to comfort me; always as being beautiful, placid, and happy, never in association with any approach to fear or distress. It was at a lonely Inn in a wide moorland place, that I halted to pass the night. When I had looked from my bedroom window over the waste of snow on which the moon was shining, I sat down by my fire to write a letter. I had always, until that hour, kept it within my own breast that I dreamed every night of the dear lost one. But in the letter that I wrote I recorded the circumstance, and added that I felt much interested in proving whether the subject of my dream would still be faithful to me, travel-tired, and in that remote place. No. I lost the beloved figure of my vision in parting with the secret. My sleep has never looked upon it since, in sixteen years, but once. I was in Italy, and awoke (or seemed to awake), the well-remembered voice distinctly in my ears, conversing with it. I entreated it, as it rose above my bed and soared up to the vaulted roof of the old room, to answer me a question I had asked touching the Future Life. My hands were still outstretched towards it as it vanished, when I heard a bell ringing by the garden wall, and a voice in the deep stillness of the night calling on all good Christians to pray for the souls of the dead; it being All Souls' Eve.

charles dickens, 'The Holly-Tree Inn', 1855

Of him I love day and night I dream'd I heard he was dead,
And I dream'd I went where they had buried him I love, but he was
   not in that place,
And I dream'd I wander'd searching among burial-places to find
   him,
And I found that every place was a burial-place;
The houses full of life were equally full of death, (this house is now,)
The streets, the shipping, the places of amusement, the Chicago,
   Boston, Philadelphia, the Mannahatta, were as full of the dead as
   of the living,
And fuller, O vastly fuller of the dead than of the living;
And what I dream'd I will henceforth tell to every person and age,
And I stand henceforth bound to what I dream'd,
And now I am willing to disregard burial-places and dispense with
   them,
And if the memorials of the dead were put up indifferently
   everywhere, even in the room where I eat or sleep, I should be
   satisfied,
And if the corpse of any one I love, or if my own corpse, be duly
   render'd to powder and pour'd in the sea, I shall be satisfied,
Or if it be distributed to the winds I shall be satisfied.

WALT WHITMAN, 'Of Him I Love Day and Night', 1860

I dreamt of Jules for the first time last night. He was just as I am, in
deep mourning for himself – and he was with me. We were walking
down a street which vaguely resembled the rue Richelieu, and I had a
feeling that we were taking a play to a director of some theatre or
other. On the way there we ran into some friends, among whom was
Théophile Gautier. The first reaction of them all was to come up and
offer me condolences. We were suddenly interrupted by an
unexpected glimpse of my brother, who, as was his habit, was
walking in my dream, behind me. And I felt searing doubt, torn
between the certainty that he was alive, borne out by his presence
beside me, and the certainty that he was dead, for I recalled instantly
my distinct memory of the announcements of his death still spread
out on the billiard table.

EDMOND DE GONCOURT, *Journal*, 27 July 1870

    I dream that the dearest I ever knew
       Has died and been entombed.
    I am sure it's a dream that cannot be true,

But I am so overgloomed
By its persistence, that I would gladly
  Have quick death take me,
Rather than longer think thus sadly;
  So wake me, wake me!

It has lasted days, but minute and hour
  I expect to get aroused
And find him as usual in the bower
  Where we so happily housed.
Yet stays this nightmare too appalling,
  And like a web shakes me,
And piteously I keep on calling,
  And no one wakes me!

THOMAS HARDY, 'Bereft, She Thinks She Dreams', 1914

In a dream an angel appeared before me, saying 'Arise, and follow me.'

'Whither will you lead me in this darkness?' I asked, and received the reply: 'Come, I will reveal to you human existence in its true reality.'

Full of foreboding, I followed my guide and we descended a number of steep steps; and rocks towered above us like gigantic arches, while spread before us lay a vast city of death with horrible remnants and tokens of mortality and transient existence – a perished grandeur, an immense, sunken world of corpses, death's silent subjects. Over all hovered a withered, ghastly twilight that enveloped churchyards, graves and sepulchres. In a stronger light row upon row of white skeletons reflected a phosphorescent glow. A fear seized me as I stood by the angel's side.

'Here, you see, all is vanity,' he said.

Then came a roar like that which heralds a storm, which grew to a raging hurricane so that the dead moved and stretched their arms towards me, and with a cry I awoke wet from the cold night-dew.

HENRIK IBSEN, quoted in R. L. Mégroz, *The Dream World*, 1939

The first night I was in bed here, i.e. after my first day in bed, I went to sleep. And suddenly I felt my whole body *breaking up*. It broke up with a violent shock – an earthquake – and it broke like glass. A long terrible shiver, you understand – and the spinal cord and the bones and every bit and particle quaking. It sounded in my ears — a low, confused din, and there was a sense of flashing greenish brilliance, like broken glass. When I woke up I thought there had been a violent earthquake. But all was still. It slowly dawned upon me — the conviction that in that dream I died. I shall go on living now — it may be for months, or for weeks or days or hours. Time is not. In that dream I died.

KATHERINE MANSFIELD, *Letters and Journals*, 15 December 1919

The dream which Pedro Henríquez Ureña dreamed close to dawn one day in 1946 consisted, oddly enough, not of images but of slow, specific words. The voice which spoke them was not his own, but resembled it. Its tone, in spite of the mournful possibilities implicit in what it said, was impersonal and matter-of-fact. During the dream, which was short, Pedro knew that he was asleep in his own room, with his wife at his side. In the dark, the dream addressed him:

Some nights ago, on a corner of the Calle Córdoba, you discussed with Borges the invocation of the Anonymous One of Seville: 'O Death come in silence as you are wont to do in the hands of the clock.' You both suspected it to be the deliberate echo of some Latin text, inasmuch as these transliterations corresponded with the habits of a particular time, totally outside our own notions of plagiarism, unquestionably less literary than practical. What you did not suspect, what you could not suspect, is that the dialogue was a prophetic one. In a few hours, you will be hurrying along the last platform of Constitution Station, to give your class at the University of La Plata. You will catch the train, put your briefcase on the rack and settle in your seat, beside the window. Someone, whose name I do not know but whose face I am seeing, will address some words to you. You will not reply, because you will be dead. You will already have said goodbye, as usual, to your wife and children. You will not remember this dream, because your forgetting is necessary to the fulfilment of these events.

JORGE LUIS BORGES, 'The Dream of Pedro Henríquez Ureña', 1975

This August I began to dream of drowning. The dying
went on and on in water as white and clear
as the gin I drink each day at half-past five.
Going down for the last time, the last breath lying,

I grapple with eels like ropes — it's ether, it's queer
and then, at last, it's done. Now the scavengers arrive,
the hard crawlers who come to clean up the ocean floor.
And death, that old butcher, will bother me no more.

ANNE SEXTON, from 'Imitations of Drowning', 1966

I suddenly found myself in a room which formed part of my grandfather's house, only it seemed to have grown larger. . . . Three women were working in the room and, without exactly resembling them, they stood for relatives and friends of my youth. Each seemed to have the features of several of them. Their facial contours changed like the flames of a lamp, and all the time something of one was passing to the other. Their smiles, the color of their eyes and hair, their figures and familiar gestures, all these were exchanged as if they had lived the same life, and each was made up of all three, like those figures painters take from a number of models in order to achieve a perfect beauty.

The eldest spoke to me in a vibrant, melodious voice which I recognized as having heard in my childhood, and whatever it was she said struck me as being profoundly true. But she drew my attention to myself and I saw I was wearing a little old-fashioned brown suit, entirely made of needlework threads as fine as a spider's web. It was elegant, graceful, and gently perfumed. I felt quite rejuvenated and most spruce in this garment which their fairy fingers had made, and I blushingly thanked them as if I had been a small boy in the presence of beautiful grown-up ladies. At that moment one of them got up and went towards the garden.

It is a well-known fact that no one ever sees the sun in a dream, although one is often aware of some far brighter light. Material objects and human bodies are illumined through their own agencies. Now I was in a little park through which ran long vine arbors, loaded with heavy clusters of black and white grapes; and as the lady, guiding me, passed beneath these arbors, the shadows of the intertwined trellis-work changed her figure and her clothes. At last we came out from these bowers of grapes to an open space. Traces of the old paths which had once divided it cross-wise were just visible. For some years the plants had been neglected and the sparse patches of clematis, hops and honeysuckle, of jasmine, ivy, and creepers, had stretched their long clinging tendrils between the sturdy growths of the trees. . . .

The lady I was following stretched her slender figure in a

movement that made the folds of her dress of shot taffeta shimmer, and gracefully she slid her bare arm about the stem of a hollyhock. Then, in a clear shaft of light, she began to grow in such a way that gradually the whole garden blended with her own form, and the flowerbeds and trees became the patterns and flounces of her clothes, while her face and arms imprinted their contours on the rosy clouds in the sky. I lost her thus as she became transfigured, for she seemed to vanish in her own immensity.

'Don't leave me!' I cried. 'For with you Nature itself dies.'

With these words I struggled painfully through the brambles trying to grasp the vast shadow that eluded me. I threw myself on a fragment of ruined wall, at the foot of which lay the marble bust of a woman. I lifted it up and felt convinced it was of *her* . . . I recognized the beloved features and as I stared around me I saw that the garden had become a graveyard, and I heard voices crying: 'The universe is in darkness.'

This dream, which began so happily, perplexed me deeply, for I did not discover what it meant until much later. Aurélia was dead.

GÉRARD DE NERVAL, *Aurélia*, 1855

Sleep never came!

I err. She came once, but in anger. Impatient of my importunity she brought with her an avenging dream. By the clock of St Jean Baptiste, that dream remained scarce fifteen minutes – a brief space, but sufficing to wring my whole frame with unknown anguish; to confer a nameless experience that had the hue, the mien, the terror, the very tone of a visitation from eternity. Between twelve and one that night a cup was forced to my lips, black, strong, strange, drawn from no well, but filled up seething from a bottomless and boundless sea. Suffering, brewed in temporal or calculable measure, and mixed for mortal lips, tastes not as this suffering tasted. Having drank and woke, I thought all was over: the end come and past by. Trembling fearfully – as consciousness returned – ready to cry out on some fellow creature to help me, only that I knew no fellow creature was near enough to catch the wild summons – Goton in her far distant attic could not hear – I rose on my knees in bed. Some fearful hours went over me: indescribably was I torn, racked and oppressed in mind. Amidst the horrors of that dream I think the worst lay here. Methought the well-loved dead, who had loved *me* well in life, met me elsewhere, alienated: galled was my inmost spirit with an unutterable sense of despair about the future. Motive there was none why I should try to recover or wish to live; and yet quite unendurable was the pitiless and haughty voice in which Death challenged me to engage his unknown terrors. When I tried to pray I could only utter these words: 'From my youth up Thy terrors have I suffered with a troubled mind.'

Most true was it.

CHARLOTTE BRONTË, *Villette*, 1853

When I awoke again, I was a baby-ape in Bornean forests, perched among fragrant trailers and fantastic orchis flowers; and as I looked down, beneath the green roof, into the clear waters paved with unknown water-lilies on which the sun had never shone, I saw my face reflected in the pool – a melancholy, thoughtful countenance, with large projecting brow – it might have been a negro child's. And I felt stirring in me, germs of a new and higher consciousness – yearnings of love towards the mother ape, who fed me and carried me from tree to tree. But I grew and grew; and then the weight of my destiny fell upon me. I saw year by year my brow recede, my neck enlarge, my jaw protrude; my teeth became tusks; skinny wattles grew from my cheeks – the animal faculties in me were swallowing up the intellectual. I watched in myself, with stupid self-disgust, the fearful degradation which goes on from youth to age in all the monkey race, especially in those which approach nearest to the human form. Long melancholy mopings, fruitless strugglings to think, were periodically succeeded by wild frenzies, agonies of lust and aimless ferocity. I flew upon my brother apes, and was driven off with wounds. I rushed howling down into the village gardens, destroying everything I met. I caught the birds and insects, and tore them to pieces with savage glee. One day, as I sat among the boughs, I saw Lillian coming along a flowery path – decked as Eve might have been, the day she turned from Paradise. The skins of gorgeous birds were round her waist; her hair was wreathed with fragrant tropic flowers. On her bosom lay a baby – it was my cousin's. I knew her, and hated her. The madness came upon me. I longed to leap from the bough and tear her limb from limb; but brutal terror, the dread of man which is the doom of beasts, kept me rooted to my place. Then my cousin came – a hunter missionary; and I heard him talk to her with pride of the new world of civilisation and Christianity which he was organising in that tropic wilderness. I listened with a dim jealous understanding – not of the words, but of the facts. I saw them instinctively, as in a dream. She pointed up to me in terror and disgust, as I sat gnashing and gibbering overhead. He threw up the muzzle of his rifle carelessly, and fired – I fell dead, but conscious still. I knew that my carcase was carried to the settlement; and I watched while a smirking, chuckling surgeon dissected me, bone by bone, and nerve by nerve. And as he was fingering at my heart . . . Eleanor glided by again, like an angel, and drew my soul out of the knot of nerves, with one velvet finger-tip.

CHARLES KINGSLEY, *Alton Locke*, 1850

I dreamed that somebody was dead. I don't know who, but it's not to the purpose. It was a private gentleman, and a particular friend; and I was greatly overcome when the news was broken to me (very delicately) by a gentleman in a cocked hat, top boots, and a sheet. Nothing else. 'Good God!' I said, 'is he dead?' 'He is dead, sir,' rejoined the gentleman, 'as a door-nail. But we must all die, Mr. Dickens, sooner or later, my dear sir.' 'Ah!' I said, 'Yes, to be sure. Very true. But what did he die of?' The gentleman burst into a flood of tears, and said, in a voice broken by emotion, 'He christened his youngest child, sir, with a toasting-fork.' I never in my life was so affected as at his having fallen a victim to this complaint. It carried a conviction to my mind that he never could have recovered. I knew that it was the most interesting and fatal malady in the world; and I wrung the gentleman's hand in a convulsion of respectful admiration, for I felt that this explanation did equal honour to his head and heart.

CHARLES DICKENS, letter to C. C. Felton, 1 September 1843

I had a dream. A wondrous thing:
It seem'd an evening in the Spring:
– A little sickness in the air
From too much fragrance everywhere: –
As I walk'd a stilly wood,
Sudden, Death before me stood:
In a hollow lush and damp,
He seem'd a dismal mirky stamp
On the flowers that were seen
His charnelhouse-grate ribs between,
And with coffin-black he barr'd the green.
'Death,' said I, 'what do you here
At this Spring season of the year?'

'I mark the flowers ere the prime
Which I may tell at Autumn-time.'
Ere I had further questions made
Death was vanish'd from the glade.
Then I saw that he had bound
Many trees and flowers round
With a subtle web of black,
And that such a sable track
Lay along the grasses green
From the spot where he had been.

   But the Spring-tide pass'd the same;
Summer was as full of flame;
Autumn-time no earlier came.
And the flowers that he had tied,
As I mark'd not always died
Sooner than their mates; and yet
Their fall was fuller of regret:
   It seem'd so hard and dismal thing,
Death, to mark them in the Spring.

GERARD MANLEY HOPKINS, 'Spring and Death', *c*.1865

It was during the winter of 1930–1931, while I was at Rishikesh. In the dream I saw myself go down toward the Ganges, where a boat I knew very well was waiting for me to take me to the other side. But once in the boat, I no longer recognized it. It was much bigger than the one I knew. Tied up along its side was another boat, which I hadn't noticed at first, and of which I could make out neither the shape nor the dimensions. Almost without realizing it, I went from my boat to this other mysterious boat. And suddenly, *I understood*: everything became extraordinarily clear and simple. Everything: life, death, the meaning of existence. And even stronger than this revelation was my surprise: how had *no one* on earth yet understood this thing, *so extraordinarily simple*? Death, that was the extraordinarily simple and *obvious* thing. While getting into that boat, I said to myself: It's unbelievable that no one has yet seen it when it's so obvious. And all of a sudden I had the feeling that a message had been transmitted to me, that I should certainly remember in what the obviousness and simplicity of this beyondness of death consisted, so as to be able to communicate it to men. I woke up . . . with this idea in mind: not to forget what I had seen. A second later, I had forgotten.

MIRCEA ELIADE, *No Souvenirs*, 20 July 1961

Presently I thought that I found myself naked, and laid at length in the niche of a catacomb, among the dust of the dead, which resembled damp snuff, or moistened bark, in colour and consistency. What was worse, I was clasped in the arms of a living skeleton, which endeavoured to break in my ribs by its grasp. Grief is as intense in dreams as in reality, but we can bear horrors in sleep which would certainly deprive us of our waking senses, if not of life. I struggled with the body of this Death, and at the same time called for help. The sexton heard my cries, for I heard him approaching to ascertain the cause. This made the skeleton renew his efforts to crush my bones, while I worked upon his with the same intent. My attempts to cry aloud disturbed Edith, and she awoke me from this singularly frightful dream, which left me with a sensation in both sides, as if they had been bruised.

ROBERT SOUTHEY, 5 October 1823

Piet dreamed . . . that he was in an airplane, a big new jet. The appointments, in beige and aqua, of the immense tubular interior were vivid to his eyes, though he had never ridden in such a plane. . . . The luxurious plane of his dream was gliding as if motionless through the sky; the backs of heads and hands receded tranquilly down the length of aqua-carpeted aisle. The pilot's voice . . . jubilantly announced over the loudspeaking system, 'I think we've slipped it, folks!' and through his little rubber-sealed porthole Piet saw a wall of gray cloud, tendrilous and writhing, slowly drift backward, revealing blue sky. They had evaded a storm. Then the plane rocked and jerked in the bumpy air currents; it sank flatly through a gap in atmosphere, grabbed for something, missed, slipped, and tilted. The angle of tilt increased; the plane began to plunge. The huge hull rushed toward the earth. The delicately engineered details – the luminous stenciled seat numbers, the chrome rivets holding the tinted head napkins – stayed weirdly static amid the rising scream of the dive. Far down the aisle, a stewardess, her ginger hair in a high stiff coiffure, gripped the seats for support, and the curtains hiding the first-class section billowed. Otherwise there was no acknowledgment of the horror, no outcry. Piet thought, *The waste.* Such ingenious fragility utterly betrayed. The cost. The plane streamed straight down. The liquid in Piet's inner ear surged, froze. He knew there could be no pulling from this dive and awoke in darkness, convinced of his death.

JOHN UPDIKE, *Couples*, 1968

He thought that he, and some one on whom his heart had long been set . . . stood in the church being married. While the ceremony was performing, and while he recognized among the witnesses some whom he knew to be living, and many whom he knew to be dead, darkness came on, succeeded by the shining of a tremendous light. It broke from one line in the table of commandments at the altar, and illuminated the building with the words. They were sounded through the church, too, as if there were voices in the fiery letters. Upon this, the whole appearance before him and around him changed, and nothing was left as it had been, but himself and the clergyman. They stood in the daylight before a crowd so vast, that if all the people in the world could have been brought together into one space, they could not have looked, he thought, more numerous; and they all abhorred him, and there was not one pitying or friendly eye among the millions that were fastened on his face. He stood on a raised stage, under his own loom; and, looking up at the shape the loom took, and hearing the burial service distinctly read, he knew that he was there to suffer death. In an instant what he stood on fell below him, and he was gone.

CHARLES DICKENS, Hard Times, 1854

He dreamt that he was lying in the room he really was in, but that he was quite well and unwounded. Many various indifferent and insignificant people appeared before him. He talked to them, and discussed something trivial. They were preparing to go away somewhere. Prince Andrew dimly realized that all this was trivial and that he had more important cares, but he continued to speak, surprising them by empty witticisms. Gradually, unnoticed, all these persons began to disappear and a single question, that of the closed door, superseded all else. He rose and went to the door to bolt and lock it. Everything depended on whether he was, or was not, in time to lock it. He went, and tried to hurry, but his legs refused to move and he knew he would not be in time to lock the door though he painfully strained all his powers. He was seized by an agonizing fear. And that fear was the fear of death. *It* stood behind the door. But just when he was clumsily creeping towards the door, that dreadful something on the other side was already pressing against it and forcing its way in. Something not human – death – was breaking in through that door and had to be kept out. He seized the door, making a final effort to hold it back – to lock it was no longer possible – but his efforts were weak and clumsy and the door, pushed from behind by that terror, opened and closed again.

Once again *it* pushed from outside. His last superhuman efforts were vain and both halves of the door noiselessly opened. *It* entered, and it was *death*, and Prince Andrew died.

But at the instant he died, Prince Andrew remembered that he was asleep, and at the very instant he died, having made an effort, he awoke.

LEO TOLSTOY, *War and Peace*, 1865–9

II

EARTHLY THINGS

Food

There is an art to make dreams as well as their interpretations, and physicians will tell us that some food makes turbulent, some gives quiet dreams. Cato who doated upon cabbage might find the crude effects thereof in his sleep; wherein the Egyptians might find some advantage by their superstitious abstinence from onions. Pythagoras might have more calmer sleeps if he totally abstained from beans. Even Daniel, that great interpreter of dreams, in his leguminous diet seems to have chosen no advantageous food for quiet sleeps according to Grecian physick.

SIR THOMAS BROWNE, 'On Dreams', c.1650

To see white meats is exceedingly advantageous.
To see black meats forebodes evil to one's children.

ASTRAMPSYCHUS, *The Oneirocriticon*, c.AD 350

[*King Gormr has three dreams prophetic of nine years of famine.*]

He dreamed that he was outside and was looking over all his kingdom. He saw that the sea had ebbed so far from land that his eye could not reach it, and that the tidal flats were so great that all the straits between the islands and the firths were dry. Next he saw that three white oxen came from the sea and ran up on to the land close to where he was, and ate all the grass down to the ground wherever they went. After that they went away.

The second dream, which was much like this, was that it again seemed to him that three oxen came up out of the sea. They were red and had large horns. They cropped the grass down to the ground as had the former ones; when they had been there for some time they went back into the sea.

He dreamed yet a third dream, and this was again like the others. The king once more saw three oxen come up out of the sea. They were all black, and with much the largest horns; they stayed a while, and left in the same way, and went back into the sea. After that he heard a crash so great that he felt that it must be heard over all Denmark; he saw that it was made by the sea as it drove against the shore.

Jomsvikinga Saga, c.AD 900

All dreams, as in old Gallen I have read,
Are from repletion and complexion bred:
From rising fumes of indigested food,
And noxious humours that infect the blood.

JOHN DRYDEN, from 'The Cock and the Fox', 1700

Three companions, of whom two were Tradesmen and Townsmen, and the third a Villager, on the score of devotion, went on pilgrimage to a noted sanctuary; and as they went on their way, their provision began to fail them, insomuch that they had nothing to eat, but a little flour, barely sufficient to make of it a very small loaf of bread. The tricking townsmen seeing this, said between themselves, we have but little bread, and this companion of ours is a great eater; on which account it is necessary we should think how we may eat this little bread without him. When they had made it and set it to bake, the tradesmen seeing in what manner to cheat the countryman, said: let us all sleep, and let him that shall have the most marvellous dream betwixt all three of us, eat the bread. This bargain being agreed upon, and settled between them, they laid down to sleep. The countryman, discovering the trick of his companions, drew out the bread half baked, eat it by himself, and turned again to sleep. In a while, one of the tradesmen, as frightened by a marvellous dream, began to get up, and was asked by his companion, why he was so frightened? he answered, I am frightened and dreadfully surprized by a marvellous dream: it seemed to me that two Angels, opening the gates of Heaven, carried me before the throne of God with great joy: his companion said: this is a marvellous dream, but I have seen another more marvellous, for I saw two Angels, who carried me over the earth to Hell. The countryman hearing this, made as if he slept; but the townsmen, desirous to finish their trick, awoke him; and the countryman, artfully as one surprized, answered: Who are these that call me? They told him, we are thy companions. He asked them: How did you return? They answered: We never went hence; why d'ye talk of our return? The countryman replied: It appeared to me that two Angels, opening the gates of Heaven, carried one of you before our Lord God, and dragged the other over the earth to Hell, and I thought you never would return hither, as I have never heard that any had returned from Paradise, nor from Hell, and so I arose and eat the bread by myself.

JUAN DE LUNA, *Life of Lazarillo de Tormes*, 1620

A diviner was consulted by a man who had dreamed that he saw an egg hanging from the bed-cords of the bed in his sleeping-room – the story is from Chrysippus' *On Dreams* – and the diviner answered, 'A treasure is buried under your bed.' The man dug, found a quantity of gold surrounded with silver and sent the diviner as much of the silver as he thought fit. The diviner then inquired, 'Do I get none of the yolk?' For, in his view, the yolk meant gold, the white of the egg, silver. Now, did no one else ever dream of an egg? If so, then why did this fellow, whoever he was, alone find a treasure by dreaming of an egg? What a lot of poor devils there are, deserving of divine assistance, who never were instructed by a dream how to find a treasure! Furthermore, why was this man given so obscure an intimation as that contained in the fancied resemblance between an egg and a treasure, instead of being as plainly directed as Simonides was when he was bidden not to go on board the ship? My conclusion is that obscure messages by means of dreams are utterly inconsistent with the dignity of the gods.

CICERO, *De Divinatione*, Book II, *c.* 70 BC

Dreamed of being in a great passion in the kitchen about a stale egg, afterwards the servant thinking I had gone crazy again. Then, of my father, and his introducing me to the sweetest and prettiest girl I ever dreamed of.

JOHN RUSKIN, *Brantwood Diary*, 23 August 1883

To hold eggs, or to eat eggs, symbolizes vexation.

ASTRAMPSYCHUS, *The Oneirocriticon*, c.AD 350

'What were you discussing with him?'
'It is not a discussion.'
'Talking about, then. Had he had any good dreams? I think Magnus has quite the most original dreams of your patients.'
'He dreamt he was an egg.'
'An egg?'
'He was a huge white egg floating in a sea of turquoise blue, and he was everything that there was.'
'It sounds a nice dream.'
'No dream is nice for Magnus. All dream experiences fill him with terror. He now feels that all his limbs are withdrawing inside his

body and his face is flattening out and his features are disappearing. He keeps looking in the mirror to make sure his nose hasn't vanished.'. . .

'Poor thing. What does the dream mean?'

'Fear of castration.'

'What a pity. It sounds so beautiful,' said Harriet. 'It's a painter's dream.' She pictured the great white egg, tinged a little with ivory, floating in the deeply saturated turquoise ocean. She saw it clearly in her mind, and the image soothed her.

'It's connected with his compulsive eating. . .'

IRIS MURDOCH, The Sacred and Profane Love Machine, 1974

Vodka gives one marvellous dreams I have discovered, but prevents one from sleeping. Every night lately I have dreamed luxuriously but slept ill.

EVELYN WAUGH, Diaries, 18 October 1925

Musty wine announces many difficulties.
To swallow bunches of grapes indicates a deluge of rain.
To feed on lettuces is a sign of disease of the body.

ASTRAMPSYCHUS, The Oneirocriticon, c.AD 350

It was the hour of night, when thus the Son
Commun'd in silent walk, then laid him down
Under the hospitable covert nigh
Of trees thick interwoven; there he slept,
And dream'd, as appetite is wont to dream,
Of meats and drinks, nature's refreshment sweet;
Him thought, he by the brook of Cherith stood
And saw the ravens with their horny beaks
Food to Elijah bringing ev'n and morn,
Though ravenous, taught to abstain from what they brought:
He saw the Prophet also how he fled
Into the desert, and how there he slept
Under a juniper; then how awak't,
He found his supper on the coals prepar'd,
And by the angel was bid rise and eat,
And eat the second time after repose,
The strength whereof suffic'd him forty days;

Sometimes that with Elijah he partook,
Or as a guest with Daniel at his pulse.
Thus wore out night, and now the herald lark
Left his ground-nest, high tow'ring to descry
The morn's approach, and greet her with his song:
As lightly from his grassy couch up rose
Our Saviour, and found all was but a dream;
Fasting he went to sleep, and fasting wak'd.

JOHN MILTON, *Paradise Regain'd*, Book II, 1671

I dreamt last night that I was at an entertainment given by Mr Coke at his house, amongst other dishes there was a faun roasted but cold, and plenty of hares roasted, and cold also, etc. Mr Coke very civil to me, on coming away I lost my hat, someone had taken it, and I thought a soldier. I thought however that I bought a second-hand one of old Mr Corbould, with many other things, all forgot.

JAMES WOODFORDE, *The Diary of a Country Parson*, 12 September 1796

I was at an inn at some watering-place with two or three people. . . . The landlady brought in a tray with drinks. For some reason or other, she knew I would not take what the others were taking, so she had brought me a glass of clear blackish brown fluid (like the water from a shingle roof in Australia, but darker) which she said was the speciality of the inn, and called 'tuccotine'. I took a mouthful of it and choked – not that I thought it exactly nasty, though it wanted sugar. What is a little remarkable is that I woke immediately after *with the clear impression of having invented a taste.*

WILLIAM ARCHER, *On Dreams*, 24–25 January 1917

Dreamed of a wonderful pie made of blackberries, thrushes' eggs, honeycomb and watercress.

HUGH WALPOLE, 1940, quoted in Rupert Hart-Davis, *Hugh Walpole: A Biography*, 1952

I shift my glance into the future of my children and can see my past. I am what I have been. I incorporate already what I am going to become. They inform me like highway markers. And here is another dream I imagine as I see myself hunched over the smoking, roasted turkey with my bone-handled carving knife, poised for severing, after separating the second joints, that first dramatic slice of white meat from the breast while they all watch and wait silently in high-backed chairs like skeptical shadows, unbreathing: they're mine. I own them. They belong to me. I'm in command (and hope the white meat will be toothsome and the dark meat juicy). Now we are frozen again and do not move. (Get the picture?) We cannot move. I stand over my turkey; they sit rigid. And I feel weirdly in that arrested dumb show in which we are all momentarily statues that even if I'd never had them, had never married, sired children, had parents, I would have had them with me anyway. . . . They wait like stumps. They sit like ruins in a coffin in their high-backed chairs. The turkey's carved; white meat, dark meat, second joints, wings, and legs lie laid out neatly like tools on a dentist's tray or surgical instruments of an ear-nose-and-throat man about to remove tonsils. But the platter's not been passed. There are spiced apples, chilled cranberry molds, and imported currant jams. It's a gelid feast, a scene of domesticity chiseled on cold and rotting stone. I'm in control, but there's not much I can do. (I can pass the platter of meat to my wife.) My mother's there with hair that's white as soap. My father's elsewhere. She'll die. I know she will because she already has.

JOSEPH HELLER, *Something Happened*, 1974

'Many's the long night I've dreamed of cheese – toasted, mostly.'

R. L. STEVENSON, *Treasure Island*, 1883

It is certain enough . . . that dreams in general proceed from indigestion; and it appears nearly as much so, that they are more or less strange according to the waking fancy of the dreamer. It is probable that a trivial degree of indigestion will give rise to very fantastic dreams in a fanciful mind; while, on the other hand, a good orthodox repletion is necessary towards a fanciful creation in a dull one. It shall make an epicure, of any vivacity, act as many parts in his sleep as a tragedian, 'for that night only.' The inspirations of veal, in particular, are accounted extremely Delphic; Italian pickles partake of the same spirit of Dante; and a butter-boat shall contain as many ghosts as Charon's.

LEIGH HUNT, 'Of Dreams', 1820

The eating of sweets portends disagreeable circumstances. The eating of figs signifies nonsensical discourse.

ASTRAMPSYCHUS, *The Oneirocriticon*, c.AD 350

The state of the stomach and liver has also a prodigious influence upon the character of dreams. Persons of bad digestion, especially hypochondriacs, are harassed with visions of the most frightful nature. This fact was well known to the celebrated Mrs. Radcliffe, who, for the purpose of filling her sleep with those phantoms of horror, which she has so forcibly embodied in the 'Mysteries of Udolpho,' and 'Romance of the Forest,' is said to have supped upon the most indigestible substances; while Dryden and Fuseli, with the opposite view of obtaining splendid dreams, are reported to have eaten raw flesh.

ROBERT MACNISH, *The Philosophy of Sleep*, 1830

A lady dreamed that she went to an entertainment which turned out to be a kind of revival meeting, presided over by a lady, and full of uproar. It was suddenly realised that Hell was underneath the hall, and a man, supposed to be a slave, was torn to pieces and cast into Hell. A lady present was so much affected by the scene that she threw herself into a pool of water, and was drowned, her body being afterwards pulled out by a working man with a pitchfork. The dreamer was so overcome by these tragic events that she felt that there was nothing left but to commit suicide. Resolving to drown herself, she went to a lighthouse (which, however, somewhat resembled a bathing machine) on a height, in order to throw herself down into the sea. It was of an exquisite green tint, extremely lovely and attractive, but she had not the courage to leap in. She thought it might give her courage if she had a good meal first, so she returned to the hall and joined the lady who had presided over the meeting. They sat down to a dish of roast mutton, but, as they were eating, suddenly looked at each other with mutual understanding; they realised that they were eating the woman who had been drowned, and, it will be remarked, had been pulled out of the water by a fork.

HAVELOCK ELLIS, *The World of Dreams*, 1911

Animals

❧

I dreamt that I had entered the body of a hog, that I could not easily get out again, and that I was wallowing in the filthiest slime. Was it a kind of reward? My dearest wish had been granted. I no longer belonged to mankind. For my part I understood this to be the correct interpretation, and I felt the deepest joy. And yet I actively inquired into this to see what deed of virtue I had done to deserve this remarkable boon from Providence. Now that I have gone over in my mind the different phases of my frightful prostration on the granite belly, during which, unknown to me, the tide flowed twice over this irreducible mixture of living flesh and dead matter, it is perhaps not unprofitable to proclaim that this degradation was only a punishment inflicted on me by divine justice. But who knows his inmost needs or the causes of his pestilential joys? The metamorphosis was always in my eyes the high and magnanimous resonance of the perfect happiness which I had long been awaiting. At last the day had come when I was a hog! I tested my teeth on the barks of trees; with pleasure I contemplated my snout. Not the slightest trace of divinity remained: I raised my soul to the excessive height of that unspeakable delight. Listen then to me, and do not blush, inexhaustible caricatures of the Beautiful, who take seriously the laughable brayings of your supremely despicable souls; and who do not understand why the Almighty, in a rare moment of excellent buffoonery which certainly did not transgress the great general laws of the grotesque, one day took amazing pleasure in peopling a planet with strange microscopic beings called humans, made of matter resembling pink coral. Certainly, flesh and bone, you have reason to blush, but listen to me. I do not invoke your understanding; it would spit blood at the horror you cause it: forget it, and be consistent with yourselves . . . There were no constraints there. Whenever I wanted to kill, I killed. I even wanted to quite often, and no one stopped me. The vengeance of human laws still pursued me, although I did not attack the race I had so calmly abandoned; but my conscience did not reproach me at all. During the day, I fought my new fellows, and the ground was often bespattered with many layers of congealed blood. I was the strongest, and I won all the victories. Biting wounds covered my body: I pretended not to notice them. The animals of the earth shunned me and I remained alone in my dazzling grandeur. What was my astonishment when, having swum across a river, leaving behind me lands which my fury had depopulated to find other countries in which to plant my customs of carnage and murder, I tried to walk on that flowery bank. My feet were paralysed; and no movement of any kind belied this enforced immobility. It was then, amid supernatural efforts to continue on my way, that I awoke and realized that I was turning back into a man. Thus Providence made clear to me, in a not inexplicable way, that she did not want my sublime projects to be realized even in a dream.

COMTE DE LAUTRÉAMONT, *Maldoror*, 1868

And there as I sat I had a dream. . . . Methought I was in Llangolen fair in the place where the pigs were sold, in the midst of Welsh drovers, immense hogs and immense men whom I took to be the gents of Wolverhampton. What huge fellows they were! One enormous fellow particularly caught my notice. I guessed he must have weighed at least eleven score, he had a half-ruddy, half-tallowy face, brown hair, and rather thin whiskers. He was higgling with the proprietor of an immense hog, and as he higgled he wheezed as if he had a difficulty of respiration, and frequently wiped off, with a dirty white pocket-handkerchief, drops of perspiration which stood upon his face. At last methought he bought the hog for nine pounds, and had no sooner concluded his bargain than turning round to me, who was standing close by staring at him, he slapped me on the shoulder with a hand of immense weight, crying with a half-piping, half-wheezing voice, 'Coom, neighbour, coom, I and thou have often dealt; gi' me noo a poon for my bargain, and it shall be all thy own.' I felt in a great rage at his unceremonious behaviour, and owing to the flutter of my spirits whilst I was thinking whether or not I should try and knock him down, I awoke, and found the fire nearly out and the ecclesiastical cat seated on my shoulders. The creature had not been turned out, as it ought to have been, before my wife and daughter retired, and feeling cold had got upon the table and thence had sprung upon my back for the sake of the warmth which it knew was to be found there; and no doubt the springing on my shoulders by the ecclesiastical cat was what I took in my dream to be the slap on my shoulders by the Wolverhampton gent.

GEORGE BORROW, *Wild Wales*, 1862

Earthly Things

He, ent'ring at the study door,
Its ample area 'gan explore;
   And something in the wind
Conjectur'd, sniffing round and round,
Better than all the books he found,
   Food chiefly for the mind.

Just then, by adverse fate impress'd,
A dream disturb'd poor Bully's rest;
   In sleep he seem'd to view
A rat fast clinging to the cage,
And, screaming at the sad presage,
   Awoke and found it true.

WILLIAM COWPER, from 'On the death of Mrs Throckmorton's
Bullfinch', 1782

. . . And up and doun as he the forest soughte,
He mette he saugh a bor with tuskes grete,
That slepte ayeyn the bryghte sonnes hete.

And by this bor, fast in his armes folde,
Lay, kissyng ay, his lady bryght, Criseyde.
For sorwe of which, whan he it gan byholde,
And for despit, out of his slep he breyde,
And loude he cride on Pandarus, and seyde:
'O Pandarus, now know I crop and roote.
I n'am but ded; ther nys non other bote.

'My lady bryght, Criseyde, hath me bytrayed,
In whom I trusted most of any wight.
She elliswhere hath now here herte apayed.
The blysful goddes, thorugh here grete myght,
Han in my drem yshewed it ful right.
Thus yn my drem Criseyde have I byholde' –
And al this thing to Pandarus he tolde. . . .

Pandare answerde and seyde, 'Allas the while
That I was born! Have I nat seyd er this,
That dremes many a maner man bigile?
And whi? For folk expounden hem amys.
How darstow seyn that fals thy lady ys,

For any drem, right for thyn owene drede?
Lat be this thought; thow kanst no dremes rede.

'Peraunter, ther thow dremest of this boor,
It may so be that it may signifie,
Hire fader, which that old is and ek hoor,
Ayeyn the sonne lith, o poynt to dye,
And she for sorwe gynneth wepe and crie,
And kisseth hym, ther he lith on the grounde.
Thus sholdestow thi drem aright expounde!'

GEOFFREY CHAUCER, *Troilus and Criseyde*, Book V, *c.*1380

In Winter in my Room
I came upon a Worm –
Pink, lank, and warm –
But as he was a worm
And worms presume
Not quite with him at home –
Secured him by a string
To something neighboring
And went along.

A Trifle afterward
A thing occurred
I'd not believe it if I heard
But state with creeping blood –
A snake with mottles rare
Surveyed my chamber floor
In feature as the worm before
But ringed with power –

The very string with which
I tied him – too
When he was mean and new
That string was there –

I shrank – 'How fair you are!'
Propitiation's claw –
'Afraid,' he hissed,
'Of me?'
'No cordiality' –

He fathomed me –
Then to a Rhythm *Slim*
Secreted in his Form
As Patterns swim
Projected him.

That time I flew
Both eyes his way
Lest he pursue
Nor ever ceased to run
Till in a distant Town
Towns on from mine
I set me down
This was a dream.

EMILY DICKINSON, *c.*1870

I saw a man whose name was Apollonius, who for some grievous sin had received a grievous punishment. A worm like a viper, about three inches in length, and proportionately thin, was fastened upon one of the nerves of a decayed tooth, and I saw it hanging therefrom, though at times it lay coiled within the cavity. The poor wretch was relating his sufferings to me with so much contrition and resignation, that his repentance was accepted, and the worm fell off. It crawled into a fire, and here the dream adapted itself to old notions, for as the creature entered the flames it put out legs like a salamander, and lay parching in that shape till it was dried up and consumed.

ROBERT SOUTHEY, 27 February 1805

Got restless – taste in mouth – and had the most horrible serpent dream I ever had yet in my life. The deadliest came out into the room under a door. It rose up like a Cobra – with horrible round eyes and had woman's, or at least Medusa's, breasts. It was coming after me, out of one room, like our back drawing room at Herne Hill, into another; but I got some pieces of marble off a table and threw at it, and that cowed it and it went back; but another small one fastened on my neck like a leech, and nothing would pull it off.

JOHN RUSKIN, *Diaries*, 1 November 1869

My dream was that there were seven butchers, dressed in white, with blue-and-white aprons, pinned by a pearl button up to their breast-bones. They opened a white door that had a big silvery handle like the hold of a ship, and inside it was all furred and frosted, and as the air came out, their breaths fogged it. They marched in and began carrying out big joints of meat, which they arranged on tables whose tops were clean timber that had been scrubbed many times, and which were hacked and notched as with much work of butchers. They carried out the joints of an animal that had been frozen, and with great skill sliced the meat off in chops and joints until the bones and gristle were bare, carrying the meat out to another place where I understood it was bought, cooked and consumed. With great ceremony one of the butchers marched out with the head of the animal. There was no skin on this head, but it had great swept-back horns, and its lidless eyes glared and its lipless teeth smiled. They scooped out the eyes and pared the cheeks, the neck and the scalp of the last remnants, and when the whole skeleton was bare and laid complete in its parts over the block, they stood back in a row, having put down their knives, and looked at me expectantly, from under their seven straw hats. At first I did not know what to do. The cold from the open door was chilling my bones, and my teeth started to chatter. I remembered your doctor and his saying 'Think of bees,' and my teeth chattering seemed like the hum of a swarm of bees, and my whole body began to tremble. A darkness was gathering round the frame of the white door and on the walls of the white room, and I saw that one of the bearded butchers was bearded with bees. My body grew warmer as the hum grew deeper, and I tasted a sweetness in my mouth. The swarm of bees launched themselves into the air, and swayed like a thick smoke in a cone or small whirlwind. I saw the butcher's beard strip itself off and he was clean-shaven. Then these bees began to line the bare bones on the table, and the bones, clothed with wings, hovered off the wood and settled themselves standing on the floor. The horned head flew to the neck and settled there. I saw the bees hanging in folds beneath the chin like a dewlap. The hum altered in pitch to the lowing of a cow. I thought of udders, that gave honey. I woke. I woke up with that idea, that we should give up drink together, come what may.

PETER REDGROVE, *The Beekeepers*, 1980

A man dreamt that a friend and associate of his, with whose daughter he was having an affair, sent him a horse. The groom brought the horse up two flights of stairs and led him into the bedchamber where the man himself was lying. Not long afterwards, the man lost all access to his mistress. For the horse signified the woman. The place, however, signified that the present arrangement would not continue, since it was impossible for a horse to be on the third floor.

ARTEMIDORUS, The Interpretation of Dreams, Book 4, <small>C.AD</small> 150

O God, in the dream the terrible horse began
To paw at the air, and make for me with his blows.
Fear kept for thirty-five years poured through his mane,
And retribution equally old, or nearly, breathed through his nose.

Coward complete, I lay and wept on the ground
When some strong creature appeared, and leapt for the rein.
Another woman, as I lay half in a swound,
Leapt in the air, and clutched at the leather and chain.

Give him, she said, something of yours as a charm.
Throw him, she said, some poor thing you alone claim.
No, no, I cried, he hates me; he's out for harm,
And whether I yield or not, it is all the same.

But, like a lion in a legend, when I flung the glove
Pulled from my sweating, my cold right hand,
The terrible beast, that no one may understand,
Came to my side, and put down his head in love.

LOUISE BOGAN, 'The Dream', 1941

[I] dreamt that I was in a room (but not my own) . . . in the room I noticed a dreadful-looking creature, a sort of monstrosity. It looked like a scorpion, but it was not a scorpion, and more hideous and much more dreadful just because, I think, there are no such creatures in nature, and because it had come to me *deliberately* and that there was some kind of mystery in that fact. I had a good look at it: it was brown and encased in a shell, a crawling reptile, about seven inches in length, two fingers thick at the head, gradually tapering off to the tail, so that the tip of the tail was no more than one-fifth of an inch thick. About two inches from the head, at an angle of forty-five degrees, two legs grew out of the body, one on each side, about three and a half inches in length, so that, if looked at from above, the animal was in the shape of a trident. I couldn't make out the head, but I saw two feelers, not very long, shaped like two strong needles, and also brown. It had a pair of identical feelers at the end of its tail and at the end of each of its legs, altogether eight feelers. The creature was running about the room very, very swiftly, supporting itself on its legs and its tail, and when it ran, its body and legs wriggled about like little snakes, with extraordinary rapidity, in spite of its shell, and it was very horrible to look at. I was terribly afraid it would sting me; I had been told that it was poisonous, but what worried me most was who could have sent it into my room, what they meant to do to me, and what was the meaning of it all. It kept hiding under the chest of drawers, under the cupboard, and crawled into corners. I sat down on a chair with my legs tucked under me. It ran quickly across the room and disappeared somewhere near my chair. I was peering round in dismay, but as I was sitting with my legs tucked up, I hoped that it would not crawl up the chair. Suddenly I heard behind me, almost on the level with my head, a faint rattling sound; I turned round, and saw that the reptile was crawling up the wall and was already on the level with my head and even touching my hair with its tail, which was twisting and wriggling with incredible rapidity. I jumped up and the creature disappeared. I was afraid to lie down on the bed for fear that it might creep under the pillow. My mother came into the room with some friend of hers. They began trying to catch the reptile, but they were much calmer than I was and were not even afraid of it. But they did not realize how dangerous it was. Suddenly the reptile crawled out again; this time it was crawling very quickly and, it seemed, with some special purpose, across the room towards the door, wriggling slowly, which was more horrible than ever. Then my mother opened the door and called our dog, Norma – a huge, shaggy black Newfoundland bitch; she died five years ago. She rushed into the room and stopped dead over the reptile. . . . But notwithstanding her fear, Norma looked very fierce, although she trembled in all her limbs. Suddenly she slowly bared her terrible teeth, opened her huge, red jaws, took careful aim, and suddenly seized the reptile with her teeth. The creature must have darted out of her mouth in order to escape, because Norma caught it once more, this time in the air, and twice got it all into her mouth, still catching it in the air, as though gobbling it up. The shell cracked between her teeth; the tail and legs of the creature, which hung out of the dog's mouth, moved about with terrible rapidity. Suddenly Norma yelped piteously: the reptile had succeeded in stinging her tongue after all. She opened her mouth wide with the pain, whining and yelping, and

I saw the horrible creature, though bitten in two, still wriggling in her mouth and out of its half-crushed body a large quantity of a white fluid, similar to the fluid of a crushed black beetle, was oozing out on to her tongue. . . . Just then I woke up and the prince came in.

FYODOR DOSTOEVSKY, *The Idiot*, 1869

To behold oxen in dreams is of evil tendency. To see black mares is a thoroughly bad sign. The sight of white horses is a vision of angels. To see lions announces the contentions of one's enemies. The sight of doves is the introduction of injury. To see a colt running denotes something mysterious.

ASTRAMPSYCHUS, *The Oneirocriticon*, c.AD 350

I dreamed that we were sitting, a party of twenty, in a big room with open windows.

Among us were women, children, old men. . . . We were all talking of some very well-known subject, talking noisily and indistinctly.

Suddenly, with a sharp, whirring sound, there flew into the room a big insect, two inches long . . . it flew in, circled round, and settled on the wall.

It was like a fly or a wasp. Its body dirt-coloured; of the same colour too its flat, stiff wings; outspread feathered claws, and a head thick and angular, like a dragon-fly's; both head and claws were bright red, as though steeped in blood.

This strange insect incessantly turned its head up and down, to right and to left, moved its claws . . . then suddenly darted from the wall, flew with a whirring sound about the room, and again settled, again hatefully and loathesomely wriggling all over, without stirring from the spot.

In all of us it excited a sensation of loathing, dread, even terror. . . . No one of us had ever seen anything like it. We all cried: 'Drive that monstrous thing away!' and waved our handkerchiefs at it from a distance . . . but no one ventured to go up to it . . . and when the insect began flying, every one instinctively moved away.

Only one of our party, a pale-faced young man, stared at us all in amazement. He shrugged his shoulders; he smiled, and positively could not conceive what had happened to us, and why we were in such a state of excitement. He himself did not see an insect at all, did not hear the ill-omened whirr of its wings.

All at once the insect seemed to stare at him, darted off, and dropping on his head, stung him on the forehead, above the eyes. . . . The young man feebly groaned, and fell dead.

The fearful fly flew out at once. . . . Only then we guessed what it was had visited us.

IVAN TURGENEV, *Poems in Prose*: 'The Insect', 1878–82

She began nightly to dream of octopi, sinister brownies, hobs, monita lizards, Jotuns, autocthons, kleagles, Lapiths, bonicons, and nests of ninnies. A sneaping frost crept over her heart. But of this anon.

ALEXANDER THEROUX, *The Great Wheadle Tragedy*, 1975

Hear now a curious dream I dreamed last night
Each word whereof is weighed and sifted truth.

I stood beside Euphrates while it swelled
Like overflowing Jordan in its youth:
It waxed and coloured sensibly to sight;
Till out of myriad pregnant waves there welled
Young crocodiles, a gaunt blunt-featured crew,
Fresh-hatched perhaps and daubed with birthday dew.
The rest if I should tell, I fear my friend
My closest friend would deem the facts untrue;
And therefore it were wisely left untold;
Yet if you will, why, hear it to the end.

Each crocodile was girt with massive gold
And polished stones that with their wearers grew:
But one there was who waxed beyond the rest,
Wore kinglier girdle and a kingly crown,
Whilst crowns and orbs and sceptres starred his breast.
All gleamed compact and green with scale on scale,
But special burnishment adorned his mail
And special terror weighed upon his frown;
His punier brethren quaked before his tail,
Broad as a rafter, potent as a flail.
So he grew lord and master of his kin:
But who shall tell the tale of all their woes?
An execrable appetite arose,

He battened on them, crunched, and sucked them in.
He knew no law, he feared no binding law,
But ground them with inexorable jaw:
The luscious fat distilled upon his chin,
Exuded from his nostrils and his eyes,
While still like hungry death he fed his maw;
Till every minor crocodile being dead
And buried too, himself gorged to the full,
He slept with breath oppressed and unstrung claw.
Oh marvel passing strange which next I saw:
In sleep he dwindled to the common size,
And all the empire faded from his coat.
Then from far off a wingèd vessel came,
Swift as a swallow, subtle as a flame:
I know not what it bore of freight or host,
But white it was as an avenging ghost.
It levelled strong Euphrates in its course;
Supreme yet weightless as an idle mote
It seemed to tame the waters without force
Till not a murmur swelled or billow beat:
Lo, as the purple shadow swept the sands,
The prudent crocodile rose on his feet
And shed appropriate tears and wrung his hands.

    What can it mean? you ask. I answer not
For meaning, but myself must echo, What?
And tell it as I saw it on the spot.

CHRISTINA ROSSETTI, 'My Dream', 1855

One hot night a leopard came into my room and lay down on the bed
beside me. I was half asleep, and did not realize at first that it was a
leopard. I seemed to be dreaming the sound of some large,
soft-footed creature padding quietly through the house, the doors of
which were wide open because of the intense heat. It was almost too
dark to see the lithe, muscular shape coming into my room, treading
softly on velvet paws, coming straight to the bed without hesitation,
as if perfectly familiar with its position. A light spring, then warm
breath on my arm, on my neck and shoulder, as the visitor sniffed me
before lying down. It was not until later, when moonlight entering
through the window revealed an abstract spotted design, that I

recognized the form of an unusually large, handsome leopard stretched out beside me.

His breathing was deep though almost inaudible, he seemed to be sound asleep. I watched the regular contractions and expansions of the deep chest, admired the elegant relaxed body and supple limbs, and was confirmed in my conviction that the leopard is the most beautiful of all wild animals. . . . While I observed him, I was all the time breathing his natural odour, a wild primeval smell of sunshine, freedom, moon and crushed leaves, combined with the cool freshness of the spotted hide, still damp with the midnight moisture of jungle plants. I found this non-human scent, surrounding him like an aura of strangeness, peculiarly attractive and stimulating.

My bed, like the walls of the house, was made of palm-leaf matting stretched over stout bamboos, smooth and cool to the touch, even in the great heat. It was not so much a bed as a room within a room, an open staging about twelve feet square, so there was ample space for the leopard as well as myself. I slept better that night than I had since the hot weather started, and he too seemed to sleep peacefully at my side. The close proximity of this powerful body of another species gave me a pleasant sensation I am at a loss to name.

When I awoke in the faint light of dawn, with the parrots screeching outside, he had already got up and left the room. . . .

ANNA KAVAN, 'The Visit', 1970

Out of what country ballad of green England,
or Persian etching, out of what secret region
of nights and days enclosed in our lost past
came the white deer I dreamed of in the dawn?
A moment's flash. I saw it cross the meadow
and vanish in the golden afternoon,
a lithe, illusory creature, half-remembered
and half-imagined, deer with a single side.
The presences which rule this curious world
have let me dream of you but not command you.
Perhaps in a recess of the unplumbed future,
again I will find you, white deer from my dream.
I too am dream, lasting a few days longer
than that bright dream of whiteness and green fields.

JORGE LUIS BORGES, 'The White Deer', 1975

And Eleanor came by, and took my soul in the palm of her hand, as the angels did Faust's, and carried it to a cavern by the seaside, and dropped it in; and I fell and fell for ages. And all the velvet mosses, rock flowers, and sparkling spars and ores, fell with me, round me, in showers of diamonds, whirlwinds of emerald and ruby, and pattered into the sea that moaned below, and were quenched; and the light lessened above me to one small spark, and vanished; and I was in darkness and turned again to my dust.

*   *   *

And I was at the lowest point of created life; a madrepore rooted to the rock, fathoms below the tide-mark; and worst of all, my individuality was gone. I was not one thing, but many things – a crowd of innumerable polypi; and I grew and grew, and the more I grew the more I divided, and multiplied thousand and ten thousand-fold. If I could have thought, I should have gone mad at it, but I could only feel. . . .

And I was a soft crab, under a stone on the sea-shore. With infinite starvation, and struggling, and kicking, I had got rid of my armour, shield by shield, and joint by joint, and cowered naked and pitiable, in the dark, among dead shells and ooze. Suddenly the stone was turned up; and there was my cousin's hated face laughing at me, and pointing me out to Lillian. She laughed too, as I looked up, sneaking, ashamed, and defenceless, and squared up at him with my soft useless claws. Why should she not laugh? Are not crabs, and toads, and monkeys, and a hundred other strange forms of animal life, jests of nature – embodiments of a divine humour, at which men are meant to laugh and be merry? But, alas! my cousin, as he turned away, thrust the stone back with his foot, and squelched me flat.

CHARLES KINGSLEY, *Alton Locke*, 1850

The sight of a mouse bespeaks propitious circumstances. Dead oxen signify times of famine. The sight of wasps marks injuries to one's foes. The sight of a hare portends an unlucky journey. To hold a sparrow, struggling to escape, forebodes mischief.

ASTRAMPSYCHUS, *The Oneirocriticon*, c.AD 350

I have had many dreams about animals, domestic, wild, and legendary, but I shall describe only one at this point, as it seems to me to throw into an imaginative shape two of the things I have been writing about: our relation to the animal world, a relation involving a predestined guilt, and our immortality. All guilt seeks expiation and the end of guilt, and our blood-guiltiness towards the animals tries to find release in visions of a day when man and the beasts will live in friendship and the lion will lie down with the lamb. My dream was connected with this vision. I dreamed that I was lying asleep, when a light in my room wakened me. A man was standing by my bedside. He was wearing a long robe, which fell about him in motionless folds, while he stood like a column. The light that filled the room came from his hair, which rose straight up from his head, burning, like a motionless brazier. He raised his hand, and without touching me, merely by making that sign, lifted me to my feet in one movement, so that I stood before him. He turned and went out through the door, and I followed him. We were in the gallery of a cloister; the moon was shining, and the shadow of the arches made black ribs on the flagstones. We went through a street, at the end of which there was a field, and while we walked on the moonlight changed to the white light of early morning. As we passed the last houses I saw a dark, shabby man with a dagger in his hand; he was wearing rags bound round his feet, so that he walked quite soundlessly; there was a stain as of blood on one of his sleeves; I took him to be a robber or a murderer and was afraid. But as he came nearer I saw that his eyes, which were fixed immovably on the figure beside me, were filled with a profound, violent adoration such as I had never seen in human eyes before. Then, behind him, I caught sight of a confused crowd of other men and women in curious or ragged clothes, and all had their eyes fixed with the same look on the man walking beside me. I saw their faces only for a moment. Presently we came to the field, which as we drew near changed into a great plain dotted with little conical hills a little higher than a man's head. All over the plain animals were standing or sitting on their haunches on these little hills; lions, tigers, bulls, deer, elephants, were there; serpents too wreathed their lengths on the knolls; and each was separate and alone, and each slowly lifted its head upward as if in prayer. This upward-lifting motion had a strange solemnity and deliberation; I watched head after head upraised as if proclaiming some truth just realized, and yet as if moved by an irresistible power beyond them. The elephant wreathed its trunk upward, and there was something pathetic and absurd in that indirect act of adoration. But the other animals raised their heads with the inevitability of the sun's rising, as if they knew, like the sun, that a new day was about to begin, and were giving the signal for its coming. Then I saw a little dog busily running about with his nose tied to the ground, as if he did not know that the animals had been redeemed. He was a friendly little dog, officiously going about his business, and it seemed to me that he too had a place in this day, and that his oblivious concern with the earth was also a sort of worship. How the dream ended I do not remember: I have now only a memory of the great animals with all their heads raised to heaven.

EDWIN MUIR, An Autobiography, 1954

I dream that I am walking in the fields. I saunter along idly, pleasantly, through level meadows, and by and by come to a narrow stream; the whole scene being just such an one as the angler resorts to in Hampshire. But I am no fisherman, and never think of rod-fishing except as a dull delight about which a vast deal of lyrical nonsense is sung to one old tune. Yet, when I look into the stream, and see there many good fish gliding, I wish for a rod and a creel. The wish is no sooner formed than it rises to eagerness, for at every moment the fish become larger and larger and still more plentiful. Before long they might be baled out with a bucket; yet a little while and they might be cast to the banks with a malt-shovel. Rapidly changing in shape and size from pretty one-pound trout to great-eyed, loose-mouthed cod-like monsters, they presently fill the whole bed of the stream – fill it pile-high in a horrible sweltering heap; which becomes more horrible still in another moment, when the ghastly creatures die and fall to pieces. An unendurable sight, instantly followed by the relief of waking, but not to shake off the squalid terror of the scene for hours after. At intervals of months, or more frequently of years, this dream has been repeated many times, with no difference of detail whatever.

FREDERICK GREENWOOD, Imagination in Dreams, 1894

That night I had a dream which I repeated to him [Bertrand Russell] next morning at breakfast. I had dreamed that I was standing with him in an aquarium looking at some fish. To my surprise I saw that they were musical fish and that they were producing the most beautiful music. What is more, they were dancing in time to it so that it was clear that they appreciated it.

GERALD BRENAN, Personal Record, 1975

'Are you both crazy?' the doctor cried shrilly, backing away in paling confusion.

'Yes, he really is crazy, Doc,' Dunbar assured him. 'Every night he dreams he's holding a live fish in his hands.'

The doctor stopped in his tracks with a look of elegant amazement and distaste, and the ward grew still. '*He does what?*' he demanded.

'He dreams he's holding a live fish in his hand.'

'What kind of fish?' the doctor inquired sternly of Yossarian.

'I don't know,' Yossarian answered. 'I can't tell one kind of fish from another.'

'In which hand do you hold them?'

'It varies,' answered Yossarian.

'It varies with the fish,' Dunbar added helpfully.

The colonel turned and stared down at Dunbar suspiciously with a narrow squint. 'Yes? And how come you seem to know so much about it?'

'I'm in the dream,' Dunbar answered without cracking a smile.

The colonel's face flushed with embarrassment. He glared at them both with cold, unforgiving resentment. 'Get up off the floor and into your bed,' he directed Dunbar through thin lips. 'And I don't want to hear another word about this dream from either one of you. I've got a man on my staff to listen to disgusting bilge like this.'

'Just why do you think,' carefully inquired Major Sanderson, the soft and thickset smiling staff psychiatrist to whom the colonel had ordered Yossarian sent, 'that Colonel Ferredge finds your dream disgusting?'

Yossarian replied respectfully. 'I suppose it's either some quality in the dream or some quality in Colonel Ferredge.'

'That's very well put. . . . This fish you dream about. Let's talk about that. It's always the same fish, isn't it?'

'I don't know,' Yossarian replied. 'I have trouble recognizing fish.'

'What does the fish remind you of?'

'Other fish.'

'And what do other fish remind you of?'

'Other fish.'

Major Sanderson sat back disappointedly. 'Do you like fish?'

'Not especially.'

'Just why do you think you have such a morbid aversion to fish?' asked Major Sanderson triumphantly.

'They're too bland,' Yossarian answered. 'And too bony.'

Major Sanderson nodded understandingly, with a smile that was agreeable and insincere. 'That's a very interesting explanation. But we'll soon discover the true reason, I suppose. Do you like this particular fish? The one you're holding in your hand?'

'I have no feelings about it either way.'

'Do you dislike the fish? Do you have any hostile or aggressive emotions toward it?'

'No, not at all. In fact, I rather like the fish.'

'Then you do like the fish.'

'Oh, no. I have no feelings toward it either way.'

'But you just said you liked it. And now you say you have no feelings toward it either way. I've just caught you in a contradiction. Don't you see?'

'Yes, sir. I suppose you have caught me in a contradiction.'

Major Sanderson proudly lettered 'Contradiction' on his pad with his thick black pencil. 'Just why do you think,' he resumed when he had finished, looking up, 'that you made those two statements expressing contradictory emotional responses to the fish?'

'I suppose I have an ambivalent attitude toward it.'

Major Sanderson sprang up with joy when he heard the words 'ambivalent attitude.' 'You do understand!' he exclaimed, wringing his hands together ecstatically. 'Oh, you can't imagine how lonely it's been for me, talking day after day to patients who haven't the slightest knowledge of psychiatry, trying to cure people who have no real interest in me or my work! . . . Do you ever have any good sex dreams?'

'My fish dream is a sex dream.'

'No, I mean real sex dreams – the kind where you grab some naked bitch by the neck and pinch her and punch her in the face until she's all bloody and then throw yourself down to ravish her and burst into tears because you love her and hate her so much you don't know what else to do. *That's* the kind of sex dreams I like to talk about. Don't you ever have sex dreams like that?'

Yossarian reflected a moment with a wise look. 'That's a fish dream,' he decided.

Major Sanderson recoiled as though he had been slapped. 'Yes, of course,' he conceded frigidly, his manner changing to one of edgy and defensive antagonism. 'But I'd like you to dream one like that anyway just to see how you react. That will be all for today. In the meantime, I'd also like you to dream up the answers to some of those questions I asked you. These sessions are no more pleasant for me than they are for you, you know.'

'I'll mention it to Dunbar,' Yossarian replied.
'Dunbar?'
'He's the one who started it all. It's his dream.'

JOSEPH HELLER, Catch-22, 1961

Travel and the Natural World

I was at a place I conceived to be Watford Junction and wanted to get to London. I saw a train about to start, which seemed to consist entirely of one very splendid car *de luxe*. I made up my mind that, cost what it might, I would go by it, and produced a 'wad' of American money wherewith to take my ticket. But just as I got to the ticket-office a queue of other people suddenly appeared at it. I thought of pushing in ahead of them, but dismissed the idea, and fell into my proper place, with the result that the train started without me. Then another more ordinary train came in, and I asked an old man who seemed to be a servant of the company whether it was bound for London. He said 'I don't know – that's what comes of democracy – no one knows anything'. And I gathered that the company, or at any rate the station, was run on some collectivist (perhaps Soviet) system which resulted in complete disorganization. I then made a rush over the metals to get into this train and succeeded in doing so, only to find that it started in the wrong direction.

WILLIAM ARCHER, *On Dreams*, 27–28 July 1921

Mr. Edmund Halley . . . was carried on with a strong impulse to take a voyage to St. Helens, to make observations of the southern constellations, being then about twenty-four years old. Before he undertook his voyage, he dreamt that he was at sea, sailing towards that place, and saw the prospect of it from the ship in his dream, which he declared to the Royal Society, to be the perfect representation of that island, even as he had it really when he approached to it.

JOHN AUBREY, *Miscellanies Upon Various Subjects*, 1696

I saw before me stretched a boundless plain
Of sandy wilderness, all black and void,
And as I looked around, distress and fear
Came creeping over me, when at my side,
Close at my side, an uncouth shape appeared
Upon a dromedary, mounted high.
He seemed an Arab of the Bedouin tribes:

A lance he bore, and underneath one arm
A stone, and in the opposite hand, a shell
Of a surpassing brightness. At the sight
Much I rejoiced, not doubting but a guide
Was present, one who with unerring skill
Would through the desert lead me; and while yet
I looked and looked, self-questioned what this freight
Which the new-comer carried through the waste
Could mean, the Arab told me that the stone
(To give it in the language of the dream)
Was 'Euclid's Elements;' and 'This,' said he,
'Is something of more worth;' and at the word
Stretched forth the shell, so beautiful in shape,
In colour so resplendent, with command
That I should hold it to my ear. I did so,
And heard that instant in an unknown tongue,
Which yet I understood, articulate sounds,
A loud prophetic blast of harmony;
An Ode, in passion uttered, which foretold
Destruction to the children of the earth
By deluge, now at hand. No sooner ceased
The song, than the Arab with calm look declared
That all would come to pass of which the voice
Had given forewarning, and that he himself
Was going then to bury those two books:
The one that held acquaintance with the stars,
And wedded soul to soul in purest bond
Of reason, undisturbed by space or time;
The other that was a god, yea many gods,
Had voices more than all the winds, with power
To exhilarate the spirit, and to soothe,
Through every clime, the heart of human kind.
While this was uttering, strange as it may seem,
I wondered not, although I plainly saw
The one to be a stone, the other a shell;
Nor doubted once but that they both were books,
Having a perfect faith in all that passed.
Far stronger, now, grew the desire I felt
To cleave unto this man; but when I prayed
To share his enterprise, he hurried on
Reckless of me: I followed, not unseen,
For oftentimes he cast a backward look,

Grasping his twofold treasure. – Lance in rest,
He rode, I keeping pace with him; and now
He, to my fancy, had become the knight
Whose tale Cervantes tells; yet not the knight,
But was an Arab of the desert too;
Of these was neither, and was both at once.
His countenance, meanwhile, grew more disturbed;
And, looking backwards when he looked, mine eyes
Saw, over half the wilderness diffused,
A bed of glittering light: I asked the cause:
'It is,' said he, 'the waters of the deep
Gathering upon us;' quickening then the pace
Of the unwieldy creature he bestrode,
He left me: I called after him aloud;
He heeded not; but, with his twofold charge
Still in his grasp, before me, full in view,
Went hurrying o'er the illimitable waste,
With the fleet waters of a drowning world
In chase of him; whereat I waked in terror,
And saw the sea before me, and the book,
In which I had been reading, at my side.

WILLIAM WORDSWORTH, *The Prelude*, Book V, 1850

Gladness of mind shows that you will live abroad.

ASTRAMPSYCHUS, *The Oneirocriticon*, c.AD 350

I dreamed that Max, Otto, and I had the habit of packing our trunks
only when we reached the railway station. There we were, carrying
our shirts, for example, through the main hall to our distant trunks.
Although this seemed to be a general custom, it was not a good one in
our case, especially since we had begun to pack only shortly before
the arrival of the train. Then we were naturally excited and had
hardly any hope of still catching the train, let alone getting good
seats.

FRANZ KAFKA, *Diaries*, 28 October 1911

Other dreams – perfectly absurd ones – filled him with an
incommunicable delight. All those that he remembered began by the
brushwood-pile. For instance, he found a small clockwork steamer

(he had noticed it many nights before) lying by the sea-road, and stepped into it, whereupon it moved with surpassing swiftness over an absolutely level sea. This was glorious, for he felt he was exploring great matters; and it stopped by a lily carved in stone, which, most naturally, floated on the water. Seeing the lily was labelled 'Hong-Kong,' Georgie said: 'Of course. This is precisely what I expected Hong-Kong would be like. How magnificent!' Thousands of miles farther on it halted at yet another stone lily, labelled 'Java'; and this again delighted him hugely, because he knew that now he was at the world's end. But the little boat ran on and on till it stopped in a deep fresh-water lock, the sides of which were carven marble, green with moss. Lily-pads lay on the water, and reeds arched above. Some one moved among the reeds – some one whom Georgie knew he had travelled to this world's end to reach. Therefore everything was entirely well with him. He was unspeakably happy, and vaulted over the ship's side to find this person. When his feet touched the still water, it changed, with the rustle of unrolling maps, to nothing less than a sixth quarter of the globe, beyond the most remote imagining of man – a place where islands were coloured yellow and blue, their lettering strung across their faces. They gave on unknown seas, and Georgie's urgent desire was to return swiftly across this floating atlas to known bearings. He told himself repeatedly that it was no good to hurry; but still he hurried desperately, and the islands slipped and slid under his feet, the straits yawned and widened, till he found himself utterly lost in the world's fourth dimension, with no hope of return.

RUDYARD KIPLING, 'The Brushwood Boy', 1898

In China, over and above what it has in common with the rest of southern Asia, I am terrified by the modes of life, by the manners, and the barrier of utter abhorrence, and want of sympathy, placed between us by feelings deeper than I can analyse. I could sooner live with lunatics, or brute animals. All this, and much more than I can say, or have time to say, the reader must enter into before he can comprehend the unimaginable horror which these dreams of Oriental imagery, and mythological tortures, impressed upon me. Under the connecting feeling of tropical heat and vertical sun-lights, I brought together all creatures, birds, beasts, reptiles, all trees and plants, usages and appearances, that are found in China or Indostan. From kindred feelings, I soon brought Egypt and all her gods under the same law. I was stared at, hooted at, grinned at, chattered at, by monkeys, by paroquets, by cockatoos. I ran into pagodas: and was fixed, for centuries, at the summit, or in secret rooms; I was the idol; I was the priest; I was worshipped; I was sacrificed. I fled from the wrath of Brama through all the forests of Asia: Vishnu hated me: Seeva laid wait for me. I came suddenly upon Isis and Osiris: I had done a deed, they said, which the ibis and the crocodile trembled at. I was buried, for a thousand years, in stone coffins, with mummies and sphinxes, in narrow chambers at the heart of eternal pyramids. I was kissed, with cancerous kisses, by crocodiles; and laid, confounded with all unutterable slimy things, amongst reeds and Nilotic mud.

I thus give the reader some slight abstraction of my Oriental dreams, which always filled me with such amazement at the monstrous scenery, that horror seemed absorbed, for a while, in sheer astonishment. Sooner or later, came a reflux of feeling that swallowed up the astonishment, and left me, not so much in terror, as in hatred and abomination of what I saw. Over every form, and threat, and punishment, and dim sightless incarceration, brooded a sense of eternity and infinity that drove me into an oppression as of madness. Into these dreams only, it was, with one or two slight exceptions, that any circumstances of physical horror entered. All before had been moral and spiritual terrors. But here the main agents were ugly birds, or snakes, or crocodiles; especially the last. The cursed crocodile became to me the object of more horror than almost all the rest. I was compelled to live with him; and (as was always the case almost in my dreams) for centuries. I escaped sometimes, and found myself in Chinese houses, with cane tables, etc. All the feet of the tables, sofas, etc., soon became instinct with life: the abominable head of the crocodile, and his leering eyes, looked out at me, multiplied into a thousand repetitions: and I stood loathing and fascinated. And so often did this hideous reptile haunt my dreams, that many times the very same dream was broken up in the very same way: I heard gentle voices speaking to me (I hear everything when I am sleeping); and instantly I awoke: it was broad noon; and my children were standing, hand in hand, at my bed-side; come to show me their coloured shoes, or new frocks, or to let me see them dressed for going out. I protest that so awful was the transition from the damned crocodile, and the other unutterable monsters and abortions of my dreams, to the sight of innocent *human* natures and of infancy, that, in the mighty and sudden revulsion of mind, I wept, and could not forbear it, as I kissed their faces.

THOMAS DE QUINCEY, *Confessions of an English Opium-Eater*, 1822

I see thee ever in my dreams,
Karaman!
Thy hundred hills, thy thousand streams,
Karaman, O Karaman!
As when thy gold-bright morning gleams,
As when the deepening sunset seams
With lines of light thy hills and streams,
Karaman!
So thou loomest on my dreams,
Karaman!
On all my dreams, my homesick dreams,
Karaman, O Karaman!

The hot bright plains, the sun, the skies,
Karaman!
Seem death-black marble to mine eyes,
Karaman, O Karaman!
I turn from summer's blooms and dyes;
Yet in my dreams thou dost arise
In welcome glory to mine eyes,
Karaman!
In thee my life of life yet lies,
Karaman!

JAMES CLARENCE MANGAN, from 'The Karamanian Exile', 1844

Last night I dreamt I went to Manderley again. It seemed to me I stood by the iron gate leading to the drive, and for a while I could not enter for the way was barred to me. There was a padlock and a chain upon the gate. I called in my dream to the lodge-keeper, and had no answer, and peering closer through the rusted spokes of the gate I saw that the lodge was uninhabited.

No smoke came from the chimney, and the little lattice windows gaped forlorn. Then, like all dreamers, I was possessed of a sudden with supernatural powers and passed like a spirit through the barrier before me. The drive wound away in front of me, twisting and turning as it had always done, but as I advanced I was aware that a change had come upon it; it was narrow and unkept, not the drive that we had known. At first I was puzzled and did not understand, and it was only when I bent my head to avoid the low swinging branch of a tree that I realised what had happened. Nature had come into her own again and, little by little, in her stealthy, insidious way had encroached upon the drive with long, tenacious fingers. The woods, always a menace even in the past, had triumphed in the end. They crowded, dark and uncontrolled, to the borders of the drive. The beeches with white, naked limbs leant close to one another, their branches intermingled in a strange embrace, making a vault above my head like the archway of a church. And there were other trees as well, trees that I did not recognise, squat oaks and tortured elms that straggled cheek by jowl with the beeches, and had thrust themselves out of the quiet earth, along with monster shrubs and plants, none of which I remembered. . . . On and on, now east now west, wound the poor thread that once had been our drive. . . . Surely the miles had multiplied, even as the trees had done, and this path led but to a labyrinth, some choked wilderness, and not to the house at all. I came upon it suddenly; the approach masked by the unnatural growth of a vast shrub that spread in all directions, and I stood, my heart thumping in my breast, the strange prick of tears behind my eyes.

There was Manderley, our Manderley, secretive and silent as it had always been, the grey stone shining in the moonlight of my dream, the mullioned windows reflecting the green lawns and the terrace. Time could not wreck the perfect symmetry of those walls, nor the site itself, a jewel in the hollow of a hand.

DAPHNE DU MAURIER, *Rebecca*, 1938

In dreams a dark château
    Stands ever open to me,
In far ravines dream-waters flow,
    Descending soundlessly;
Above its peaks the eagle floats,
    Lone in a sunless sky;
Mute are the golden woodland throats
    Of the birds flitting by.

No voice is audible. The wind
    Sleeps in its peace.
No flower of the light can find
    Refuge beneath its trees;
Only the darkening ivy climbs
    Mingled with wilding rose,
And cypress, morn and evening, time's
    Black shadow throws.

All vacant, and unknown;
   Only the dreamer steps
From stone to hollow stone,
   Where the green moss sleeps,
Peers at the river in its deeps,
   The eagle lone in the sky,
While the dew of evening drips,
   Coldly and silently.

Would that I could steal in! –
   Into each secret room;
Would that my sleep-bright eyes could win
   To the inner gloom;
Gaze from its high windows,
   Far down its mouldering walls,
Where amber-clear still Lethe flows,
   And foaming falls.

But ever as I gaze,
   From slumber soft doth come
Some touch my stagnant sense to raise
   To its old earthly home;
Fades then that sky serene;
   And peak of ageless snow;
Fades to a paling dawn-lit green,
   My dark château.

WALTER DE LA MARE, 'Dark Château', 1912

For the credit of my imagination, I am almost ashamed to say how tame and prosaic my dreams are grown. They are never romantic, seldom even rural. They are of architecture and of buildings – cities abroad, which I have never seen and hardly have hoped to see. I have traversed, for the seeming length of a natural day, Rome, Amsterdam, Paris, Lisbon – their churches, palaces, squares, market-places, shops, suburbs, ruins, with an inexpressible sense of delight – a map-like distinctness of trace, and a day-light vividness of vision, that was all but being awake. – I have formerly travelled among the Westmorland fells – my highest Alps, – but they are objects too mighty for the grasp of my dreaming recognition; and I have again and again awoke with ineffectual struggles of the inner eye, to make out a shape, in any way whatever, of Helvellyn.

Methought I was in that country, but the mountains were gone. The poverty of my dreams mortifies me.

CHARLES LAMB, 'Witches, and Other Night Fears', 1823

To creep up a mountain signifies the difficulty of business.

ASTRAMPSYCHUS, *The Oneirocriticon*, c.AD 350

Anna slept and dreamed. She was standing on the edge of a wide yellow desert at midday. The sun was darkened by the dust hanging in the air. The sun was a baleful orange colour over the yellow dusty expanse. Anna knew she had to cross the desert. Over it, on the far side, were mountains – purple and orange and grey. The colours of the dream were extraordinarily beautiful and vivid. But she was enclosed by them, enclosed by these vivid dry colours. There was no water anywhere. Anna started off to walk across the desert, so that she might reach the mountains.

That was the dream she woke with in the morning; and she knew what it meant. The dream marked a change in Anna, in her knowledge of herself. In the desert she was alone, and there was no water, and she was a long way from the springs. She woke knowing that if she was to cross the desert she must shed burdens.

DORIS LESSING, *The Golden Notebook*, 1962

For many years after leaving Wyre I never dreamed about it once; it was as if that part of my life had been forgotten. My first dream of it came twenty-five years later, when I was being psychoanalysed in London. I dreamed that I was standing at the bow of a boat; it was early morning, and the sky and the sea were milk-white. The ship went on with a rustling motion, and cut more deeply into the ever-deepening round of the horizon. A spire rose above the rim of the sea, and at once, as the ship rushed smoothly on, I could see the little streets, the prickly weeds growing out of the walls, the tangle dripping from the pier. The houses opened out, melted and ran together; in a moment I would be there; but then I saw that this was not the town I knew, and that the people walking about the streets were strangers. Then, the ship clean gone, I was wandering along the top of a high, craggy coast. Far beneath me the sea snarled in the caves, which like marine monsters gnashed at it and spat it out again; opposite, across the boiling strait, so near that I felt I could touch it,

was Rousay with its towering black mountain. I had never thought
that this coast of Wyre was so wild and rocky, and even as this
thought formed in my mind the isle grew tamer, grew quite flat, and I
was walking along a brown path level with the sea, picking great,
light, violet-hued, crown-shaped flowers which withered at once in
my hands. I came to a little chapel or shrine on the shore. On one wall
a brown clay image was hanging: a weatherbeaten image of an old
woman naked to the waist, with sun-burned, wrinkled dugs. I went
up to the image, and as if I were fulfilling some ritual pressed one of
the nipples with my finger. A trembling flowed over the figure, and
like a wave running across another in counter-motion, the texture
changed; the clay quivered and rippled with life, all the marks of age
vanishing in that transparent flood; the breasts shone smooth and
round, and rose and fell with living breath. At the same time in the
centre of my breast I felt a hot, tingling fire, and I knew that a yellow
sun was blazing there, and with its beams, which filled my body with
light and soft power, was raising the image from the dead. The figure
came down from the wall, a dark brown girl, and stood beside me.
That is all I remember about the dream.

EDWIN MUIR, *Autobiography*, 1954

During one summer holidays my father took us to the salt-mines. We
went on an outside car, clopping of hoofs and scuttling of pebbles,
the country a prism for the sun was shining on the patchwork, but
Elizabeth and I were impatient till we got there; we had always
wanted to go down under the earth to the caves of crystal and
man-made thunder, to the black labyrinth of galleries under the
carefree fields, under the tumbledown walls, the whins and the
ragweed. We descended a pitch-black shaft in a great bucket, at the
bottom was a cross of fire and there sure enough was the
subterranean cathedral and men like gnomes in the clerestories,
working with picks.

Some time later I dreamed the gnomes had caught me, imprisoned
me under the ground until I should find a certain jewel. A hopeless
task; I wandered under the vaults groping through heaps of
shattered quartzite rocks. Then met another prisoner, a girl; we
decided to give up the hunt, to brave the gnomes and make our
escape to daylight. No sooner decided than we found ourselves in a
lift, an enormous lift fitted up as a teashop; a middle-aged man was
eating bacon and eggs; no one took any notice of us. So there we
were going up, sometimes the lift would stop, people come in and get

out, but no one took any notice. It was frightening but almost hilarious. Then as we rose to the light I do not know what became of the girl but I woke up.

LOUIS MacNEICE, *The Strings Are False*, 1965

I had a dream about the ninth year of my age as follows: I saw the moon rise near the west and run a regular course eastward, so swift that in about a quarter of an hour she reached our meridian, where there descended from her a small cloud on a direct line to the earth, which lighted on a pleasant green about twenty yards from the door of my father's house (in which I thought I stood) and was immediately turned into a beautiful green tree. The moon appeared to run on with equal swiftness and soon set in the east, at which time the sun arose at the place where it commonly does in the summer, and shining with full radiance in a serene air, it appeared as pleasant a morning as ever I saw.

    All this time I stood still in the door in an awful frame of mind, and I observed that as heat increased by the rising sun, it wrought so powerfully on the little green tree that the leaves gradually withered; and before noon it appeared dry and dead. There then appeared a being, small of size, full of strength and resolution, moving swift from the north, southward, called a sun worm.

JOHN WOOLMAN, *Journal*, 1729

I had a sort of dream-trance the other day, in which I saw my favourite trees step out and promenade up, down and around, very curiously – with a whisper from one, leaning down as he pass'd me, *We do all this on the present occasion, exceptionally, just for you.*

WALT WHITMAN, 'Thoughts Under an Oak', from *Specimen Days*, 1875

The sight of withered trees declares the uselessness of labours.

ASTRAMPSYCHUS, *The Oneirocriticon*, c.AD 350

Rarely were my dreams tinctured with happiness. As a rule they were stuffed with fear – and with a fear so strange and alien that it had no ponderable quality. No fear that I experienced in my waking life resembled that fear that possessed me in my sleep. It was of a quality and kind that transcended all my experiences.

For instance, I was a city boy, a city child, rather, to whom the country was an unexplored domain. Yet I never dreamed of cities; nor did a house ever occur in any of my dreams. Nor, for that matter, did any human being ever break through the wall of my sleep. I, who had seen trees only in parks and illustrated books, wandered in my sleep through interminable forests. And further, these dream trees were not a mere blur on my vision. They were sharp and distinct. I was on terms of practised intimacy with them. I saw every branch and twig; I saw and knew every different leaf.

Well do I remember the first time in my waking life that I saw an oak tree. As I looked at the leaves, and branches, and gnarls, it came to me with distressing vividness that I had seen that same kind of tree many and countless times in my sleep. So I was not surprised, still later on in my life, to recognize instantly, the first time I saw them, trees such as the spruce, the yew, the birch, and the laurel. I had seen them all before, and was seeing them even then, every night, in my sleep.

JACK LONDON, *Before Adam*, 1908

One of my dreams was the synthesis of what my imagination had often sought to depict, in my waking hours, of a certain seagirt place and its mediæval past. In my sleep I saw a gothic city rising from a sea whose waves were stilled as in a stained-glass window. An arm of the sea divided the town into two; the green water stretched to my feet; on the opposite shore it washed round the base of an oriental church, and beyond it houses which existed already in the fourteenth century, so that to go across to them would have been to ascend the stream of time. This dream in which nature had learned from art, in which the sea had turned Gothic, this dream in which I longed to attain, in which I believed that I was attaining the impossible, was one that I felt I had often dreamed before. But as it is the nature of what we imagine in sleep to multiply itself in the past, and to appear, even when new, to be familiar, I supposed that I was mistaken.

MARCEL PROUST, *The Guermantes Way*, 1920

Maybe I shouldn't breathe a word about the most beautiful, the most mysterious dream I ever had. I dream it once or twice a year. Suddenly, I see myself on a road that skirts the top of a cliff and I know that the dream is beginning and with it, a feeling of happiness such that human speech cannot give the faintest idea of it. Farther on, there will be a big iron gate, so difficult to turn on its hinges, then the long avenue of trees, then once again the cliff and I pause to look at the sea, but instead of water I see an immense forest that stretches to the horizon and covers the whole countryside, and at that moment I feel as happy as someone who has passed beyond death. Is that all? It is.

JULIAN GREEN, *Diary*, 12 December 1934

A man dreamt that he turned into the River Xanthus in Troy. He bled for ten years. . . . Still, he did not die, which was quite understandable, since the river is immortal.

ARTEMIDORUS, *The Interpretation of Dreams*, Book 5, *c.*AD 150

I have beheld scenes, with the intimate and unaccountable connexion of which with the obscure parts of my own nature, I have been irresistibly impressed. I have beheld a scene which has produced no unusual effect on my thoughts. After the lapse of many years I have dreamed of this scene. It has hung on my memory, it has haunted my thoughts, at intervals, with the pertinacity of an object connected with human affections. I have visited this scene again. Neither the dream could be dissociated from the landscape, nor the landscape from the dream, nor feelings, such as neither singly could have awakened, from both. But the most remarkable event of this nature, which ever occurred to me, happened five years ago at Oxford. I was walking with a friend, in the neighbourhood of that city, engaged in earnest and interesting conversation. We suddenly turned the corner of a lane, and the view, which its high banks and hedges had concealed, presented itself. The view consisted of a windmill, standing in one among many plashy meadows, inclosed with stone walls; the irregular and broken ground, between the wall and the road on which we stood; a long low hill behind the windmill, and a grey covering of uniform cloud spread over the evening sky. It was that season when the last leaf had just fallen from the scant and stunted ash. The scene surely was a common scene; the season and the hour little calculated to kindle lawless thoughts, such as would drive the imagination for refuge in serious and sober talk, to the evening fireside, and the dessert of winter fruits and wine. The effect which it produced on me was not such as could have been expected. I

suddenly remembered to have seen that exact scene in some dream of
long *——

* *Here I was obliged to leave off, overcome by thrilling horror.*— This remark
closes this fragment, which was written in 1815. I remember well his coming to me
from writing it, pale and agitated, to seek refuge in conversation from the fearful
emotions it excited. [*Note by Mrs Shelley*]

PERCY BYSSHE SHELLEY, 'Speculations on Metaphysics', 1815

Worn out with emotion, I soon fell asleep. Can anyone guess of what
I dreamed? Why, of my iris flowers! . . . In a lovely stream of water
which wound all round the farmhouse, a limpid, transparent, azure
stream like the waters of the fountain at Vaucluse, I beheld the most
beautiful clumps of iris covered with a perfect wonder of golden
blossoms! Little dragon-flies with blue silk wings came and settled
on the flowers, while I swam about naked in the laughing rivulet and
plucked by handfuls and armsful those enchanting yellow blooms.
And the more I picked the more sprang up. All at once I heard a voice
calling me, 'Frédéric!' I awoke and to my joy I saw a great bunch of
golden iris shining by my side. The master himself, my worshipful
sire, had actually gone to pick those flowers I so longed for and the
mistress, my dear sweet mother, had placed them on my bed.

FRÉDÉRIC MISTRAL, *Memoirs*, 1906

Lady. If I be sure I am not dreaming now,
    I should not doubt to say it was a dream.
    Methought a star came down from heaven,
    And rested mid the plants of India,
    Which I had given a shelter from the frost
    Within my chamber. There the meteor lay,
    Panting forth light among the leaves and flowers,
    As if it lived, and was outworn with speed;
    Or that it loved, and passion made the pulse
    Of its bright life throb like an anxious heart,
    Till it diffused itself, and all the chamber
    And walls seemed melted into emerald fire
    That burned not; in the midst of which appeared
    A spirit like a child, and laughed aloud
    A thrilling peal of such sweet merriment
    As made the blood tingle in my warm feet:
    Then bent over a vase, and murmuring

Low, unintelligible melodies,
Placed something in the mould like melon-seeds,
And slowly faded, and in place of it
A soft hand issued from the veil of fire,
Holding a cup like a magnolia flower
And poured upon the earth within the vase
The element with which it overflowed,
Brighter than morning light, and purer than
The water of the springs of Himalah.

Indian. You waked not?

Lady.   Not until my dream became
Like a child's legend on the tideless sand,
Which the first foam erases half, and half
Leaves legible.

> PERCY BYSSHE SHELLEY, from 'Fragments of an Unfinished Drama',
> 1822

I couldn't get to sleep last night. When I shut my eyes *gardens* drifted
by – the most incredible sort of tropical gardens with glimpses of
palaces through the rich green. Trees I've never seen or imagined –
trees like feathers and silver trees and others quite white with huge
transparent leaves passed and passed. My heart just fluttered: I
scarcely had to breathe at all. It was like a vision brought about by
drugs. I couldn't stop it and yet it frightened me; but it was too
beautiful to stop. One is almost in a state of coma – very strange. I've
often got *near* this condition before, but never like last night. Perhaps
if one gives way to it and gives way to it one may even be able to get
there . . . Oh, I don't know, but it *was* a vision, not a memory.

> KATHERINE MANSFIELD, *Letters and Journals*, 29 November 1919

I dreamed such a vivid little dream of you last night. I dreamed you
came to Cromford, and stayed there. You were not coming on here
because you weren't well enough. You were quite clear from the
consumption – quite, you told me. But there was still something that
made you that you couldn't come up the hill here.

So you went out with me as I was going. It was night, and very
starry. We looked at the stars, and they were different. All the
constellations were different, and I, who was looking for Orion, to
show you, because he is rising now, was very puzzled by these thick,
close, brilliant new constellations. Then suddenly we saw one planet,

so beautiful, a large, fearful, strong star, that we were both pierced by it, possessed, for a second. Then I said, 'That's Jupiter' – but I felt that it wasn't Jupiter – at least not the everyday Jupiter.

Ask Jung or Freud about it? Never! It was a star that blazed for a second on one's soul.

I wish it was spring for us all.

D. H. LAWRENCE, letter to Katherine Mansfield, March 1919

More drowsy dreams the moon tonight. She rests
Like a proud beauty on heaped cushions pressing,
With light and absent-minded touch caressing,
Before she sleeps, the contour of her breasts.

On satin-shimmering, downy avalanches
She dies from swoon to swoon in languid change,
And lets her eyes on snowy visions range
That in the azure rise like flowering branches.

When sometimes to this earth her languor calm
Lets streak a stealthy tear, a pious poet,
The enemy of sleep, in his cupped palm,

Takes this pale tear, of liquid opal spun
With rainbow lights, deep in his heart to stow it
Far from the staring eyeballs of the Sun.

CHARLES BAUDELAIRE, 'Sorrow of the Moon', c.1850

Once in a dream a message came speeding over land and sea that winter was descending upon the world from the North Pole, that the Arctic zone was shifting to our mild climate. Far and wide the message flew. The ocean was congealed in midsummer. Ships were held fast in the ice by thousands, the ships with large, white sails were held fast. Riches of the Orient and the plenteous harvests of the Golden West might no more pass between nation and nation. For some time the trees and flowers grew on, despite the intense cold. Birds flew into the houses for safety, and those which winter had overtaken lay on the snow with wings spread in vain flight. At last the foliage and blossoms fell at the feet of Winter. The petals of the flowers were turned to rubies and sapphires. The leaves froze into emeralds. The trees moaned and tossed their branches as the frost pierced them through bark and sap, pierced into their very roots. I shivered myself awake, and with a tumult of joy I breathed the many sweet morning odours wakened by the summer sun.

HELEN KELLER, *The World I Live In*, 1908

Real People

✄

Dozing off subsequently, I saw, through the red cobwebs of a nightmare, a clean, empty room, brilliantly lit, which was next to ours though I had not noticed it earlier. Through a wide, open door, I saw Totochabo disguised as an ostrich like some African bush-hunter; he had kept this room for himself – it was a bit like the armoury, but without the arms, of a feudal castle – for receiving visitors of note.

There were three men with him, walking and talking. I recognised François Rabelais straight off even though he was disguised under a nun's habit which featured a large, floating coif like a sea manta, the ominous sting-ray, except that its dark colouring was the result of Hebrew inscriptions covering the white starch like so many fly-spottings. Instead of the customary bunch of keys and rosary there hung in the blue folds of the cloth an extremely common-looking pigsticker. The second person had a thin, oval belly like a long fish, the white clothes of a fencer, a waspish eye, a heroic honey-coloured moustache with the ends painted green, and a foil with the button removed: it was Alfred Jarry. I heard him explaining that 'the reason why his trouser-bottoms were not held in by lobster claws was that he was wearing shorts and white stockings' and that was all I could catch of what the four men were saying. The third was Léon-Paul Fargue in the uniform of an admiral which he had decked out with a lot of extra gold braid; he wore the two-pointed hat the wrong way and instead of the sword was carrying a boarding cutlass. One minute on his chin and the next in his hand was a false Armenian beard and, depending on the various phases, curves and knots of the conversation, his face went from smooth to hairy and from hirsute to shaved just like the amazing evolutions of a human shooting star.

It's a pity I was able to hear so little of what they said to each other. Nobody else noticed the three visitors nor even the room in which they chatted. When I told the others about it, they simply laughed at me.

RENÉ DAUMAL, *A Night of Serious Drinking*, 1938

I was in Bonaparte's palace, where some sort of contest was taking place between him and Sir Sidney Smith, who came to me for a knife to cut something which prevented him from drawing his sword.

Bonaparte struck me; I had an axe in my hand; he saw that I was half inclined to cut him down, and attempted to kill me. I struck him with the axe, and brought him down, and dragged him out into a public hall, not being yet dead, and there beheaded him. This is the first time I ever killed him in self-defence, though I have more than once done it upon the pure principle of tyrannicide.

ROBERT SOUTHEY, 8 November 1804

I dreamed the other night that I was paying a visit to Marshal Lyautey. He was receiving me in an office of vast proportions, with some magnificent rugs on the floor; and it was a strange office, for in the place where one would have expected to see a window, there was an archway of rock. And beneath this archway was the blue water of the Mediterranean, and the floor, covered with seaweed, sloped gently down toward it. I could not see the horizon, the archway being too low for that, but I saw the reflection of the sun in the water. Neither of us spoke for some moments. Then I asked my host: 'Are you comfortable here, Marshal?' 'Oh, yes, quite,' he answered, 'quite comfortable. . . .' What struck me when I awoke was the element of reality in all this; the plausible had mingled with the improbable. Perhaps we shall be talking just like that when we awake from this life. Who could say that all our waking life was not a dream?

JULIAN GREEN, *Personal Record 1928–1939*, 5 February 1939

Good people give attention, and listen for a while,
To an interesting ditty, which cannot fail to make you smile,
So all draw near, and lend an ear, while I relate a theme,
Concerning of Victoria, a strange and funny dream.

Chorus.

So these are dreams and visions
Of old England's blooming Queen.

At the Isle of Wight, the other night, as Vic lay in her bed,
Strange visions did to her appear, and dreams came in her head;
She drew Prince Albert by the nose, and gave a dreadful scream,
Oh, dear, she said, I'm filled with dread, I'd such a dreadful dream.

Says Albert, Vic, what are you at? you've made my nose quite sore,
I'm in a mind, for half a pin, to kick you on the floor,
Such dreams for me will never do, you pepper'd me with blows.
I never knew a wife to dream, and pull her husband's nose.

O, don't be vex'd, the Queen replied, you know I love you well,
So listen awhile dear Albert, and my dreams to you I'll tell:
Last night, she said, I had a dream, as soon as I lay down,
I thought Napoleon had come o'er, to steal away my crown.

The vision of Napoleon appeared at my bed side,
He said that by my subjects he had been greatly belied,
But now, said he, I'll be revenged, I'll quickly make you rue,
And I'll take away the laurels that were won at Waterloo.

When the vision of Napoleon, from my view did disappear,
To escape the French, I thought that we came to lodge here,
I thought that we were so held down, by cursed poverty,
That I was forc'd to labour hard in a cotton factory.

Prince Albert, he stood quite amazed, and listened to the Queen,
And said, dear Vic, I little thought that you had such a dream,
Cheer up your heart, don't look so sad, you need not be afraid,
For I'm sure the French will ne'er attempt, Old England to invade.

The Queen to Albert then replied, I have not told you all,
For I dream't that Lord John Russell, altho' but very small,
Just like a Briton bold, then so nobly did advance,
And with his fist, knocked out the eye, of the Emperor of France.

I dreamed that I was weaving on a pair of patent looms,
And I thought that you were going through the streets a-selling
    brooms,
And I thought our blooming Prince of Wales was selling milk and
    cream,
But, Albert dear, when I awoke, it was nothing but a dream.

Indeed, said Albert, dream no more, you fill my heart with pain,
And I hope that you will never have such frightful dreams again,
We've English and Irish soldiers, we can conquer all our foes,
So, whenever you dream again Vic, pray don't you pull my nose.

                                    ANON., 'The Queen's Dream'

Before the Coronation [of King Edward VII] I had a remarkable dream. The State coach had to pass through the Arch at the Horse Guards on the way to Westminster Abbey. I dreamed that it stuck in the Arch, and that some of the Life Guards on duty were compelled to hew off the Crown upon the coach before it could be freed. When I told the Crown Equerry, Colonel Ewart, he laughed and said, 'What do dreams matter?' 'At all events,' I replied, 'let us have the coach and Arch measured.' So this was done, and, to my astonishment, we found that the Arch was nearly two feet too low to allow the coach to pass through. I returned to Colonel Ewart in triumph, and said, 'What do you think of dreams now?' 'I think it's damned fortunate you had one,' he replied. It appears that the State coach had not been driven through the Arch for some time, and that the level of the road had since been raised during repairs. So I am not sorry that my dinner disagreed with me that night; and I only wish all nightmares were as useful.

WILLIAM CAVENDISH-BENTINCK, DUKE OF PORTLAND, *Men, Women and Things*, 1937

Lunching with King and Queen. I gave imitations of the Royal Family which were well received. The King's eyes very bloodshot, voice very loud. I walked with him along a street. 'There's the police station! Ha, ha! We all know what *that* means. There's the cemetery – cremation in my dominions is not obligatory, though advisable. I am told I have a remarkable facial resemblance to the late Dr Pusey!' A footman arrives – we were now on a terrace. 'I am to tell your Majesty that Her Majesty is waiting in the carriage.' K. to footman 'I prefer to walk!' To me – 'That's the way to treat women!' – pause – 'You are a bachelor, Benson?' 'Yes, sir', 'Remain one, Ha, ha!' 'You are a writer, Benson?' 'Yes, sir', 'These remarks of mine would make good copy!' This all written down on waking.

A. C. BENSON, November 1923, quoted in David Newsome, *On the Edge of Paradise*, 1980

I was to lunch with the King and Queen, but on coming into a large saloon where I was to meet them, they had gone into lunch. A huge hall with many people. The Q. waved her hand to me, and the K. beckoned me to a small side-table where he had turned down a chair. He said, 'You see I have kept you a place. The Q. wanted to send up to you, but I said we wouldn't disturb you at your writing.' Then after a little he said, 'Do you ever reflect that I am the only King who has ever inherited *all* the virtues and *none* of the faults of his ancestors. I have the robustness of the Normans, the activity of the Plantagenets, the romance of the Stewarts, the common sense of the Guelphs.' Then he said, 'I want you to look at the roof of my mouth. That will show you. That is how you tell a well-bred spaniel.' He turned to me, threw his head back and opened his mouth – but I cd see nothing except that it was of enormous extent, cavernous and dark. I said I couldn't see, and he called an attendant, who brought an electric torch. Then I saw it was as black as jet. I thanked him, and he said, 'I particularly wish you to look at the roof of the Queen's mouth – do so afterwards.' I said I could hardly do that, but he said 'Tell her I wished you to do so.' Events followed which I can't recollect, but I was eventually in a small sitting-room with the Queen, who said 'Mind, it is only because the K. desires it that I show you my mouth.' She threw her head back, and it was an enormous cavity of a dark purple, as if enamelled. I said, 'It's very remarkable', and she said with a smile, 'You are right. You are about the only person to whom we have ever shown our mouths!' This did not appear either strange or ludicrous – only a solemn privilege.

A. C. BENSON, August 1923, quoted in David Newsome, On the Edge of Paradise, 1980

Mr. Gawber was asleep. He had the elderly commuter's habit of being able to sleep without shifting position; sleep took him and embalmed him lightly like a touch of sadness he would soon shake off. He was dreaming of having tea with the Queen in a sunny room of Buckingham Palace. Jammed in the corner, the standing passengers' coats brushing his head, the lunch pail of the shirtless man next to him nudging his thigh, he dreamed. Around him, travelers slapped and shook their evening papers, but Mr. Gawber slept on. The Queen suddenly smiled and leaned forward and plucked open the front of her dress. Her full breasts tumbled out and Mr. Gawber put his head between them and sobbed with shame and relief. They were so cool; and he felt her nipples against his ears.

PAUL THEROUX, The Family Arsenal, 1966

What would you give to have such a dream about Milton as I had about a week since? I dreamed that being in a house in the city and with much company, looking toward the lower end of the room from the upper end of it, I descried a figure which I immediately knew to be Milton's. He was very gravely but very neatly attired in the fashion of his day, and had a countenance which filled me with those feelings that an affectionate child has for a beloved father. . . . My first thought was wonder where he could have been concealed so many years, my second a transport of joy to find him still alive, my third, another transport to find myself in his company, and my fourth a resolution to accost him. I did so, and he received me with a complacence in which I saw equal sweetness and dignity. I spoke of his *Paradise Lost* as every man must who is worthy to speak of it at all, and told him a long story of the manner in which it affected me when I first discovered it, being at that time a schoolboy. He answered me by a smile and a gentle inclination of his head. I told him we had poets in *our* days, and no mean ones, and that I was myself intimate with the best of them. He replied – I know Mr Hayley very well by his writings. He then grasped my hand affectionately and with a smile that charmed me said – Well, you, for your part, will do well also. At last, recollecting his great age, for I understood him to be about 200 years old, I said that I might fatigue him by much talking and took my leave, and he took his with an air of the most perfect good breeding. His person, his features, his dress, his manner, were all so perfectly characteristic, that I am persuaded an apparition of him could not represent him more completely.

WILLIAM COWPER, letter to William Hayley, 24 February 1793

Returning from Skelwith Fold . . . in the autumn of 1906, where he had visited the Severns in Ruskin's house (Brantwood) at Coniston, [A. C. Benson] has a characteristically vivid dream with scene-changes of mounting absurdity. It started with the strange predicament of having to sleep in the same room as Ruskin and Mrs Arthur Severn. Arthur worried through the night how he could manage to get dressed without embarrassment, but found, in his dream, that he was actually fully dressed at the time. Then all of them – Ruskin, Mrs Severn, Arthur and countless visitors – executed a strange old English morris-dance, with Ruskin playing an instrument like a bassoon, dancing very slowly. 'We all moved about absurdly.' Ruskin then had a fit and collapsed on the sofa, from which vantage point he discoursed to the assembly 'for hour after hour'.

DAVID NEWSOME, *On the Edge of Paradise*, 1980

Yesterday a most pleasant bustling dream of driving through a superb town, seeing a superb piece of 14th century sculpture, and being introduced to the Pope, with Mr. Collingwood, who sang the Pope a song in a red cap. Afterwards the Pope gave me his blessing, and on my kneeling down to receive it, knelt down too. But it is all darker and more vague than life, with *me*. I never dream really bright dreams unless I'm ill.

JOHN RUSKIN, *Diaries*, 12 July 1885

Shaw and I – I was dreaming – were, owing to scarcity of accommodation in some remote country sanatorium, confined within one bed. The war was in full swing, men were sunk in the mud of trenches only a few yards away, so we deemed our accommodation ample. Shaw was very benevolent and smiling, and admitted me into his bed with the courtesy of a true socialist who saw nothing private in it, but regarded it as a national institution. Any scruples that I might have had on account of being confined under the same blanket with an octogenarian vanished when I remembered that he was also a vegetarian – and so scrupulously clean. We each had our pillow at opposite ends of the bed, and Shaw's feet hardly ever got in the way. The whole thing was so civilized – Shaw so benignant. I told him a long story which I thought might interest him. But Shaw, I realized, was a very old man; his attention, though he knitted his brows, tended to relax, he wearied of the story, missed the point, yet received it with courtesy. We lay like this in the dark, and at last I asked Shaw how old he was. He said he was ninety-seven, and as he said it he realized he couldn't have much longer to live, three years at most; but it was all right and he was prepared for it, still it rather tended to distort one's sense of values, make one throw one's whole weight into the remaining three years; and when, to take off his thoughts from his impending death, I came out with another story, he said he could not listen, he had only three years left to himself, but he lay quite still with the same expression of benevolence on his aged face, passing the brief balance of his life in gentle courtesy.

WILLIAM GERHARDIE, *Memoirs of a Polyglot*, 1931

I was standing somewhere with someone when a leopard came into our field of vision. I said to my neighbour, 'You mightn't think it, but that is Gilbert Chesterton'. Then the leopard hung himself by his tail upon something which I vaguely conceived as the opening of an arbour or pergola; and I thought (and I believe said) that Chesterton was lying in wait for Bernard Shaw, and that by thus looking as if he were hanging dead, he was lulling Shaw's suspicions. Then Shaw appeared, I think also in animal form, but what form I cannot say. At all events the leopard fell upon him and it seemed that, in a moment, he had not only killed him but sucked all his blood and left him like a squeezed-out rag. Then the leopard disappeared and I rushed to the scene of the tragedy in an agony of grief and remorse. I somehow felt that I had regarded it all as a joke, and that, if I had had my wits about me, I might have interfered to avert this fatal and horrible termination.

WILLIAM ARCHER, *On Dreams*, 6–7 April 1920

Interview with two men who are a sort of bogus publishers. . . . Gilbert Murray and another Oxford professor, both in disguise (Murray wearing a beard), come to interview these publishers, while Lady Mary and I sit in a gallery and look on. Murray wears over his head in a sort of rack, supported on his shoulders, a large book entitled *Italian Drainage Systems*.

WILLIAM ARCHER, *On Dreams*, 27–28 November 1920

In a dream I once had, I saw a vessel on the sea, at midnight, in a storm. It was no great full-rigg'd ship, nor majestic steamer, steering firmly through the gale, but seem'd one of those superb little schooner yachts I had often seen lying anchor'd rocking so jauntily, in the waters around New York, or up Long Island sound – now flying uncontroll'd with torn sails and broken spars through the wild sleet and winds and waves of the night. On the deck was a slender, slight, beautiful figure, a dim man, apparently enjoying all the terror, the murk, and the dislocation of which he was the centre and the victim. That figure of my lurid dream might stand for Edgar Poe, his spirit, his fortunes, and his poems – themselves all lurid dreams.

WALT WHITMAN, *Washington Star*, 16 November 1875

In a café Gertler [Mark Gertler the painter] met me. 'Katherine, you must come to my table. I've got Oscar Wilde there. He's the most marvellous man I ever met. He's splendid!' Gertler was flushed. When he spoke of Wilde he began to cry – tears hung on his lashes, but he smiled.

Oscar Wilde was very shabby. He wore a green overcoat. He kept tossing and tossing back his long greasy hair with the whitest hand. When he met me he said: 'Oh *Katherine*!' – very affected.

But I did find him a fascinating talker. So much so that I asked him to come to my home. He said would 12.30 tonight do? When I arrived home it seemed madness to have asked him. Father and Mother were in bed. What if Father came down and found that chap Wilde in one of the chintz armchairs? Too late now. I waited by the door. He came with Lady Ottoline. I saw he was disgustingly pleased to have brought her. 'Dear *Lady* Ottoline!' and Ottoline in a red hat on her rust hair houynhyming along. He said, 'Katherine's hand – the same gentle hand!' as he took mine. But again when we sat down – I couldn't help it. He *was* attractive – as a curiosity. He was fatuous *and* brilliant.

'You know, Katherine, when I was *in that dreadful place* I was haunted by the memory of a *cake*. It used to float in the air before me – a little delicate thing *stuffed* with cream and with the cream there was something *scarlet*. It was made of pastry and I used to call it my little Arabian Nights cake. But I couldn't remember the name. Oh, Katherine, it was *torture*. It used to *hang* in the air and *smile* at me. And every time I resolved that next time *they let someone* come and see me I would ask them to tell me what it was but every time, Katherine, I was *ashamed*. Even now . . .'

I said, 'Mille feuilles à la crême?'

At that he turned round in the armchair and began to sob, and Ottoline who carried a parasol, opened it and put it over him . . .

KATHERINE MANSFIELD, *Letters and Journals*, 1920

Creativity

❧

In the course of my life I have often had the same dream, appearing in different forms at different times, but always saying the same thing, 'Socrates, practise and cultivate the arts.' In the past I used to think that it was impelling and exhorting me to do what I was actually doing; I mean that the dream, like a spectator encouraging a runner in a race, was urging me on to do what I was doing already, that is, practising the arts, because philosophy is the greatest of the arts, and I was practising it. But ever since my trial, while the festival of the god has been delaying my execution, I have felt that perhaps it might be this popular form of art that the dream intended me to practise, in which case I ought to practise it and not disobey. I thought it would be safer not to take my departure before I had cleared my conscience by writing poetry and so obeying the dream.

PLATO, *Phaedo*, c.380 BC

Fanatics have their dreams, wherewith they weave
A paradise for a sect, the savage too
From forth the loftiest fashion of his sleep
Guesses at Heaven; pity these have not
Traced upon vellum or wild Indian leaf
The shadows of melodious utterance.
But bare of laurel they live, dream, and die;
For Poesy alone can tell her dreams,
With the fine spell of words alone can save
Imagination from the sable charm
And dumb enchantment. Who alive can say,
'Thou art no poet; may'st not tell thy dreams'?
Since every man whose soul is not a clod
Hath visions, and would speak, if he had loved
And been well nurtured in his mother tongue.
Whether the dream now purposed to rehearse
Be poet's or fanatic's will be known
When this warm scribe my hand is in the grave.

JOHN KEATS, from 'The Fall of Hyperion', I, 1819

During the night of November 11 in this year [Descartes] had three dreams. . . . The first of his dreams was one of acute physical distress and terror, a dream of darkness haunted by strange and spectral beings and a tempestuous wind. He awoke in pain, afflicted by the horror that an evil spirit had aspired to seduce him. He prayed to God to protect him against any evil consequences of this dream, and that He would preserve him from ills which might menace him as a punishment for his sins. These, he realised, had been grave enough to draw down the thunderbolts of heaven upon his head: although he had hitherto led a life which, in the eyes of his fellow men, had been irreproachable enough. After prolonged meditation, he fell asleep again.

Terror, caused by the sound as of a clap of thunder, awoke him suddenly from the dream that then followed. On opening his eyes, he perceived a multitude of fiery sparks scattered about the room. This was not a new experience. He had frequently awaked at night with his eyes so filled with sparks of light that in a confused fashion he had been able to discern the objects around him. Now, however, after opening and shutting his eyes, and observing the qualities of what was represented to him, he wished to explain this phenomenon by philosophic reasoning, and he drew from it conclusions favourable to his soul. His fears left him, and he fell asleep again in peace.

There was nothing terrible in the dream which immediately followed this. It was concerned with two books, one a dictionary with which he was delighted; the other, also new to him, an anthology of poems entitled *Corpus Poetarum*. On opening the book to read in it, he chanced on the verse, 'Quod vitae sectabor iter?' At this moment in his dream he saw a stranger, who gave him a poem beginning with the words, 'Est et non', declaring that it was an excellent poem. Descartes told the stranger that he knew the poem, that it was one of the Idylls of Ausonius. While he was searching for it in the *Corpus*, with which he declared he was familiar, he discovered that the dictionary had vanished. He was explaining this to the stranger when it reappeared at the other end of the table. But it was no longer complete. Unable to find 'Est et non' among the poems of Ausonius, he told the stranger of an even lovelier poem by the same poet, 'Quod vitae', but failed to find it, discovering instead several little portraits engraved '*en taille douce*'. Both books and stranger then vanished from his imagination. Still asleep, and doubting whether this experience had been a vision or a dream, Descartes decided that it had been a dream and, still asleep, proceeded to interpret it.

He concluded that the dictionary represented the Sciences, and that the *Corpus* represented Philosophy and Wisdom in union; for even foolish and superficial poets may be full of sentences more serious, more weighty, and better expressed than those in the writings of the philosophers. He attributed this marvel to the divinity of Enthusiasm and to the force of the Imagination, which puts forth the seeds of wisdom that are to be found in the spirit of all men—as sparks of fire may be found in pebbles—much more easily and brilliantly than does the Reason of the Philosophers. He concluded that the poem on the uncertainty as to what kind of life one ought to lead represented the counsel of a wise man or even Moral Theology. He then awoke, continued his interpretation, and was finally convinced that the Spirit of Truth had in this dream intended to open the treasures of all the Sciences to him. As for the little portraits, next day an Italian painter called on him, and Descartes sought no further explanation.

WALTER DE LA MARE, *Behold, This Dreamer*, 1939

A propos of dreams, is it not a strange thing if writers of fiction never dream of their own creations; recollecting, I suppose, even in their dreams, that they have no real existence? *I* never dream of any of my own characters, and I feel it is so impossible that I would wager Scott never did of his, real as they are.

CHARLES DICKENS, letter to C. C. Felton, 1 September 1843

By the end of 1788, the first portion of that singularly original and significant series of Poems, by which of themselves Blake established a claim, however unrecognized, on the attention of his own and after generations, had been written; and the illustrative designs in colour to which he wedded them in inseparable loveliness, had been executed. The *Songs of Innocence* form the first section of the series he afterwards, when grouping the two together, suggestively named *Songs of Innocence and of Experience*. But how publish? for standing with the public, or credit with the trade, he had none. . . . He had not the wherewithal to publish on his own account, and though he could be his own engraver, he could scarcely be his own compositor. . . .

The subject of anxious daily thought passed – as anxious meditation does with us all – into the domain of dreams and (in his case) of visions. In one of these a happy inspiration befell, not, of course, without supernatural agency. After intensely thinking by day and dreaming by night, during long weeks and months, of his cherished object, the image of the vanished pupil and brother at last blended with it. In a vision of the night, the form of Robert stood before him, and revealed the wished-for secret, directing him to the technical mode by which could be produced a facsimile of song and design. On his rising in the morning Mrs. Blake went out with half-a-crown, all the money they had in the world, and of that laid out 1s. 10d. on the simple materials necessary for setting in practice the new revelation. Upon that investment of 1s. 10d. he started what was to prove the principal means of support of his future life – the series of poems and writings illustrated by coloured plates, often highly finished afterwards by hand – which became the most efficient and durable means of revealing Blake's genius to the world.

ALEXANDER GILCHRIST, *Life of Blake*, 1863

The poet and the dreamer are distinct,
Diverse, sheer opposite, antipodes.
The one pours out a balm upon the world,
The other vexes it.

JOHN KEATS, from 'The Fall of Hyperion', I, 1819

So I have this recurring dream. My publisher tells me that a new Editor has been put in charge of me and all my works; and I go along to the publisher's office and there, lo and behold!, the Editor turns out to be an Editress, and she is sitting there ready to discuss my new book of poems – which lies in typescript before her.

She is a neat, tidy, well-turned-out lady of fifty or so, with gaudily rimmed spectacles and an owl-like look, blue rinse hair. She explains that the Poetry Readers' Association, of which she is President, will not like a lot of the poems in this book (which she has photostatted and circulated to all her membership). She quotes a letter received from a housewife in Esher, which says: 'This book is sheer filth. I tremble to think what would happen if it were left lying about the house for young children to read!'. A domesticated Professor has written: 'This kind of pornography is anti-life.'

The Editress picks up a big blue pencil, about a foot long, and begins – with the utmost savagery – to score great diagonal lines through the poems not approved of. In the end one poem only is left, its innocence established. This is about feeding a horse with lumps of sugar. I leave the office feeling I am lucky not to be arrested.

The other form of the dream (for this is a serial dream and exists in two parts) is exactly as above except that the Editor turns out to be a very serious smartly dressed American. He is called Chuck. 'Glad to meet up with you!' and 'I'm mighty pleased to have the opportunity to talk with you!' he says, and 'Hopefully, now we can get some place!'

His view is that all the poems should be rewritten by him and then re-presented to me for a joint consultation. He starts to go through them: 'The end of this one ought to be at the beginning!' and (when he comes to the word 'expedient') 'The kids'll never understand this!' He explains to me that in Iowa nobody has ever heard of Telemann or Ronald Firbank – nor has he ('Who they?' he asks). He criticises the poems for lack of positive thinking. 'These are all negative poems, Gavin!' (we have been on first name terms since the first moment of meeting). In the end no poems are left unscathed; they are all bowdlerised, simplified, run through the cliché-machine. No one line is more than two words long.

As in the first dream, I wake up drowned in sweat, with a feeling of criminal inadequacy.

GAVIN EWART, 'Dreams', 1980

[*There are many accounts of Tartini's dream. The following one is taken from Havelock Ellis's* The World of Dreams.]

In old age he told Lalande the astronomer . . . that he had a dream in which he sold his soul to the Devil, and it occurred to him in his dream to hand his fiddle to the Devil to see what he could do with it. 'But how great was my astonishment when I heard him play with consummate skill a sonata of such exquisite beauty as surpassed the boldest flights of my imagination. I felt enraptured, transported, enchanted; my breath was taken away, and I awoke. Seizing my violin I tried to retain the sounds I had heard. But it was in vain. The piece I then composed, the "Devil's Sonata", was the best I ever wrote, but how far below the one I had heard in my dream!'

When I placed my head on my pillow, I did not sleep, nor could I be said to think. My imagination, unbidden, possessed and guided me, gifting the successive images that arose in my mind with a vividness far beyond the usual bounds of reverie. I saw — with shut eyes, but acute mental vision, — I saw the pale student of unhallowed arts kneeling beside the thing he had put together. I saw the hideous phantasm of a man stretched out, and then, on the working of some powerful engine, show signs of life, and stir with an uneasy, half vital motion. Frightful must it be; for supremely frightful would be the effect of any human endeavour to mock the stupendous mechanism of the Creator of the world. His success would terrify the artist; he would rush away from his odious handwork, horror-stricken. He would hope that, left to itself, the slight spark of life which he had communicated would fade; that this thing, which had received such imperfect animation, would subside into dead matter; and he might sleep in the belief that the silence of the grave would quench for ever the transient existence of the hideous corpse which he had looked upon as the cradle of life. He sleeps; but he is awakened; he opens his eyes; behold the horrid thing stands at his bedside, opening his curtains, and looking on him with yellow, watery, but speculative eyes.

I opened mine in terror. The idea so possessed my mind, that a thrill of fear ran through me, and I wished to exchange the ghastly image of my fancy for the realities around. . . .

Swift as light and as cheering was the idea that broke in upon me. 'I have found it! What terrified me will terrify others; and I need only describe the spectre which had haunted my midnight pillow.' On the morrow I announced that I had *thought of a story*.

MARY SHELLEY, Introduction to *Frankenstein*, 1831

The fifth canto of Dante pleases me more and more — it is that one in which he meets with Paulo and Francesca — I had passed many days in rather a low state of mind and in the midst of them I dreamt of being in that region of Hell. The dream was one of the most delightful enjoyments I ever had in my life — I floated about the whirling atmosphere as it is described with a beautiful figure to whose lips mine were joined as it seem'd for an age — and in the midst of all this cold and darkness I was warm — even flowery tree tops sprung up and we rested on them sometimes with the lightness of a cloud till the wind blew us away again — I tried a Sonnet upon it — there are fourteen lines but nothing of what I felt in it — O that I could dream it every night . . .

JOHN KEATS, letter to George and Georgiana Keats, 1819

Tennyson told us he had often dreamed long passages of poetry, and believed them to be good at the time, though he could never remember them after waking except four lines which he dreamed at ten years old:

> May a cock sparrow
> Write to a barrow?
> I hope you'll excuse
> My infantile muse;

— which as an unpublished fragment of the Poet Laureate may be thought interesting, but not affording much promise of his after powers.

He also told us he once dreamed an enormously long poem about fairies, which began with very long lines that gradually got shorter, and ended with fifty or sixty lines of two syllables each!

> LEWIS CARROLL, Journal for 1859, quoted in S. D. Collingwood, *The Life and Letters of Lewis Carroll*, 1899

I can but give an instance or so of what part is done sleeping and what part awake . . . and to do this I will first take . . . *Dr. Jekyll and Mr. Hyde*. I had long been trying to write a story on this subject. . . . For two days I went about wracking my brains for a plot of any sort; and on the second night I dreamed the scene at the window, and a scene afterward split in two, in which Hyde, pursued for some crime, took the powder and underwent the change in the presence of his pursuers. All the rest was made awake, and consciously.

> R. L. STEVENSON, 'A Chapter on Dreams', 1892

William Morris wanted for a long time to dream a poem. At last he did and was asked if he could remember it. 'Only the first line,' he said sadly, 'and it went like this:

> *The moonlight slept on a treacle sea.*

> R. L. MÉGROZ, *The Dream World*, 1939

[Archbishop Benson] told me that he had had a very vivid dream, in which it appeared that he had been himself appointed Poet Laureate. He said, 'I thought that I was standing before the Queen, reciting a poem, and I was very uncomfortable, partly because the Lord Chamberlain had just placed the laurel wreath on my head, and it fell a little over one eye, and partly because I was not at all sure that I ought to be dressed, as I was, in full Archiepiscopal robes. But I tried to forget all that, and concentrate my mind on my poem, and I was getting on nicely with it, when I suddenly woke, and went on, saying out loud: –

> Your latest atmosphere device
> Is all composed of dust and lice.'

SIR EDMUND GOSSE, quoted in A. C. Benson, *The Life of Edward White Benson*, 1899

[*The ring structure of benzene was revealed in a dream to the German chemist F. A. Kekulé. He reported this to a convention in 1890.*]

Again the atoms were juggling before my eyes . . . my mind's eye, sharpened by repeated sights of a similar kind, could now distinguish larger structures of different forms and in long chains, many of them close together; everything was moving in a snake-like and twisting manner. Suddenly, what was this? One of the snakes got hold of its own tail and the whole structure was mockingly twisting in front of my eyes. As if struck by lightning, I awoke. . . . Let us learn to dream, gentlemen, and then we may perhaps find the truth.

Sir John Squire confessed that when he dreamed the following lines they seemed marvellous, until he woke up:

> There was a boy grew twenty inch, yes,
> > Twenty inch a year,
> It might have made his mother flinch, but
> > She was quite a dear;
> > Yes, she was excellent,
> > And she was well content
> To watch her offspring forge ahead in his
> > Peculiar sphere.

R. L. MÉGROZ, *The Dream World*, 1939

I dreamed the whole poem in a dream, in 1894 I think, and wrote it down in the middle of the night on a scrap of paper by my bedside. I have never had a similar experience, and, what is more curious, it is a lyric of a style which I have never attempted before or since. . . . I really can offer no explanation either of the idea of the poem or its interpretation. It came to me so (apparently) without any definite

volition of my own that I don't profess to understand or be able to
interpret the symbolism. . . .

> By feathers green, across Casbeen,
>   The pilgrims track the Phoenix flown,
> By gems he strewed in waste and wood
>   And jewelled plumes at random thrown.
>
> Till wandering far, by moon and star,
>   They stand beside the fruitful pyre,
> Whence breaking bright with sanguine light,
>   The impulsive bird forgets his sire.
>
> Those ashes shine like ruby wine,
>   Like bag of Tyrian murex spilt;
> The claw, the jowl of the flying fowl
>   Are with the glorious anguish gilt.
>
> So rare the light, so rich the sight,
>   Those pilgrim men, on profit bent,
> Drop hands and eyes and merchandise,
>   And are with gazing most content.

A. C. BENSON, quoted in A. J. J. Ratcliff, *A History of Dreams*, 1923

I *dreamed* a short story last night, even down to its name, which was
Sun and Moon. It was very light. I dreamed it all – about children. I
got up at 6.30 and wrote a note or two because I knew it would fade.
I'll send it some time this week. It's so nice. I didn't dream that I read
it. No, I was in it, part of it, and it played round invisible me. But the
hero is not more than 5. In my dream I saw a supper table with the
eyes of 5. It was awfully queer – especially a plate of half-melted
ice-cream . . .

KATHERINE MANSFIELD, *Letters and Journals*, 10 February 1918

Dream that I write a one-act comic opera in the early Mozartian
manner called *Lesbien et Lesbienne*.

JAMES AGATE, *Ego 5*, 25 December 1941

The following fragment is here published at the request of a poet of
great and deserved celebrity [Lord Byron], and, as far as the Author's
own opinions are concerned, rather as a psychological curiosity,
than on the ground of any supposed *poetic* merits.

In the summer of the year 1797, the Author, then in ill health, had retired to a lonely farm-house between Porlock and Linton, on the Exmoor confines of Somerset and Devonshire. In consequence of a slight indisposition, an anodyne had been prescribed, from the effects of which he fell asleep in his chair at the moment that he was reading the following sentence, or words of the same substance, in 'Purchas's Pilgrimage': 'Here the Khan Kubla commanded a palace to be built, and a stately garden thereunto. And thus ten miles of fertile ground were inclosed with a wall.' The Author continued for about three hours in a profound sleep, at least of the external senses, during which time he has the most vivid confidence, that he could not have composed less than from two to three hundred lines; if that indeed can be called composition in which all the images rose up before him as *things*, with a parallel production of the correspondent expressions, without any sensation or consciousness of effort. On awaking he appeared to himself to have a distinct recollection of the whole, and taking his pen, ink, and paper, instantly and eagerly wrote down the lines that are here preserved. At this moment he was unfortunately called out by a person on business from Porlock, and detained by him above an hour, and on his return to his room, found, to his no small surprise and mortification, that though he still retained some vague and dim recollection of the general purport of the vision, yet, with the exception of some eight or ten scattered lines and images, all the rest had passed away like the images on the surface of a stream into which a stone has been cast, but, alas! without the after restoration of the latter!

> In Xanadu did Kubla Khan
> A stately pleasure-dome decree:
> Where Alph, the sacred river, ran
> Through caverns measureless to man
>   Down to a sunless sea.
> So twice five miles of fertile ground
> With walls and towers were girdled round:
> And there were gardens bright with sinuous rills,
> Where blossomed many an incense-bearing tree;
> And here were forests ancient as the hills,
> Enfolding sunny spots of greenery.
>
> But oh! that deep romantic chasm which slanted
> Down the green hill athwart a cedarn cover!
> A savage place! as holy and enchanted

As e'er beneath a waning moon was haunted
By woman wailing for her demon-lover!
And from this chasm, with ceaseless turmoil seething,
As if this earth in fast thick pants were breathing,
A mighty fountain momently was forced:
Amid whose swift half-intermitted burst
Huge fragments vaulted like rebounding hail,
Or chaffy grain beneath the thresher's flail:
And 'mid these dancing rocks at once and ever
It flung up momently the sacred river.
Five miles meandering with a mazy motion
Through wood and dale the sacred river ran,
Then reached the caverns measureless to man,
And sank in tumult to a lifeless ocean:
And 'mid this tumult Kubla heard from far
Ancestral voices prophesying war!
    The shadow of the dome of pleasure
    Floated midway on the waves;
    Where was heard the mingled measure
    From the fountain and the caves.
It was a miracle of rare device,
A sunny pleasure-dome with caves of ice!

    A damsel with a dulcimer
    In a vision once I saw:
    It was an Abyssinian maid,
    And on her dulcimer she played,
    Singing of Mount Abora.
    Could I revive within me
    Her symphony and song,
    To such a deep delight 'twould win me,
That with music loud and long,
I would build that dome in air,
That sunny dome! those caves of ice!
And all who heard should see them there,
And all should cry, Beware! Beware!
His flashing eyes, his floating hair!
Weave a circle round him thrice,
And close your eyes with holy dread,
For he on honey-dew hath fed,
And drunk the milk of Paradise.

S. T. COLERIDGE, 'Kubla Khan', 1798

Violence

❧

Dreamed I was going up a lovely mountain ravine and met a party of Germans, four very ugly women and their papa and mamma – indefinite – and they were arranging themselves to pic-nic, as I thought, with their backs to the beautiful view. But when I looked, I saw they were settling themselves to see Punch, and wanted me out of the way lest I should get any of it gratis; and I was going on up the ravine contemptuously, when, Punch appearing on the stage, I looked back for a minute and was startled by his immediately knocking down his wife without dancing with her first, which new reading of the play made me stop to see how it went on; and then I saw it was an Italian Punch, modernized, and that there was no idea of humour in it, but all the interest was in a mad struggle of the wife for the stick, and in her being afterwards beaten slowly, crying out, and with a stuffed body, which seemed to bruise under the blows, so as to make the whole as horrible and nasty as possible.

JOHN RUSKIN, *Diaries*, 24 October 1869

On the night before [Caligula's] assassination he dreamed that he was standing beside Jupiter's heavenly throne, when the God kicked him with the great toe of his right foot and sent him tumbling down to earth.

SUETONIUS, *The Twelve Caesars*, c.AD 120

[*A few days before his assassination, Abraham Lincoln recounted the following dream.*]

About ten days ago, I retired very late. I had been up waiting for important dispatches from the front. I could not have been long in bed when I fell into a slumber, for I was weary. I soon began to dream. There seemed to be death-like stillness about me. Then I heard subdued sobs, as if a number of people were weeping. I thought I left my bed and wandered downstairs. There the silence was broken by the same pitiful sobbing, but the mourners were invisible. I went from room to room; no living person was in sight, but the same mournful sounds of distress met me as I passed along. It was light in all the rooms; every object was familiar to me; but where

were all the people who were grieving as if their hearts would break?
I was puzzled and alarmed. What could be the meaning of all this?
Determined to find the cause of a state of things so mysterious and so
shocking, I kept on until I arrived at the East Room, which I entered.
There I met with a sickening surprise. Before me was a catafalque, on
which rested a corpse wrapped in funeral vestments. Around it were
stationed soldiers who were acting as guards; and there was a throng
of people, some gazing mournfully upon the corpse, whose face was
covered, others weeping pitifully. 'Who is dead in the White House?'
I demanded of one of the soldiers. 'The President,' was his answer;
'he was killed by an assassin!' Then came a loud burst of grief from
the crowd, which awoke me from my dream.

> WARD HILL LAMON, *Recollections of Abraham Lincoln, 1847–1865,*
> 1911

Vittoria. To pass away the time, I'll tell your grace
  A dream I had last night.
Brachiano. Most wishedly.
Vittoria. A foolish idle dream:
  Methought I walked about the mid of night
  Into a churchyard, where a goodly yew-tree
  Spread her large root in ground: under that yew,
  As I sat sadly leaning on a grave,
  Chequer'd with cross-sticks, there came stealing in
  Your duchess and my husband; one of them
  A pickaxe bore, th'other a rusty spade,
  And in rough terms they 'gan to challenge me
  About this yew.
Brachiano. That tree?
Vittoria. This harmless yew;
  They told me my intent was to root up
  That well-grown yew, and plant i' the stead of it
  A wither'd blackthorn, and for that they vow'd
  To bury me alive. My husband straight
  With pickaxe 'gan to dig, and your fell duchess
  With shovel, like a fury, voided out
  The earth and scatter'd bones: Lord, how methought
  I trembled! and yet for all this terror
  I could not pray.
Flamineo. No; the devil was in your dream.

Vittoria. When to my rescue there arose, methought,
  A whirlwind, which let fall a massy arm
  From that strong plant;
  And both were struck dead by that sacred yew,
  In that base shallow grave that was their due.

Flamineo. Excellent devil!
  She hath taught him in a dream
  To make away his duchess and her husband.

Brachiano. Sweetly shall I interpret this your dream.
  You are lodg'd within his arms who shall protect you
  From all the fevers of a jealous husband,
  From the poor envy of our phlegmatic duchess.
  I'll seat you above law, and above scandal;
  Give to your thoughts the invention of delight,
  And the fruition; nor shall government
  Divide me from you longer, than a care
  To keep you great: you shall to me at once
  Be dukedom, health, wife, children, friends, and all.

JOHN WEBSTER, The White Devil, Act I, c.1608

Last night I had a strange and horrible dream. It was one of those curious things, a dream within a dream, like a picture within a picture. I dreamt that I dreamt that Mr. and Mrs. Venables tried to murder me. We were all together in a small room and they were both trying to poison me, but I was aware of their intention and baffled them repeatedly. At length, Mr. Venables put me off my guard, came round fondling me, and suddenly clapping his hand on my neck behind said, 'It's of no use, Mr. Kilvert. You're done for'. I felt the poison beginning to work and burn in my neck. I knew it was all over and started up in fury and despair. I flew at him savagely. The scene suddenly changed to the organ loft in Hardenhuish Church. Mr. Venables, seeing me coming at him, burst out at the door. Close behind the door was standing the Holy Ghost. He knocked him from the top to the bottom of the stairs, rolling over head over heels, rushed downstairs himself, mounted his horse and fled away, I after him.

    This dream within a dream excited me to such a state of fury, that in the outer dream I determined to murder Mr. Venables. Accordingly I lay in wait for him with a pickaxe on the Vicarage lawn at Clyro, hewed an immense and hideous hole through his head, and kicked his face till it was so horribly mutilated, crushed and disfigured as to be past recognition. Then the spirit of the dream changed. Mrs. Venables became her old natural self again. 'Wasn't it enough,' she said, looking at me reproachfully, 'that you should have hewed that hole through his head, but you must go and kick his face so that I don't know him again?' At this moment, Mr. Bevan, the Vicar of Hay, came in. 'Well,' he said to me, 'you *have* done it now. You have made a pretty mess of it.'

All this time I was going about visiting the sick at Clyro and preaching in Clyro Church. But I saw that people were beginning to look shy at me and suspect me of the murder which had just been discovered. I became so wretched and conscience-stricken that I could bear my remorse no longer in secret and I went to give myself up to a policeman, who immediately took me to prison where I was kept in chains. Then the full misery of my position burst upon me and the ruin and disgrace I had brought on my family. 'It will kill my father,' I cried in an agony of remorse and despair.

I knew it was no dream. This at last was a reality from which I should never awake. I had awaked from many evil dreams and horrors and found them unreal, but this was a reality and horror from which I should never awake. It was all true at last. I had committed a murder. I calculated the time. I knew the Autumn Assizes were over and I could not be tried till the Spring. 'The Assizes,' I said, 'will come on in March and I shall be hung early in April.' And at the words I saw Mrs. Venables give a shudder of horror.

When I woke I was so persuaded of the reality of what I had seen and felt and done in my dreams that I felt for the handcuffs on my wrists and could not believe I was in bed at home till I heard the old clock on the stairs warn and then strike five.

REVD FRANCIS KILVERT, *Diary*, 14 October 1872

I was sitting in an arm-chair turning over the leaves of a largish book. . . . It contained three stories – 'All rather morbid subjects,' I thought – and as I read on my dream changed and I became one of the characters in the first story. It was about a husband and a wife and was rather a prosy narrative, but I remember little of the events of it or of the part I played in it, for I thought it dull, and in my capacity as reader I turned over the pages to read the second story.

This was concerned with a murder – a murder that had taken place before the story opened. The man who had committed it was convinced, for reasons that seemed to him wholly adequate, that he was guiltless, and merited no blame for what he had done. I slipped then and there into the person of this man. I remember passionately justifying to myself and to God the righteousness of the act that I had committed. I never felt more certain of anything in my life than I felt then, that my conscience was clear of guilt, and that the dreadful deed that I had done had been right. It was all intensely real to me. I remembered the murderer's haunted journey described in *Oliver Twist*. 'People who write about a murderer's mind can know very little about it,' I thought. Again I turned over a page – 'Oh, but these stories are very morbid,' I was saying when I woke.

MARY ARNOLD-FORSTER, *Studies in Dreams*, 1921

I went on with my dream and, although I was standing up, I imagined myself enclosed in a sort of Oriental pavilion. I felt all the corners and found it to be octagonal. A divan ran around the walls, which seemed to me to be of thick plate-glass, beyond which I could see shining treasures, shawls, and tapestries. Across a street, a landscape was visible through the latticed door, and it seemed to me that I could distinguish the shapes of trees and rocks. I had already lived there in some other existence, and I thought I recognized the deep grottoes of Ellora. Gradually a bluish light penetrated the pavilion and brought out strange apparitions inside. I thought I was in the midst of some vast charnel-house where the history of the universe was written in characters of blood. Opposite me was painted the body of an enormous woman; but various parts of her had been sliced off, as if by a sword; on the other walls, other women of different races, whose bodies dominated me more and more, made a bloody jumble of limbs and heads, ranging from empresses and queens to the humblest peasants. It was the history of all crime, and I only had to keep my eyes on any one spot to see depicted there some tragic scene.

'There,' I told myself, 'is what has resulted from power bestowed on man. Man has little by little destroyed and cut up the eternal type of beauty into a thousand little pieces, so that his races are more and more losing strength and perfection . . .' And indeed, on a line of shadow creeping in through a chink in the door, I saw the descending generations of future races.

GÉRARD DE NERVAL, *Aurélia*, 1855

I was with an unknown, brown-skinned man, a savage, in a lonely, rocky mountain landscape. It was before dawn; the eastern sky was already bright, and the stars fading. Then I heard Siegfried's horn sounding over the mountains and I knew that we had to kill him. We were armed with rifles and lay in wait on a narrow path over the rocks.

Then Siegfried appeared high up on the crest of the mountain, in the first ray of the rising sun. On a chariot made of the bones of the dead he drove at furious speed down the precipitous slope. When he turned a corner, we shot at him, and he plunged down, struck dead.

Filled with disgust and remorse for having destroyed something so great and beautiful, I turned to flee, impelled by the fear that the murder might be discovered. But a tremendous downfall of rain began, and I knew that it would wipe out all traces of the dead. I had escaped the danger of discovery; life could go on, but an unbearable feeling of guilt remained.

C. G. JUNG, *Memories, Dreams, Reflections*, 1963

He lost consciousness; it seemed strange to him that he didn't remember how he got into the street. It was late evening. . . . Raskolnikov walked along, mournful and anxious; he was distinctly aware of having come out with a purpose, of having to do something in a hurry, but what it was he had forgotten. Suddenly he stood still and saw a man standing on the other side of the street, beckoning to him. He crossed over to him, but at once the man turned and walked away with his head hanging, as though he had made no sign to him. 'Stay, did he really beckon?' Raskolnikov wondered, but he tried to overtake him. When he was within ten paces he recognised him and was frightened; it was the same man with stooping shoulders in the long coat. Raskolnikov followed him at a distance; his heart was beating; they went down a turning; the man still did not look round. 'Does he know I am following him?' thought Raskolnikov. The man went into the gateway of a big house. Raskolnikov hastened to the gate and looked in to see whether he would look round and sign to him. In the courtyard the man did turn round and again seemed to beckon him. Raskolnikov at once followed him into the yard, but the man was gone. He must have gone up the first staircase. Raskolnikov rushed after him. He heard slow measured steps two flights above. The staircase seemed strangely familiar. . . . He reached the third storey, should he go on? There was a stillness that was dreadful. . . . But he went on. The sound of his own footsteps scared and frightened him. How dark it was! The man must be hiding in some corner here. Ah! the flat was standing wide open, he hesitated and went in. . . . He noticed in the corner between the window and the little cupboard something like a cloak hanging on the wall. 'Why is that cloak here?' he thought, 'it wasn't there before. . . .' He went up to it quietly and felt that there was some one hiding behind it. He cautiously moved the cloak and saw, sitting on a chair in the corner, the old woman bent double so that he couldn't see her face; but it was she. He stood over her. 'She is afraid,' he thought. He stealthily took the axe from the noose and struck her one blow, then another on the skull. But strange to say she did not stir, as though she were made of wood. He was frightened, bent down nearer and tried to look at her; but she, too, bent her head lower. He bent right down to the ground and peeped up into her face from below, he peeped and turned cold with horror: the old woman was sitting and laughing, shaking with noiseless laughter, doing her utmost that he should not hear it. Suddenly he fancied that the door from the bedroom was opened a little and that there was laughter and whispering within. He was overcome with frenzy and he began hitting the old woman on the head with all his force, but at every blow of the axe the laughter and whispering from the bedroom grew louder and the old woman was simply shaking with mirth. He was rushing away, but the passage was full of people, the doors of the flats stood open and on the landing, on the stairs and everywhere below there were people, rows of heads, all looking, but huddled together in silence and expectation. Something gripped his heart, his legs were rooted to the spot, they would not move. . . . He tried to scream and woke up.

FYODOR DOSTOEVSKY, *Crime and Punishment*, 1866

I find myself quietly talking with a dark-eyed friend whom I have met by chance in a narrow deserted London street just before summer nightfall. . . . My friend enquires if I have heard that the house, not many streets distant, in which I live alone, has been sold—over my head. Instantly I see the house, known only too well; its grimed lightless windows, its obscure façade, its dingy interior; and also a huddled, black-skirted body dwindled by the ravages of decay and locked up in an empty room on its first floor. It has lain there for at least a year, shut in, unvisited. Appalled at this information, I stare mutely into the face of my guileless informant, conscious that in the darkness the blood in my body is steadily mounting into my face and head, and in a desperate confusion of heart and brain. The news has come too late; discovery of my vile secret, and the sequel, is now inevitable. . . .

And yet, the identity of the victim, the motive for the murder, what preceded its dreadful hour, and what had passed in the intervening months—of all this the dream, as it was remembered, recorded not a trace.

WALTER DE LA MARE, Behold, This Dreamer, 1939

Methought my brother, my Uncle Antony, and Mr. Solmes, had formed a plot to destroy Mr. Lovelace; who discovering it, and believing I had a hand in it, turned all his rage against me. I thought he made them all fly into foreign parts upon it; and afterwards seizing me, carried me into a churchyard; and there, notwithstanding all my prayers and tears, and protestations of innocence, stabbed me to the heart, and then tumbled me into a deep grave ready dug, among two or three half-dissolved carcasses; throwing in the dirt and earth upon me with his hands, and trampling it down with his feet.

I awoke in a cold sweat, trembling, and in agonies; and still the frightful images raised by it remain upon my memory.

But why should I, who have such *real* evils to contend with, regard *imaginary* ones?

SAMUEL RICHARDSON, Clarissa Harlowe, 1748

I stretched myself on the mattress and put out the light; but the swarm of new images that rushed on my mind set me again instantly in motion. . . .

What chiefly occupied me was a nameless sort of terror. What shall I compare it to? Methinks, that one falling from a tree overhanging a torrent, plunged into the whirling eddy, and gasping and struggling while he sinks to rise no more, would feel just as I did then. . . .

Midnight it was, my chamber's solitude was not to be supported. After a few turns across the floor, I left the room, and the house. I walked without design and in a hurried pace. I posted straight to the house of Mrs. Fielding. I lifted the latch, but the door did not open. It was, no doubt, locked.

'How comes this?' said I, and looked around me. . . . 'Locked upon *me*! but I will summon them, I warrant me,' – and rung the bell, not timidly or slightly, but with violence. Some one hastened from above. I saw the glimmer of a candle through the keyhole.

'Strange,' thought I; 'a candle at noonday!' – The door was opened, and my poor Bess, robed in a careless and hasty manner, appeared. . . .

She led the way into the parlour. – 'Wait a moment here: I will tell her you are come:' – and she tripped away.

Presently a step was heard. The door opened again, and then entered a man. He was tall, elegant, sedate to a degree of sadness; something in his dress and aspect that bespoke the foreigner, the Frenchman.

'What,' said he, mildly, 'is your business with my wife? She cannot see you instantly, and has sent me to receive your commands.'

'Your *wife*! I want Mrs. Fielding.'

'True; and Mrs. Fielding is my wife. Thank Heaven, I have come in time to discover her, and claim her as such.'

I started back. I shuddered. My joints slackened, and I stretched my hand to catch something by which I might be saved from sinking on the floor. Meanwhile, Fielding changed his countenance into rage and fury. He called me villain! bade me avaunt! and drew a shining steel from his bosom, with which he stabbed me to the heart. I sunk upon the floor, and all, for a time, was darkness and oblivion! At length, I returned as it were to life. I opened my eyes. The mists disappeared, and I found myself stretched upon the bed in my own chamber. I remembered the fatal blow I had received. I put my hand upon my breast; the spot where the dagger entered. There were no traces of a wound. All was perfect and entire. Some miracle had made me whole.

I raised myself up. I re-examined my body. All around me was hushed, till a voice from the pavement below proclaimed that it was 'past three o'clock.'

'What!' said I; 'has all this miserable pageantry, this midnight wandering, and this ominous interview, been no more than – *a dream*?'

CHARLES BROCKDEN BROWN, *Arthur Mervyn*, 1799

Last night, one of the most curious dreams I ever had. I had gone to sleep in anguish. . . . After a moment, I saw myself (which never happens to me in dreams) in our rue Cortambert flat, the one where I spent part of my youth. In the hall was a glass sentry box, very much like the telephone booths to be seen in the streets here. Motionless in this glass sentry box was a man in a raincoat belted in at the waist; his hat was pulled down and almost hid his eyes, but his expression could be guessed. His face expressed nothing but extraordinary brutality, with something blind about it that made him most alarming. I knew that he had been living with us for years and years and that he usually stayed in his sentry box. . . . I also knew that he possessed superhuman strength but had only the intellect of a child of five, a brute who had always obeyed me, although he had obeyed less perfectly for some time, because it had dawned on him that he was stronger than I. If I told the man to go here or there, he carried out my orders, but with an ever-increasing and threatening sullenness. Usually, I chased him from my room and he returned to his sentry box, but I was afraid of him and my fright grew greater by the second. Finally, I saw him coming toward me, to kill me. Having taken refuge in my room, I turned the key in the lock, but when I awoke, my heart thumping, he was already shaking down the door with his powerful shoulder.

JULIAN GREEN, *Diary*, 29 August 1947

A dream: Two groups of men were fighting each other. The group to which I belonged had captured one of our opponents, a gigantic naked man. Five of us clung to him, one by the head, two on either side by his arms and legs. Unfortunately we had no knife with which to stab him, we hurriedly asked each other for a knife, no one had one. But since for some reason there was no time to lose and an oven stood near by whose extraordinarily large cast-iron door was red-hot, we dragged the man to it, held one of his feet close to the oven until the foot began to smoke, pulled it back again until it stopped smoking, then thrust it close to the door again. We monotonously kept this up until I awoke, not only in cold sweat but with my teeth actually chattering.

FRANZ KAFKA, *Diaries*, 20 April 1916

I dreamed that I found myself underground in a vault artificially lighted. Tables were ranged along the walls of the vault, and upon these tables were bound down the living bodies of half-dissected and mutilated animals. Scientific experts were busy at work on their victims with scalpel, hot iron and forceps. But, as I looked at the creatures lying bound before them, they no longer appeared to be mere rabbits, or hounds, for in each I saw a human shape, the shape of a man, with limbs and lineament resembling those of their torturers, hidden within the outward form. And when they led into the place an old worn-out horse, crippled with age and long toil in the service of man, and bound him down, and lacerated his flesh with their knives, I saw the human form within-him stir and writhe as though it were an unborn babe moving in its mother's womb. And I cried aloud – 'Wretches! you are tormenting an unborn man!' But they heard not, nor could they see what I saw. Then they brought in a white rabbit, and thrust its eyes through with heated irons. And as I gazed, the rabbit seemed to me like a tiny infant, with human face, and hands which stretched themselves towards me in appeal, and lips which sought to cry for help in human accents. And I could bear no more, but broke forth into a bitter rain of tears, exclaiming – 'O blind! blind! not to see that you torture a child, the youngest of your own flesh and blood!'

And with that I woke, sobbing vehemently.

> ANNA KINGSFORD, *Dreams and Dream-Stories*: 'The Laboratory Underground', 1888

Up in good time after sound sleep, though first disturbed by the ghastliest nightmare of dream I ever had in my life. After some pleasant, or at least natural dreaming about receiving people in a large house, I went to *rest* myself into a room full of fine old pictures; the first of which, when I examined it – and it was large – was of an old surgeon dying by dissecting himself! It was worse than dissecting – *tearing*: and with circumstances of horror about the treatment of the head which I will not enter.

> JOHN RUSKIN, *Diaries*, 27 December 1875

On the night between the 28th and 29th, 5th month, 1770, I dreamed a man had been hunting and brought a living creature to Mount Holly of a mixed breed, part fox and part cat. It appeared active in various motions, especially with its claws and teeth. I beheld and lo! many people gathering in the house where it was talked one to another, and after some time I perceived by their talk that an old Negro man was just now dead, and that his death was on this wise. They wanted flesh to feed this creature, and they wanted to be quit of the expense of keeping a man who through great age was unable to labour; so raising a long ladder against the house, they hanged the old man.

One woman spake lightly of it and signified she was sitting at the tea table when they hung him up, and though neither she nor any present said anything against their proceedings, yet she said at the sight of the old man a dying, she could not go on with tea drinking.

I stood silent all this time and was filled with extreme sorrow at so horrible an action and now began to lament bitterly, like as some lament at the decease of a friend, at which lamentation some smiled, but none mourned with me.

One man spake in justification of what was done and said the flesh of the old Negro was wanted, not only that this creature might have plenty, but some other creatures also wanted his flesh, which I apprehended from what he said were some hounds kept for hunting. I felt matter on my mind and would have spake to the man, but utterance was taken from me and I could not speak to him. And being in great distress I continued wailing till I began to wake, and opening my eyes I perceived it was morning.

JOHN WOOLMAN, *Journal*, 1770

Blaise remembered that he had not fed the dogs. He had had these two dogs since he was quite a little boy, both of them smooth-haired fox terriers, named Tango and Rumba by Blaise's father, who was fond of dancing. Blaise felt terrible guilt and fear because he remembered that the dogs were shut into the old stables and no one knew they were there and no one would hear them barking. They had been there for days and days, for weeks. How could he possibly have forgotten them, and what would his father say? He began to run, but his feet had become large and heavy and were cleaving to the earth. At last he reached the stables and unbarred the top half of the door of the last loosebox and peered into the obscure interior. There was no movement within. He looked and looked. Then with horror he saw the two dogs. They had become dark and dried up and elongated and were hanging from hooks upon the wall. He thought: When I did not come they must have hanged themselves. Then he thought: No, they have died and become something else, and the gardener thought they were some sort of tools or implements and hung them up. But what sort of tools or implements have they become?

'Wake up, damn you, wake up!'

IRIS MURDOCH, *The Sacred and Profane Love Machine*, 1974

I had the following dream, which was cut short by my own cries of terror, as often happens to me. I am at the salle Gaveau, in the dress circle. The hall is full, but the musicians have not yet appeared. There is general conversation all around me, but I am reading my programme and do not listen to it. At that moment someone murmurs in my ear: 'There is a change in the programme.' Almost immediately, the lights are dimmed and complete silence reigns. Then the little door on the left of the organ opens, and in the subdued light someone enters. He is being pushed from behind. Several men dressed in black follow him closely, directing his footsteps, for his head is enclosed in a sort of monk's hood, without the usual holes for eyes and mouth. Someone throws towards the ceiling a long rope which becomes attached – I cannot see how – to an iron hook. This rope seems as though it were alive, happy, quivering with joy in the hands of the men who now make a loop at its end. It was then that I realized that they were going to hang the man in the cowl, and I cried aloud with all my strength.

JULIAN GREEN, *Personal Record 1928–1939*, 5 February 1929

Chess last night – or stale tea . . . gave me comfortless waking with horrid nightmare about a man's being pitched at a fortress wall out of a catapult and splitting in two.

JOHN RUSKIN, *Diaries*, 11 February 1876

She must have been awakened by protesting cries from other voices. It was the same room, except that all but the essentials of furniture had been removed. In this bare, clinical interior the light did not come from the bedside lamp, which she could remember switching on and off, nor was it related to normal daylight. As the room was windowless, she saw, the light falling around her could only have been shed from within, yet from no visible light fittings.

Throughout this flesh-coloured, infra-natural light, she became aware of a fluttering of the bird-voices, moth-like hands, of a brood of children she did not attempt to count. They were too many and too unearthly, also too frightening, in particular the eyes and mouths, which were those of flesh-and-blood children, probing, accusing the room's focal point, herself.

She understood by degrees that the children wanted out; the safe, windowless room (its walls even upholstered, she noticed) was the cause of their distress and she the one they held responsible for their unreasonable imprisonment.

'But my darlings,' her voice sounded as odd as her use of a term she had always tended to avoid, 'here you'll be safe, don't you see?'

But the children continued battering with flat hands on the unresponsive walls, a drumming to which was added, she could hear, sounds of gathering confusion outside, as of wind rising, waves pounding, and worse, human voices screaming hatred and destruction as some monstrous act, explosive and decisive, was being prepared.

She, too, had begun screaming as she tore free from the hospital sheets pinning her down. 'Can't I make you realise?' She lunged among the milling children, trying to gather them into her arms as though they had been flowers. 'Safe – as you'll never be outside.'

Almost all of them eluded her. Only one little crop-headed boy she succeeded in trapping. She was holding his pink head against her breast, when he tore the nightdress she was wearing, and it fell around her, exposing a chest, flat and hairy, a dangling penis and testicles. To express his disgust, the pink-stubbled boy bit into one of the blind nipples, then reeled back, pointing, as did all the children, laughing vindictively as their adult counterparts might have, at the blood flowing from the wound opened in the source of their deception, down over belly and thighs, gathering at the crotch in such quantities that it overflowed and hid the penis. The dripping and finally coagulating blood might have gushed from a torn womb.

PATRICK WHITE, The Twyborn Affair, 1979

I dreamed that my wife's dog – a dog who, in real life, was constantly getting into trouble – had killed a child in the neighbouring town. On going thither I entered a butcher's shop, and saw the child lying on a table, mutilated and bleeding. After a time, however, I learned that it was not a child, but a pig that had been killed, and what I had previously taken for a child was now visibly a dead pig. I felt ashamed of my mistake, and the sympathy I had experienced now seemed excessive, especially when the butcher remarked that it was all right as he had been fattening the pig and meant to kill it soon anyhow. Then the pig was cut open, though it made daring attempts to come to life again, during which I awoke.

HAVELOCK ELLIS, The World of Dreams, 1911

Ann. Last night I had a wonderful dream. We were walking arm in arm. A perfect day. Suddenly rain bucketed down. We sheltered under a tree. Wind howled in the branches – and a bolt of lightning hit it. It crashed down, struck my husband on the head and drove him straight into the ground like a hammer striking a nail. He weren't there! Vanished! Killed and buried at one blow! I wasn't even brushed. Then the sun came out. Well it would, wouldn't it? And Lucy and Peg – my best school chums – rode up in a carriage sat on top of a great mountain of my luggage. And I'm whisked off to a gala given by royalty at Covent Garden for all the people to celebrate my release. Ee I was that happy!

EDWARD BOND, *Restoration*, 1981

When on the following night, much to his dismay, [Caesar] had a dream of raping his own mother, the soothsayers greatly encouraged him by their interpretation of it: namely, that he was destined to conquer the earth, our Universal Mother.

SUETONIUS, *The Twelve Caesars*, c.AD 120

Caesar. Calphurnia, here, my wife, stays me at home.
　She dreamt to-night she saw my statue,
　Which like a fountain with an hundred spouts
　Did run pure blood; and many lusty Romans
　Came smiling, and did bathe their hands in it.
　And these does she apply for warnings and portents
　And evils imminent; and on her knee
　Hath begg'd that I will stay at home to-day.

Decius. This dream is all amiss interpreted;
　It was a vision fair and fortunate:
　Your statue spouting blood in many pipes,
　In which so many smiling Romans bath'd,
　Signifies that from you great Rome shall suck
　Reviving blood, and that great men shall press
　For tinctures, stains, relics, and cognizance.
　This by Calphurnia's dream is signified.

WILLIAM SHAKESPEARE, *Julius Caesar*, c.1599

　Now slept the gods, and those who fought at Troy –
　horse-handlers, charioteers – the long night through,
　but slumber had no power over Zeus,

who pondered in the night how to exalt
Akhilleus, how in his absence to destroy
Akhaians in windrows at the ships.
He thought it best to send to Agamemnon
that same night a fatal dream.
Calling the dream he said:

            'Sinister Dream,
go down amid the fast ships of Akhaia,
enter Lord Agamemnon's quarters, tell him
everything, point by point, as I command you:
Let him prepare the long-haired carls of Akhaia
to fight at once. Now he may take by storm
the spacious town of Troy. The Olympians, tell him,
are of two minds no longer: Hera swayed them,
and black days overhang the men of Troy.'

The dream departed at his word, descending
swift as wind to where the long ships lay,
and sought the son of Atreus. In his hut
he found him sleeping, drifted all about
with balm of slumber. At the marshal's pillow
standing still, the dream took shape
as Neleus' son, old Nestor. Agamemnon
deferred to Nestor most, of all his peers;
so in his guise the dream spoke to the dreamer:

'Sleeping, son of Atreus, tamer of horses?
You should not sleep all night, not as a captain
responsible for his men, with many duties,
a great voice in the conferences of war.
Follow me closely: I am a messenger
from Zeus, who is far away but holds you dear.
"Prepare the troops," he said, "to take the field
without delay: now may you take by storm
the spacious town of Troy. The Olympian gods
are of two minds no longer: Hera's pleading
swayed them all, and bitter days from Zeus
await the Trojans." Hold on to this message
against forgetfulness in tides of day
when blissful sleep is gone.'

> On this the dream
> withdrew into the night, and was left the man
> to envision, rapt, all that was not to be,
> thinking that day to conquer Priam's town.
> Oh childish trust! What action lay ahead
> in the mind of Zeus he could not know – what grief
> and wounds from shock of combat in the field,
> alike for Trojans and Akhaians.
>
> HOMER (*c*.9th century BC), *The Iliad*, Book 2

In midnight sleep of many a face of anguish,
Of the look at first of the mortally wounded, (of that indescribable look,)
Of the dead on their backs with arms extended wide,
       I dream, I dream, I dream.

Of scenes of Nature, fields and mountains,
Of skies so beauteous after a storm, and at night the moon so unearthly bright,
Shining sweetly, shining down, where we dig the trenches and gather the heaps,
       I dream, I dream, I dream.

Long have they pass'd, faces and trenches and fields,
Where through the carnage I moved with a callous composure, or away from the fallen,
Onward I sped at the time – but now of their forms at night,
       I dream, I dream, I dream.

WALT WHITMAN, 'Old War-Dreams', 1865–6

Your Majesty's communication encourages me to relate a dream which I had in the spring of 1863, in the hardest days of the conflict, from which no human could see any possible way out. I dreamt (as I related the first thing next morning to my wife and other witnesses) that I was riding on a narrow Alpine path, precipice on the right, rocks on the left. The path grew narrower, so that the horse refused to proceed, and it was impossible to turn round or dismount, owing to lack of space. Then, with my whip in my left hand, I struck the smooth rock and called on God. The whip grew to an endless length, the rocky wall dropped like a piece of stage scenery and opened out a broad path, with a view over hills and forests, like a landscape in Bohemia; there were Prussian troops with banners, and even in my dream the thought came to me at once that I must report it to your Majesty. This dream was fulfilled, and I woke up rejoiced and strengthened.

OTTO VON BISMARCK, letter to Emperor William I, 18 December 1881

I dreamed that in a city dark as Paris
I stood alone in a deserted square.
The night was trembling with a violet
Expectancy. At the far edge it moved
And rumbled; on that flickering horizon
The guns were pumping colour in the sky.

There was the Front. But I was lonely here,
Left behind, abandoned by the army.
The empty city and the empty square
Was my inhabitation, my unrest.
The helmet with its vestige of a crest,
The rifle in my hands, long out of date,
The belt I wore, the trailing overcoat
And hobnail boots, were those of a *poilu*.
I was the man, as awkward as a bear.

Over the rooftops where cathedrals loomed
In speaking majesty, two aeroplanes,
Forlorn as birds, appeared. Then growing large,
The German *Taube* and the *Nieuport Scout*,
They chased each other tumbling through the sky,
Till one streamed down on fire to the earth.

These wars have been so great, they are forgotten
Like the Egyptian dynasts. My confrere
In whose thick boots I stood, were you amazed
To wander through my brain four decades later
As I have wandered in a dream through yours?

The violence of waking life disrupts
The order of our death. Strange dreams occur,
For dreams are licensed as they never were.

LOUIS SIMPSON, 'I Dreamed that in a City Dark as Paris', 1959

While looking for a flat I stayed with my sister in Highgate, dreamed that a bomb was falling plumb on the bed. Crossing my arms tightly I threw myself out of bed, fell like a log on the floor, triumphantly thought 'It has missed me.' But no, it was a time bomb, there it was on the bed and about to go off. Hastily, I seized the rubber hot-water bottle by the neck, threw it with all my force through the open window, went to sleep self-satisfied. In the morning there was no hot-water bottle, I had to go down to breakfast, say to my sister, 'I'm awfully sorry but I've thrown your hot-water bottle into the neighbour's garden.'

LOUIS MacNEICE, *The Strings Are False*, 1965

A dream dreamt by Maury has become famous. He was ill and lying in his room in bed, with his mother sitting beside him, and dreamt that it was during the Reign of Terror. After witnessing a number of frightful scenes of murder, he was finally himself brought before the revolutionary tribunal. . . . He was questioned by them, and, after a number of incidents which were not retained in his memory, was condemned, and led to the place of execution surrounded by an immense mob. He climbed on to the scaffold and was bound to the plank by the executioner. It was tipped up. The blade of the guillotine fell. He felt his head being separated from his body, woke up in extreme anxiety – and found that the top of the bed had fallen down and had struck his cervical vertebrae just in the way in which the blade of the guillotine would actually have struck them.

SIGMUND FREUD, *The Interpretation of Dreams*, 1900

I dreamt I was standing in the Rue St. Honoré. A melancholy darkness spread around me; all was still. Nevertheless, a slow and uncertain sound soon arose. All of a sudden, I perceived at the bottom of the street, and advancing towards me, a troop of cavalry – the men and horses, however, all flayed. The men held torches in their hands, the red flames of which illuminated faces without skins, and bloody muscles. Their hollow eyes rolled fearfully in their sockets, their mouths opened from ear to ear, and helmets of hanging flesh covered their hideous heads. The horses dragged along their own skins in the kennels, which overflowed with blood on all sides. Pale and dishevelled women appeared and disappeared at the windows in dismal silence; low, inarticulate groans filled the air, and

I remained in the street, alone, petrified with horror, and deprived of strength sufficient to seek safety in flight. This horrible troop continued passing along rapidly in a gallop, and casting frightful glances upon me. Their march continued, I thought, for five hours, and they were followed by an immense number of artillery waggons, full of bleeding corpses, whose limbs still quivered; a disgusting smell of blood and bitumen almost choked me. At length the iron gates of the prison, shutting with great force, awoke me again.

COUNT DE LAVALETTE *c.*1830, quoted in Frank Seafield, *The Literature and Curiosities of Dreams*, 1865

              ... Turnus lay
asleep, beneath his high roof, in black night.
Allecto sets aside her savage features
and Fury's body; she transforms herself,
becoming an old woman, furrowing
her filthy brow with wrinkles, putting on
white hair and headband, then an olive bough;
she now is Calybe, the aged priestess
of Juno and her temple. And she shows
herself before the young man with these words:
'O Turnus, can you let all you have done
run down to uselessness, your sceptre pass
to Dardan colonists? The king denies
your bride, the dowry you have won by blood.
He seeks a foreign son to take the kingdom.
Scorned one, set out to face ungrateful dangers;
go now to lay the Tuscan armies low,
to give the Latins peace beneath your shield.
This is the message that the very presence
of Saturn's mighty daughter ordered me
to bring you while you lay in tranquil night.
Rise up and gladly call your men to ready
their arms, to march beyond the gates to battle,
to burn the Phrygian chieftains who have settled
by this fair river and their painted fleet.
So does the urgent force of gods command.
If King Latinus does not grant the marriage,
does not hold fast to his old promise, let
him learn at last what Turnus is in arms.'

At this, the young man mocks the prophetess:
'I am well aware that ships are in the Tiber –
no need to conjure up for me such terrors.
Queen Juno has not been forgetful of me.
But old age, mother, overcome by rust,
fruitless of truth, has made you waste your cares;
among the quarrels of kings, it plays on your
prophetic spirit with false tears. Your task:
to guard the shrines and images of gods.
Let men run war and peace: war is their work.'

Allecto blazed in anger at his words.
But even as he spoke, a sudden trembling
clutched at the limbs of Turnus, his eyes stared:
the Fury hisses with so many serpents,
so monstrous is the face she shows. She turned
her flaming eyes and thrust him, faltering, back,
as he tried to say more. She lifted up
two vipers from her hair; her lash was loud;
with maddened lips she added this: 'Then look
at me – undone by rust, fruitless of truth,
whom old age plays upon with cheating terrors
among the quarrels of kings! Just look at me!
I come here from the home of the dread Sisters,
and in my hand I carry death and wars.'

And saying this, she cast a torch at Turnus,
fixing the firebrand within his breast,
and there it smoked with murky light. Great fear
shatters his sleep, sweat bursts from all his body
and bathes his bones and limbs. Insane, he raves
for arms, he searches beds and halls for weapons. . . .

VIRGIL, *The Aeneid*, Book VII, *c*.20 BC

Happy Endings

The old woman sighed sympathetically. 'My pretty dear,' she said, 'you must be cheerful and stop worrying about dreams. The dreams that come in daylight are not to be trusted, everyone knows that, and even night-dreams often go by contraries. For example, that one is weeping or being beaten or even having one's throat cut, is good luck and usually means prosperous change, whereas to dream that one is laughing, stuffing oneself with sweets or having fun under the bedclothes is bad luck and a sure sign of illness or unhappiness. Now let me tell you a fairy tale or two to make you feel a little better.'

APULEIUS, *The Golden Ass*, c.AD 180

Domitian dreamed, the night before he was slain, that a golden head was growing out of the nape of his neck; and indeed, the succession that followed him, for many years, made golden times.

SIR FRANCIS BACON, 'Of Prophecies', 1625

I went to Ambleside; where . . . the congregation was waiting. . . . Among them were a gentleman and his wife, who gave me a remarkable relation. She said she had often heard her mother relate what an intimate acquaintance had told her, that her husband was concerned in the Rebellion of 1745. He was tried at Carlisle, and found guilty. The evening before he was to die, sitting and musing in her chair, she fell fast asleep. She dreamed one came to her and said, 'Go to such a part of the wall, and among the loose stones you will find a key, which you must carry to your husband.' She waked; but, thinking it a common dream, paid no attention to it. Presently she fell asleep again, and dreamed the very same dream. She started up, put on her cloak and hat, and went to that part of the wall, and among the loose stones found a key. Having, with some difficulty, procured admission into the jail, she gave this to her husband. It opened the door of his cell, as well as the lock of the prison door. So at midnight he escaped for life.

JOHN WESLEY, *Journals*, 19 April 1784

'I dreamt about the winner of the Derby,' said Lola.

A swift reaction of attentive interest set in.

'Do tell us what you dreamt,' came in a chorus.

'The really remarkable thing about it is that I've dreamt it two nights running,' said Lola, finally deciding between the allurements of sausages and kedgeree . . . 'I saw the finish of the race as clearly as anything; and one horse won easily, almost in a canter, and everybody cried out "Bread and Butter wins! Good old Bread and Butter." I heard the name distinctly, and I've had the same dream two nights running.'

'Bread and Butter,' said Mrs. de Claux, 'now, whatever horse can that point to? Why – of course; Nursery Tea!'

She looked round with the triumphant smile of a successful unraveller of mystery.

'How about Le Five O'Clock?' interposed Sir Lulworth.

'It would fit either of them equally well,' said Odo; 'can you remember any details about the jockey's colours? That might help us.'

'I seem to remember a glimpse of lemon sleeves or cap, but I can't be sure,' said Lola, after due reflection.

'There isn't a lemon jacket or cap in the race,' said Bertie, referring to a list of starters and jockeys; 'can't you remember anything about the appearance of the horse? If it were a thick-set animal, thick bread and butter would typify Nursery Tea; and if it were thin, of course, it would mean Le Five O'Clock.'

'That seems sound enough,' said Mrs. de Claux; 'do think, Lola dear, whether the horse in your dream was thin or stoutly built.'

'I can't remember that it was one or the other,' said Lola; 'one wouldn't notice such a detail in the excitement of a finish.'

'But this was a symbolic animal,' said Sir Lulworth; 'if it were to typify thick or thin bread and butter, surely it ought to have been either as bulky and tubby as a shire cart-horse, or as thin as a heraldic leopard.'

'I'm afraid you are rather a careless dreamer,' said Bertie resentfully.

SAKI (H. H. MUNRO), 'A Bread and Butter Miss', 1919

While I was editing *The Academy* in 1908, I dreamt the winner of the Derby. . . .

At that time I was immersed in my paper, and I never went near a race-course or took any interest in racing. In fact when I had the dream, I did not even know the name of the Derby favourite of that year. I simply dreamt that I saw a grey filly winning the Derby. 'But Signorinetta was not grey,' any racing man would reply. I know she was not grey, but my dream made me back her in the following way.

At lunch-time on the day after I had the dream I was lunching by myself in a little restaurant. . . . This was just a week before the Derby.

At another table, also lunching by himself, I saw a friend of mine, Charlie Owen, a racing man, and I called over to him to come and lunch with me. He came over at once and I said, 'Charlie, is there a grey filly running in the Derby, because last night I dreamt that I saw a grey filly win the Derby?' He replied, 'I'm sorry, your dream is a wash-out. Not only is there no grey filly running in the Derby this year, but there is no filly at all of any colour running.' I laughed and said, 'Well, there goes my chance of backing the winner.'

I thought no more about it till that day week, Derby Day, when I was once more lunching by myself at the same restaurant, and there again was Charlie Owen. . . . I got a paper and began looking through the horses and their performances, and after a minute I said, 'Look here, you distinctly told me last week that there was no filly in the race, and here I see there is one, Signorinetta.' He said, 'Yes, quite right. I forgot all about her when you asked me, but she isn't grey and she hasn't got a million to one chance.' 'I don't care,' I replied; 'you said there was no filly and there is one, and I am going to have a fiver on her.' He said, 'Don't be a b----- fool.'

Well, to cut a long story short, I went out directly after lunch and put a 'fiver' on her, and she won at 100 to 1.

ALFRED DOUGLAS, *Without Apology*, 1938

There is surely a nearer apprehension of any thing that delights us in our dreams, than in our waked senses: without this I were unhappy; for my awaked judgement discontents me, ever whispering unto me, that I am from my friend; but my friendly dreams in the night requite me, and make me think I am within his arms. I thank God for my happy dreams, as I do for my good rest; for there is a satisfaction in them unto reasonable desires, and such as can be content with a fit of happiness; and surely it is not a melancholy conceit to think we are all asleep in this world, and that the conceits of this life are as mere dreams to those of the next; as the phantasms of the night, to the conceits of the day. There is an equal delusion in both, and the one doth but seem to be the emblem or picture of the other: we are somewhat more than our selves in our sleeps, and the slumber of the body seems to be but the waking of the soul. . . . In one dream I can compose a whole comedy, behold the action, apprehend the jests, and laugh my self awake at the conceits thereof. Were my memory as faithful as my reason is then fruitful, I would never study but in my dreams; and this time also would I chuse for my devotions: but our grosser memories have then so little hold of our abstracted understandings, that they forget the story, and can only relate to our awaked souls, a confused and broken tale of that that hath passed.

SIR THOMAS BROWNE, *Religio Medici*, 1643

Bottom. I have had a most rare vision. I have had a dream, past the wit of man to say what dream it was: man is but an ass, if he go about to expound this dream. Methought I was – there is no man can tell what. Methought I was, – and methought I had, – but man is but a patched fool, if he will offer to say what methought I had. The eye of man hath not heard, the ear of man hath not seen, man's hand is not able to taste, his tongue to conceive, nor his heart to report, what my dream was. I will get Peter Quince to write a ballad of this dream: it shall be called Bottom's dream, because it hath no bottom; and I will sing it in the latter end of a play, before the duke: peradventure, to make it the more gracious, I shall sing it after death.

WILLIAM SHAKESPEARE, *A Midsummer Night's Dream*, c.1595

III

THE DREAM WORLD

Into Sleep

❧

The world in which we live when we are asleep is so different that people who have difficulty in going to sleep seek first of all to escape from the waking world. After having desperately, for hours on end, with their eyes closed, revolved in their minds thoughts similar to those which they would have had with their eyes open, they take heart again on noticing that the preceding minute has been weighed down by a line of reasoning in strict contradiction to the laws of logic and the reality of the present, this brief 'absence' signifying that the door is now open through which they may perhaps presently be able to escape from the perception of the real, to advance to a resting-place more or less remote from it, which will mean their having a more or less 'good' night. But already a great stride has been made when we turn our backs on the real, when we reach the outer caves in which 'auto-suggestions' prepare – like witches – the hell-broth of imaginary illnesses or of the recurrence of nervous disorders, and watch for the hour when the spasms which have been building up during the unconsciousness of sleep will be unleashed with sufficient force to make sleep cease.

Not far thence is the secret garden in which the kinds of sleep, so different one from another, induced by datura, by Indian hemp, by the multiple extracts of ether – the sleep of belladonna, of opium, of valerian – grow like unknown flowers whose petals remain closed until the day when the predestined stranger comes to open them with a touch and to liberate for long hours the aroma of their peculiar dreams for the delectation of an amazed and spellbound being.

MARCEL PROUST, *The Guermantes Way*, 1921

They did not become alarmed until the third day, when no one felt sleepy at bedtime and they realized that they had gone more than fifty hours without sleeping. . . .

They had indeed contracted the illness of insomnia. Ursula, who had learned from her mother the medicinal value of plants, prepared and made them all drink a brew of monkshood, but they could not get to sleep and spent the whole day dreaming on their feet. In that state of hallucinated lucidity, not only did they see the images of their own dreams, but some saw the images dreamed by others. It was as if the house were full of visitors.

GABRIEL GARCÍA MÁRQUEZ, *One Hundred Years of Solitude*, 1967

The Spanish language makes no distinction between the act of sleeping and the act of dreaming.

CARLOS FUENTES, *The Hydra Head*, 1978

. . . I have dreams. I don't see what you're supposed to do about dreams. You're always asleep when they happen. Perhaps sleep is to blame, pulling the wool over your eyes in that deceitful way it has. Dreams wouldn't dare do what they do to me when I'm awake. That's why they wait until I'm asleep before they do it.

MARTIN AMIS, *Success*, 1978

Dreams are merciless; they come upon you when you're asleep.

*   *   *

I want to keep my dreams, even bad ones, because without them, I might have nothing all night long.

JOSEPH HELLER, *Something Happened*, 1974

> Those dreams that on the silent night intrude,
> And with false flitting shades our minds delude,
> Jove never sends us downward from the skies,
> Nor can they from infernal mansions rise;
> But all are mere productions of the brain,
> And fools consult interpreters in vain.
>
> For, when in bed we rest our weary limbs,
> The mind unburthen'd sports in various whims,
> The busy head with mimic art runs o'er
> The scenes and actions of the day before.
>
> The drowsy tyrant, by his minions led,
> To regal rage devotes some patriot's head.
> With equal terrors, not with equal guilt,
> The murd'rer dreams of all the blood he spilt.

JONATHAN SWIFT, from 'On Dreams', 1727

Sleepers lie under the rails.
They travel backward, the hard crossties that could
Crack hatchets, lying under the singing track.
The rails dream of rhyming; they
Turn into verse, endless lines
Not measured in sevens or in elevens,
Say, but continuing on
Into a converging strip.
They dream the epic of gleaming and distant
Vanishing, and diminution of time, and
They sleep dreamlessly under phrases of roar
And passages of clicking
Wheels. And these soft rails, the two
Dreamers, are being children of eleven,
Say, and of seven, and their funny dreams are
Of boxcars loaded with chattering white dice
(Seven meanwhile awakens,
Trembling, in the matter of a skull, or so
The shorter dreamer remembers). Remember
That they are poised yet in their
Sojourn of waking: they do
Not dream of these dreams. But as
The pliant engine gathers its wits back from
A sweet dream deep in the tunnel in the hill
As if drawn by its tender
Out of the inner lamplit red into blue
Light of outer night, one recalled an old dream. . . .

JOHN HOLLANDER, from 'The Train', 1979

Dreams are the agitations, the egressions or sallyings out of the soul in thoughts of the mind, while the body lieth bound by sleep in the bed. A dream indefinitely and at large is the transacting of the reasonable soul in the sleeping body, through the coassisting help of those admirable faculties: *The Fantasy*, and *The Memory*. Both which faculties are found most active in the season of sleep; for in sleep the outward senses as hearing, seeing, etc. being bound from their organical and extrinsical exercises and ordinary conveyances. The inward senses and powers of the soul as the Fantasy and Memory, are at the more liberty and freedom from such external attendances, and so being at better leisure, they within themselves fall to reflectings, to new forming and erecting new frames of things that are vented in dreams. The Fantasy and the Memory are the soul's working shops wherein strange things be wrought, when the soul (as I may say) goes not abroad, but stays at home and works within itself, strange things it does which be drawn out in dreams.

PHILIP GOODWIN, *The Mystery of Dreams*, 1658

Nightmare

❧

I remembered I was lying in the oak closet, and I heard distinctly the gusty wind, and the driving of the snow; I heard, also, the fir-bough repeat its teasing sound, and ascribed it to the right cause: but it annoyed me so much, that I resolved to silence it, if possible; and, I thought, I rose and endeavoured to unhasp the casement. The hook was soldered into the staple: a circumstance observed by me when awake, but forgotten. 'I must stop it, nevertheless!' I muttered, knocking my knuckles through the glass, and stretching an arm out to seize the importunate branch; instead of which, my fingers closed on the fingers of a little, ice-cold hand! The intense horror of nightmare came over me: I tried to draw back my arm, but the hand clung to it, and a most melancholy voice sobbed, 'Let me in – let me in!' 'Who are you?' I asked, struggling, meanwhile, to disengage myself. 'Catherine Linton,' it replied shiveringly (why did I think of *Linton*? I had read *Earnshaw* twenty times for Linton). 'I'm come home: I'd lost my way on the moor!' As it spoke, I discerned, obscurely, a child's face looking through the window. Terror made me cruel; and, finding it useless to attempt shaking the creature off, I pulled its wrist on to the broken pane, and rubbed it to and fro till the blood ran down and soaked the bedclothes: still it wailed, 'Let me in!' and maintained its tenacious gripe, almost maddening me with fear. 'How can I!' I said at length. 'Let *me* go, if you want me to let you in!' The fingers relaxed, I snatched mine through the hole, hurriedly piled the books up in a pyramid against it, and stopped my ears to exclude the lamentable prayer. I seemed to keep them closed above a quarter of an hour; yet, the instant I listened again, there was the doleful cry moaning on! 'Begone!' I shouted, 'I'll never let you in, not if you beg for twenty years.' 'It is twenty years,' mourned the voice: 'twenty years. I've been a waif for twenty years!' Thereat began a feeble scratching outside, and the pile of books moved as if thrust forward. I tried to jump; but could not stir a limb; and so yelled aloud, in a frenzy of fright.

EMILY BRONTË, *Wuthering Heights*, 1847

A most frightful dream of a woman whose features were blended with darkness catching hold of my right eye and attempting to pull it out – I caught hold of her arm fast – a horrid feel – Wordsworth cried out aloud to me hearing my scream – heard his cry and thought it cruel he did not come / but did not wake till his cry was repeated a third time – the woman's name Ebon Ebon Thalud – When I awoke, my right eyelid swelled.

S. T. COLERIDGE, *Notebooks*, 28 November 1800

She thought she was bewildered in some winding passages of the abbey; that it was almost dark, and that she wandered about a considerable time, without being able to find a door. . . . she saw a man enter the passage, habited in a long black cloak, like those usually worn by attendants at funerals, and bearing a torch. He called her to follow him, and led her through a long passage to the foot of a staircase. Here she feared to proceed, and was running back, when the man suddenly turned to pursue her, and with the terror, which this occasioned, she awoke.

Shocked by those visions, and more so by their seeming connection, which now struck her, she endeavoured to continue awake, lest their terrific images should again haunt her mind: after some time, however, her harassed spirits again sunk into slumber, though not to repose.

She now thought herself in a large old gallery, and saw at one end of it a chamber-door standing a little open, and a light within: she went towards it, and perceived the man she had before seen, standing at the door, and beckoning her towards him. With the inconsistency so common in dreams, she no longer endeavoured to avoid him, but advancing, followed him into a suite of very ancient apartments, hung with black, and lighted up as if for a funeral. Still he led her on, till she found herself in the same chamber she remembered to have seen in her former dreams; a coffin, covered with a pall, stood at the farther end of the room: some lights, and several persons surrounded it, who appeared to be in great distress.

Suddenly she thought these persons were all gone, and that she was left alone; that she went up to the coffin, and while she gazed upon it, she heard a voice speak as if from within, but saw nobody. The man she had before seen, soon after stood by the coffin, and lifting the pall, she saw beneath it a dead person, whom she thought to be the dying chevalier she had seen in her former dream: his features were sunk in death, but they were yet serene. While she looked at him, a stream of blood gushed from his side, and descending to the floor, the whole chamber was overflowed; at the same time more words were uttered in the voice she heard before;

but the horror of the scene so entirely overcame her, that she started and awoke.

ANN RADCLIFFE, The Romance of the Forest, 1791

The same nightmare returned persistently: he fancied he fell from the ardent clasp of Thérèse into the cold, sticky arms of Camille. He dreamt, first of all, that his sweetheart was stifling him in a warm embrace, and then that the corpse of the drowned man pressed him to his chest in an icelike strain. These abrupt and alternate sensations of voluptuousness and disgust, these successive contacts of burning love and frigid death, set him panting for breath, and caused him to shudder and gasp in anguish.

EMILE ZOLA, Thérèse Raquin, 1867

A pale demon with black hair came in, followed by four gnome-like creatures carrying a great black trunk. They set it down and opened it, and the Demon, crying out: 'Here's your year – here are all the horrors that have happened to you and that are still going to happen' dragged out a succession of limp black squirming things and threw them on the floor before me. They were not rags or creatures, not living or dead – they were Black Horrors, shapeless, and that seemed to writhe about as they fell at my feet, and yet were as inanimate as bits of stuff. But none of these comparisons occurred to me, for I *knew* what they were: the hideous, the incredible things that had happened to me in this dreadful year, or were to happen to me before its close; and I stared, horror-struck, as the Demon dragged them out, one by one, more and more, till finally, flinging down a blacker, hatefuller one, he said laughing: 'There – that's the last of them!'

The gnomes laughed too; but I, as I stared at the great black pile and the empty trunk, said to the Demon: '*Are you sure it hasn't a false bottom?*'

EDITH WHARTON, October 1913, quoted in R. W. B. Lewis, Edith Wharton, 1975

The amputation of the feet is a bar to a contemplated journey. The burning of the body indicates a very evil reputation.

ASTRAMPSYCHUS, The Oneirocriticon, c.AD 350

When on my bed my limbs I lay,
It hath not been my use to pray
With moving lips or bended knees;
But silently, by slow degrees,
My spirit I to love compose,
In humble trust my eyelids close,
With reverential resignation,
No wish conceiv'd, no thought exprest,
Only a *sense* of supplication,
A *sense* o'er all my soul imprest
That I am weak, yet not unblest;
Since *round* me, *in* me, every where,
Eternal strength and goodness are! —

But yesternight I pray'd aloud
In anguish and in agony,
Awaking from the fiendish crowd
Of shapes and thoughts that tortur'd me!
Desire with loathing strangely mixt,
On wild or hateful objects fixt;
Pangs of revenge, the powerless will,
Still baffled, and consuming still,
Sense of intolerable wrong,
And men whom I despis'd made strong
Vain-glorious threats, unmanly vaunting,
Bad men my boasts and fury taunting
Rage, sensual passion, mad'ning brawl,
And shame and terror over all!
Deeds to be hid that were not hid,
Which, all confus'd I might not know,
Whether I suffer'd or I did:
For all was horror, guilt and woe,
My own or others, still the same,
Life-stifling fear, soul-stifling shame!

Thus two nights pass'd: the night's dismay
Sadden'd and stunn'd the boding day.
I fear'd to sleep: sleep seem'd to be
Disease's worst malignity.
The third night when my own loud scream
Had freed me from the fiendish dream,

O'ercome by sufferings dark and wild,
I wept as I had been a child –
And having thus by tears subdued
My trouble to a milder mood –
Such punishments, I thought, were due
To natures, deepliest stain'd with sin,
Still to be stirring up anew
The self-created hell within;
The horror of their crimes to view,
To know and loathe, yet wish and do!
With such let fiends make mockery –
But I – Oh wherefore this on *me*?
Frail is my soul, yea, strengthless wholly,
Unequal, restless, melancholy;
But free from hate, and sensual folly!
To love beloved is all I need,
And whom I love, I love indeed.

S. T. COLERIDGE, 'The Pains of Sleep', 1803

It is a curious proof of the concern which body has in these vagaries, that when you dream of any particular limb being in pain, you shall most likely have gone to sleep in a posture that affects it. A weight on the feet will produce dreams in which you are rooted to the ground, or caught by a goblin out of the earth. A cramped hand or leg shall get you tortured in the Inquisition; and a head too much thrown back give you the sense of an interminable visitation of stifling. The nightmare, the heaviest punisher of repletion, will visit some persons merely for lying on their backs; which shows how much it is concerned in a particular condition of the frame. Sometimes it lies upon the chest like a vital lump. Sometimes it comes in the guise of a horrid dwarf, or malignant little hag, who grins in your teeth, and will not let you rise. Its most common enormity is to pin you to the ground with excess of fear, while something dreadful is coming up, a goblin or a mad bull. Sometimes the horror is of a very elaborate description, such as being spell-bound in an old house, which has a mysterious and shocking possessor. He is a gigantic deformity, and will pass presently through the room in which you are sitting. He comes, not a giant, but a dwarf of the most strange and odious description, hairy, spider-like, and chuckling. His mere passage is unbearable. The agony arises at every step. You would protest against so malignant a sublimation of the shocking, but are unable to move or speak. At length you give loud and long-drawn groans, and start up with a præternatural effort, awake.

LEIGH HUNT, 'Of Dreams', 1820

When I say, My bed shall comfort me, my couch shall ease my complaint; then thou scarest me with dreams, and terrifiest me through visions: so that my soul chooseth strangling, and death rather than my life.

Job 7

The Galerie d'Apollon became for years what I can only term a splendid scene of things, even of the quite irrelevant or, as might be, almost unworthy; and I recall to this hour, with the last vividness, what a precious part it played for me, and exactly by that continuity of honour, on my awaking, in a summer dawn many years later, to the fortunate, the instantaneous recovery and capture of the most appalling yet most admirable nightmare of my life. The climax of this extraordinary experience – which stands alone for me as a dream-adventure founded in the deepest, quickest, clearest act of cogitation and comparison, act indeed of life-saving energy, as well as in unutterable fear – was the sudden pursuit, through an open door, along a huge high saloon, of a just dimly-descried figure that retreated in terror before my rush and dash (a glare of inspired reaction from irresistible but shameful dread,) out of the room I had a moment before been desperately, and all the more abjectly, defending by the push of my shoulder against hard pressure on lock and bar from the other side. The lucidity, not to say the sublimity, of the crisis had consisted of the great thought that I, in my appalled state, was probably still more appalling than the awful agent, creature or presence, whatever he was, whom I had güessed, in the suddenest wild start from sleep, the sleep within my sleep, to be making for my place of rest. The triumph of my impulse, perceived in a flash as I acted on it by myself at a bound, forcing the door outward, was the grand thing, but the great point of the whole was the wonder of my final recognition. Routed, dismayed, the tables turned upon him by my so surpassing him for straight aggression and dire intention, my visitant was already but a diminished spot in the long perspective, the tremendous, glorious hall, as I say, over the far-gleaming floor of which, cleared for the occasion of its great line of priceless vitrines down the middle, he sped for *his* life, while a great storm of thunder and lightning played through the deep embrasures of high windows at the right. The lightning that revealed the retreat revealed also the wondrous place and, by the same amazing play, my young imaginative life in it of long before, the sense of which, deep within me, had kept it whole, preserved it to this thrilling use; for what in the world were the deep embrasures and the so polished floor but those of the Galerie d'Apollon of my childhood? The 'scene of something' I had vaguely then felt it? Well I might, since it was to be the scene of that immense hallucination.

HENRY JAMES, *A Small Boy and Others*, 1913

In the morning that preceded his death, Bergotte suffered from insomnia, and what was worse, whenever he did fall asleep, from nightmares which, if he awoke, made him reluctant to go to sleep again. He had long been a lover of dreams, even bad dreams, because thanks to them, thanks to the contradiction they present to the reality which we have before us in our waking state, they give us, at the moment of waking if not before, the profound sensation of having slept. But Bergotte's nightmares were not like that. When he spoke of nightmares, he used in the past to mean unpleasant things that happened in his brain. Latterly, it was as though from somewhere outside himself that he would see a hand armed with a damp cloth which, rubbed over his face by an evil woman, kept trying to wake him; or an intolerable itching in his thighs; or the rage – because Bergotte had murmured in his sleep that he was driving badly – of a raving lunatic of a cabman who flung himself upon the writer, biting and gnawing his fingers. Finally, as soon as it had grown sufficiently dark in his sleep, nature would arrange a sort of undress rehearsal of the apoplectic stroke that was to carry him off. Bergotte would arrive in a carriage beneath the porch of Swann's new house, and would try to get out. A shattering attack of dizziness would pin him to his seat; the concierge would try to help him out; he would remain seated, unable to lift himself up or straighten his legs. He would cling to the stone pillar in front of him, but could not find sufficient support to enable him to stand.

MARCEL PROUST, *The Captive*, 1925

Perhaps because he was used to a bedtime drink but not to sleeping medicine, he was quickly pulled into sleep. He had a dream. He was in the embrace of a woman, but she had four legs. The four legs were entwined about him. She had arms as well. Though half awake, he thought the four legs odd, but not repulsive. Those four legs, so much more provocative than two, were still with him. It was a medicine to make one have such dreams, he thought absently. The girl had turned away from him, her hips toward him. He seemed to find something touching about the fact that her head was more distant than her hips. Half asleep and half awake, he took the long hair spread out toward him and played with it as if to comb it; and so he fell asleep.

His next dream was most unpleasant. One of his daughters had borne a deformed child in a hospital. Awake, the old man could not remember what sort of deformity it had been. Probably he did not want to remember. It was hideous, in any case. The baby was immediately taken from the mother. It was behind a white curtain in the maternity room, and she went over and commenced hacking it to pieces, getting it ready to throw away. The doctor, a friend of Eguchi's, was standing beside her in white. Eguchi too was beside her. He was wide awake now, groaning from the horror of it. The crimson velvet on the four walls so startled him that he put his hands to his face and rubbed his forehead. It had been a horrible nightmare. There could scarcely be a monster hidden in the sleeping medicine. Was it that, having come in search of misshapen pleasure, he had had a misshapen dream? He did not know which of his three daughters he had dreamed of, and he did not try to know.

YASUNARI KAWABATA, *House of the Sleeping Beauties,* 1962

My dreams were of the most terrific description. Every species of calamity and horror befell me. Among other miseries, I was smothered to death between huge pillows, by demons of the most ghastly and ferocious aspect. Immense serpents held me in their embrace, and looked earnestly in my face with their fearfully shining eyes. Then deserts, limitless, and of the most forlorn and awe-inspiring character, spread themselves out before me. Immensely tall trunks of trees, gray and leafless, rose up in endless succession as far as the eye could reach. Their roots were concealed in widespreading morasses, whose dreary water lay intensely black, still, and altogether terrible, beneath. And the strange trees seemed endowed with a human vitality, and waving to and fro their skeleton arms, were crying to the silent waters for mercy, in the shrill and piercing accents of the most acute agony and despair.

EDGAR ALLAN POE, *The Narrative of Arthur Gordon Pym,* 1838

I was in the market-place of a town. It was filled with people, talking, buying and selling, all very happy and busy. Suddenly, as though a cloud came over the sun, the air was cold and the noise died down to the twittering of birds. Men and women looked about them. Everyone was silent. I myself felt a trembling expectant fear. I looked about me, wondering why I was so apprehensive, and found that the place was emptied like a bowl of water. It was dark and cold. Not a sound. Something told me to run for my life but I could not move. Then, from a side street, a little procession came into the square. A woman was carried on a kind of stretcher that also resembled a barrow. Two men in black carried it. They were followed by a small group of quite silent persons. And in front of the stretcher was a tall, thin man with a sallow face. But what was especially horrible about him was that his head was twisted to one side as though his neck was broken.

They advanced without a sound, their feet making no apparent contact with the pavement. There was a cold silence everywhere and great but crowded emptiness as though somewhere hundreds of people were holding their breath.

I was exactly in the path of the little procession. I knew that if the yellow-faced man touched me something appalling would follow. But I could not move.

The man and the stretcher and the followers advanced nearer and nearer. I was in an agony of terror. I woke and my pyjamas were soaked with sweat. I have never had a more horrible dream.

HUGH WALPOLE, Journal, 1933, quoted in Rupert Hart-Davis, *Hugh Walpole: A Biography*, 1952

About ten days ago a very valuable dream which I had has induced me to commence this record. I was haunted by evil spirits, of whose presence, though unseen, I was aware. There were also dead bodies near me, though I saw them not. Terrified as I was, far beyond any fear that I ever experienced in actual life, still I reasoned and insisted to myself that all was delirium and weakness of mind, and even sent away the person who I thought was present with me, that I might be left alone to exert myself. When alone the actual presence of the tormentors was more certain, and my horrors increased, till at length an arm appeared through the half-opened door, or rather a long hand. Determined to convince myself that all was unsubstantial and visionary, though I saw it most distinctly, I ran up and caught it. It was a hand, and a lifeless one. I pulled at it with desperate effort, dragged in a sort of shapeless body into the room, trampled upon it, crying out aloud the while for horror. The extreme efforts I made to call for help succeeded so far as to awake Edith, who immediately delivered me from the most violent fear that ever possessed me.

ROBERT SOUTHEY, 7 November 1804

Half sleepless night again – and entirely disgusting dream, about men using flesh and bones, *hands of children especially*, for fuel – being out of wood and coals. I took a piece to put on someones fire, and found it the side of an animals face, with the jaw and teeth in it.

JOHN RUSKIN, *Brantwood Diary*, 29 October 1877

One night I dreamt that, making a call on some matter of business I was shown into a fine great drawing-room and asked to wait. Accordingly, I went over to the fire-place in the usual English way, proposing to wait there. And there, after the same fashion, I lounged with my arm upon the mantel-piece; but only for a few moments. For feeling that my fingers had rested on something strangely cold, I looked, and saw that they lay on a dead hand: a woman's hand newly cut from the wrist.

Though I woke in horror on the instant, this dream was quite forgotten – at any rate for the time – when I did next day make a call on some unimportant matter of business, was shown into a pretty little room adorned with various knick-knacks, and then was asked to wait. Glancing by chance toward the mantel-piece (the dream of the previous night still forgotten), what should I see upon it but the hand of a mummy, broken from the wrist. It was a very little hand, and on it was a ring that would have been a 'gem ring' if the dull red stone in it had been genuinely precious. Wherefore I concluded that it was a woman's hand.

FREDERICK GREENWOOD, *Imagination in Dreams*, 1894

> Most melancholy at that time, O Friend!
> Were my day-thoughts, – my nights were miserable;
> Through months, through years, long after the last beat
> Of those atrocities, the hour of sleep
> To me came rarely charged with natural gifts,
> Such ghastly visions had I of despair
> And tyranny, and implements of death;

And innocent victims sinking under fear,
And momentary hope, and worn-out prayer,
Each in his separate cell, or penned in crowds
For sacrifice, and struggling with forced mirth
And levity in dungeons, where the dust
Was laid with tears. Then suddenly the scene
Changed, and the unbroken dream entangled me
In long orations, which I strove to plead
Before unjust tribunals, — with a voice
Labouring, a brain confounded, and a sense,
Death-like, of treacherous desertion, felt
In the last place of refuge — my own soul.

WILLIAM WORDSWORTH, *The Prelude*, Book X, 1850

The implications of auspices, of omens old and new, and of his own dreams, began to terrify Nero. In the past he had never known what it was to dream, but after killing his mother he dreamed that he was steering a ship and that someone tore the tiller from his hands. Next, his wife Octavia pulled him down into thick darkness, where hordes of winged ants swarmed over him. Then, the statues of the nations, which had been dedicated in the Theatre of Pompey, began to hem him in and prevent him from getting away; while his favourite Asturian horse turned into an ape, or all except the head, which whinnied a tune. Finally the doors of the Mausoleum opened by themselves and a voice from inside called: 'Enter, Nero!'

SUETONIUS, *The Twelve Caesars*, c.AD 120

There was a picture in the outer hall — one of those full-length gentlemen of George II's time, with a dark peruke flowing on his shoulders, a cut velvet coat, and lace cravat and ruffles. This picture was pale, and had a long chin, and somehow had impressed my boyhood with a singular sense of fear. The foot of my bed lay towards the window, distant at least five-and-twenty-feet; and before the window stood my dressing-table, and on it a large looking-glass.

I dreamed that I was arranging my toilet before this glass — just as I had done that evening — when on a sudden the face of the portrait I have mentioned was presented on its surface, confronting me like a real countenance, and advancing towards me with a look of fury; and at the instant I felt myself seized by the throat and unable to stir or to breathe. After a struggle with this infernal garotter, I succeeded in awaking myself; and as I did so, I felt a rather cold hand really resting on my throat, and quietly passed up over my chin and face. I jumped out of bed with a roar, and challenged the owner of the hand, but received no answer, and heard no sound. I poked up my fire and lighted my candle. Everything was as I had left it except the door, which was the least bit open.

In my shirt, candle in hand, I looked out into the passage. There was nothing there in human shape, but in the direction of the stairs the green eyes of a large cat were shining. I was so confoundedly nervous that even 'a harmless, necessary cat' appalled me, and I clapped my door, as if against an evil spirit.

SHERIDAN LE FANU, *Wylder's Hand*, 1864

I had a dream last night. An amputated head had been stuck on to a man's trunk, making him look like a drunken actor. The head began to talk. I was terrified and knocked over my folding screen in trying to push a Russian in front of me against the furious creature's onslaught.

AUGUST STRINDBERG, *Inferno*, 1897

The nightmares returned – one terrible one in February 1896 about a tramp, seen holding over a well 'washing, but with a kind of amused tenderness, an object that I thought was a rabbit, but I presently saw that it was a small deformed hairy child, with a curious lower jaw, very shallow: over the face it had a kind of horny carapace . . . made of some material resembling *pottery*. I was disgusted at this but went on, and it grew dark: I heard behind me an odd sound, and turning round saw this horrible creature only a foot or two high, walking complacently after me, with its limbs involved in ugly and shapeless clothes, made, it seemed to me, of oakum, or some more distressing material. The horror of it exceeded all belief.'

A. C. BENSON, quoted in David Newsome, *On the Edge of Paradise*, 1980

When I sleep away from home with my wife, I will have a nightmare the first or second night, usually the same one: a strange man is entering illegally through the door, which I have locked, and drawing near, a burglar, rapist, kidnapper, or assassin; he seems to be Black but changes; I think he is carrying a knife; I try to scream but can make no sound. I have this same bad dream at home often, even though I carefully lock all my doors before going to sleep. I have had it dozens and dozens of times. I have always had it. I must make some sound, though, while I am having the dream and trying in vain to scream, for my wife awakens with the noise of my struggles and rouses me by calling my name and tells me, as though I didn't know, that I was having a nightmare. Sometimes, even when I am trapped deep in my agony and whatever menaces me is moving right up to my bedside, some different section of me is tuned in omnisciently to the nature of the experience, knows and reassures me it is all just a very bad dream and watches from outside it tranquilly and smugly and waits expectantly, with enjoyment, for my wife to be disturbed by my noises and motions and to call to me by name and shake me awake by the shoulder to tell me I was having a nightmare. I think people have more than one brain. I like the idea of scaring my wife with my nightmares. Sometimes, when *she* is having a nightmare, I revenge myself on her by *not* waking her up and allowing it to torture her for as long as it wants to, while I watch her from outside, idly and smugly, leaning on my elbow.

JOSEPH HELLER, *Something Happened*, 1974

A beautiful girl once told me of a recurring nightmare in which she lay in the center of a large dark room and felt her face expand until it filled the whole room, becoming a formless mass while her eyes ran in bilious jelly up the chimney.

RALPH ELLISON, *Invisible Man*, 1952

A dream is nothing else but a bubbling scum or froth of the fancy, which the day hath left undigested; or an after-feast made of the fragments of idle imaginations.

How many sorts there be of them no man can rightly set down, since it scarce hath been heard there were ever two men that dreamed alike. Divers have written diversely of their causes, but the best reason among them all that I could ever pick out was this: that as an arrow which is shot out of a bow is sent forth many times with such force that it flieth far beyond the mark whereat it was aimed, so our thoughts, intensively fixed all the daytime upon a mark we are to hit, are now and then overdrawn with such force that they fly beyond the mark of the day into the confines of the night. There is no man put to any torment, but quaketh and trembleth a great while after the executioner hath withdrawn his hand from him. In the daytime we torment our thoughts and imaginations with sundry cares and devices; all the night-time they quake and tremble after the terror of their late suffering, and still continue thinking of the perplexities they have endured. To nothing more aptly can I compare the working of our brains after we have unyoked and gone to bed than to the glimmering and dazzling of a man's eyes when he comes newly out of the bright sun into the dark shadow.

Even as one's eyes glimmer and dazzle when they are withdrawn out of the light into darkness, so are our thoughts troubled and vexed when they are retired from labour to ease, and from skirmishing to surgery.

You must give a wounded man leave to groan while he is in dressing. Dreaming is no other than groaning, while sleep our surgeon hath us in cure.

He that dreams merrily is like a boy new breeched, who leaps and danceth for joy his pain is passed. But long that joy stays not with him, for presently after, his master, the day, seeing him so jocund and pleasant, comes and does as much for him again, whereby his hell is renewed.

No such figure of the first chaos whereout the world was extraught, as our dreams in the night. In them all states, all sexes, all places, are confounded and meet together.

Our cogitations run on heaps like men to part a fray where every one strikes his next fellow. From one place to another without consultation they leap, like rebels bent on a head. Soldiers just up and down they imitate at the sack of a city, which spare neither age nor beauty: the young, the old, trees, steeples and mountains, they confound in one gallimaufry.

Of those things which are most known to us, some of us that have moist brains make to ourselves images of memory. On those images of memory whereon we build in the day, comes some superfluous humour of ours, like a jackanapes, in the night, and erects a puppet stage or some ridiculous idle childish invention.

A dream is nothing else but the echo of our conceits in the day.

But otherwhile it falls out that one echo borrows of another; so our dreams, the echoes of the day, borrow of any noise we hear in the night.

As for example: if in the dead of the night there be any rumbling, knocking or disturbance near us, we straight dream of wars or of thunder. If a dog howl, we suppose we are transported into hell, where we hear the complaint of damned ghosts. If our heads lie double or uneasy, we imagine we uphold all heaven with our shoulders, like Atlas. If we be troubled with too many clothes, then we suppose the night mare rides us.

I knew one that was cramped, and he dreamed that he was torn in pieces with wild horses; and another, that having a black sant [black sanctus: discordant singing] brought to his bedside at midnight, dreamt he was bidden to dinner at Ironmongers' Hall.

Any meat that in the daytime we eat against our stomachs, begetteth a dismal dream. Discontent also in dreams hath no little predominance; for even as from water that is troubled, the mud dispersingly ascendeth from the bottom to the top, so when our blood is chased, disquieted and troubled all the light imperfect humours of our body ascend like mud up aloft into the head.

The clearest spring a little touched is creased with a thousand circles; as those momentary circles for all the world, such are our dreams.

When all is said, melancholy is the mother of dreams, and of all terrors of the night whatsoever.

THOMAS NASHE, *The Terrors of the Night*, 1594

I did not sleep very well these days. In bed in a big yellow room with a ten-foot skylight (we had had this room built to our own design) I felt the skylight encroaching, tried to dodge it; sometimes it was a falling tent and sometimes it was the gap that cannot be closed. The room too was sometimes too silent and sometimes full of voices; I would open the door quickly and no one would be there. In this room I had two precise visions, both by electric light, both solidly planted in the air about five foot up from the floor. The first was a human eye a yard or so long; the rest of the face was invisible but on both the upper and the under eyelid there were worms instead of eyelashes, transparent worms curling and wriggling. The second vision was of a sky-blue little beast like a jackal but with horns; he sat there pat on the air, his front feet firmly together.

LOUIS MacNEICE, *The Strings Are False*, 1965

I am tolerably well, meaning, the day time, for my last night was just such a noisy night of horrors, as 3 nights out of 4 are, with me. O God! when a man blesses the loud scream of agony that awakes him, night after night; night after night! – and when a man's repeated

night-screams have made him a nuisance in his own house, it is better
to die than to live.

s. t. coleridge, letter to Robert Southey, September 1803

Ah, God! what trances of torments does that man endure who is
consumed with one unachieved revengeful desire. He sleeps with
clenched hands; and wakes with his own bloody nails in his palms.

Often when forced from his hammock by exhausting and
intolerably vivid dreams of the night, which, resuming his own
intense thoughts through the day, carried them on amid a clashing of
phrensies, and whirled them round and round in his blazing brain,
till the very throbbing of his life-spot becomes insufferable anguish;
and when, as was sometimes the case, these spiritual throes in him
heaved his being up from its base, and a chasm seemed opening in
him, from which forked flames and lightnings shot up, and accursed
fiends beckoned him to leap down among them; when this hell in
himself yawned beneath him, a wild cry would be heard through the
ship; and with glaring eyes Ahab would burst from his state room, as
though escaping from a bed that was on fire. Yet these, perhaps,
instead of being the unsuppressable symptoms of some latent
weakness, or fright at his own resolve, were but the plainest tokens
of its intensity. For, at such times, crazy Ahab, the scheming,
unappeasedly steadfast hunter of the White Whale; this Ahab that
had gone to his hammock, was not the agent that so caused him to
burst from it in horror again. The latter was the eternal, living
principle or soul in him; and in sleep, being for the time dissociated
from the characterizing mind, which at other times employed it for
its outer vehicle or agent, it spontaneously sought escape from the
scorching contiguity of the frantic thing, of which, for the time, it
was no longer an integral. But as the mind does not exist unless
leagued with the soul, therefore it must have been that, in Ahab's
case, yielding up all his thoughts and fancies to his one supreme
purpose; that purpose, by its own sheer inveteracy of will, forced
itself against gods and devils into a kind of self-assumed,
independent being of its own. Nay, could grimly live and burn, while
the common vitality to which it was conjoined, fled horror-stricken
from the unbidden and unfathered birth. Therefore, the tormented
spirit that glared out of bodily eyes, when what seemed Ahab rushed
from his room, was for the time but a vacated thing, a formless
somnambulistic being, a ray of living light, to be sure, but without an
object to color, and therefore a blankness in itself. God help thee, old

man, thy thoughts have created a creature in thee; and he whose intense thinking thus makes him a Prometheus; a vulture feeds upon that heart for ever; that vulture the very creature he creates.

· HERMAN MELVILLE, Moby Dick, 1851

I dreamed that I was standing on a footway of some kind, consisting of transverse planks flanked on my left side by some sort of railing, beyond which was a deep gulf filled with thick fog. Overhead, I had an impression of an awning. But this last was not clearly seen, for the fog partly hid everything except three or four yards of the planking ahead of me with its attendant portion of railing and gulf. Suddenly I noticed, projecting upwards from somewhere far down in the gulf, an immensely long, thin, shadowy thing like a gigantic lath. It reached above the plankway, and was slanted so that it would, had the upper end been visible through the fog, have impinged upon the awning. As I stared at it, it began to wave slowly up and down, brushing the railing. A moment later I realized what the object was. I had seen just such a thing once before in a cinema picture of a fire, in the early days of cinematography. Then, as now, I had undergone the same puzzlement as to what this sort of waving lath might be, until I had realized that it was the long water-jet from a fire-engine hose, as photographed through intervening smoke. Somewhere down in that gulf, then, there must be a fire-engine, and it was playing a stream of water upon the smoke-hidden, railed structure where I stood. As I perceived this, the dream became perfectly abominable. The wooden plankway became crowded with people, dimly visible through the smoke. They were dropping in heaps; and all the air was filled with horrible, choking, gasping ejaculations. Then the smoke, which had grown black and thick, rolled heavily over everything, hiding the entire scene. But a dreadful, suffocated moaning continued—and I was entirely thankful when I awoke. . . .

I carefully recalled every detail of the dream after waking, and not till I had done this did I open the morning papers. There was nothing in these. But the evening editions brought the expected news.

There had been a big fire in a factory somewhere near Paris. I think it was a rubber factory, though I cannot be sure. At any rate it was a factory for some material which gave off vile fumes when burning. A large number of workgirls had been cut off by the flames, and had made their way out on to a *balcony*. There, for the moment, they had been comparatively safe, but the ladders available had been too short to admit of any rescue. While longer ones were being obtained, the fire-engines had directed streams of water on to the balcony to keep that refuge from catching alight. And then there happened a thing which must, I imagine, have been unique in the history of fires. From the broken windows behind the balcony the smoke from the burning rubber or other material came rolling out in such dense volumes that, although the unfortunate girls were standing actually in the open air, every one of them was suffocated before the new ladders could arrive.

                              J. W. DUNNE, *An Experiment with Time*, 1927

All the events of the day, distorted and exaggerated and jumbled together after the usual manner of dreams, wove themselves into a kind of nightmare and oppression. I was on my way to my old abode; everything that I met or saw was grotesque and impossible, yet had now the strange, vague charm of association and reminiscence, now the distressing sense of change and loss and desolation.

As I got near to the avenue gate, instead of the school on my left there was a prison; and at the door a little thick-set jailer, three feet high and much deformed, and a little deformed jaileress no bigger than himself, were cunningly watching me out of the corners of their eyes, and toothlessly smiling. Presently they began to waltz together to an old, familiar tune, with their enormous keys dangling at their sides; and they looked so funny that I laughed and applauded. But soon I perceived that their crooked faces were not really funny; indeed, they were fatal and terrible in the extreme, and I was soon conscious that these deadly dwarfs were trying to waltz between me and the avenue gate for which I was bound—to cut me off, that they might run me into the prison, where it was their custom to hang people of a Monday morning.

In an agony of terror I made a rush for the avenue gate, and there stood the Duchess of Towers, with mild surprise in her eyes and a kind smile—a heavenly vision of strength and reality.

'You are not dreaming true!' she said. 'Don't be afraid—those little people don't exist! Give me your hand and come in here.'

And as I did so she waved the troglodytes away, and they vanished; and I felt that this was no longer a dream, but something else—some strange thing that had happened to me, some new life that I had woke up to.

                              GEORGE DU MAURIER, *Peter Ibbetson*, 1891

Last night I had a recurrence of that dream which . . . was the most frightening of all the different types of cycles of dreams. . . .

The first time I dreamed it, the principle, or figure, took form in a certain vase I had then, a peasant wooden vase from Russia, that someone had brought back. It was bulbous, rather jolly and naive in shape, and covered with crude red and black and gilt patterns. This vase, in my dream, had a personality, and the personality was the nightmare, for it represented something anarchistic and uncontrollable, something destructive. This figure, or object, for it was not human, more like a species of elf or pixie, danced and jumped with a jerky cocky liveliness and it menaced not only me, but everything that was alive, but impersonally, and without reason. This was when I 'named' the dream as about destruction. The next time I dreamed, months later, but instantly recognized it as the same dream, the principle or element took shape in an old man, almost dwarf-like, infinitely more terrifying than the vase-object, because he was part human. This old man smiled and giggled and sniggered, was ugly, vital and powerful, and again, what he represented was pure spite, malice, joy in malice, joy in a destructive impulse. This was when I 'named' the dream as about joy in spite. And I dreamed the dream again, always when particularly tired, or under stress, or in conflict, when I could feel that the walls of myself were thin or in danger. The element took a variety of shapes, usually that of a very old man or woman (yet there was a suggestion of a double sex, or even sexlessness) and the figure was always very lively, in spite of having a wooden leg, or a crutch, or a hump, or being deformed in some way. And the creature was always powerful, with an inner vitality which I knew was caused by a purposeless, undirected, causeless spite. It mocked and jibed and hurt, wished murder, wished death. And yet it was always vibrant with joy.

DORIS LESSING, *The Golden Notebook*, 1962

I find myself alone in a narrow cell or chamber; its polished walls ebony black. In an intense blaze of light, I am scrutinising an intricate machine consisting of many solid wheels of specklessly smooth and glittering steel and brass. They range in size from a monster of some seven feet down to a midget of a few inches. They are inert, motionless. And yet, yet—an inward whisper has bidden me watch the largest of them. *Is* it or is it not, beginning to revolve? In acute foreboding, I continue to gaze at it. Yes, inchmeal, almost beyond perception, it *is*. Instant by instant, without (as I fancy) the faintest audible sound, the momentum of the wheels is continually increasing; and—horror of horrors—I am now *myself* become, as it were, the machine. And the degree of its speed is the degree of my own exquisite bodily pangs and mental anguish as its wheels ever more rapidly spin on and on and on. It reaches an appalling crisis and then, instant by instant, its hideous velocity begins to diminish again, until at length every wheel and every nerve in my body is once more at rest. But *is* it? Again, in that pitiless glare, I watch; again the gigantic wheel begins to stir. . . . And yet again. . . . Words can no more than hint at the agony thus endured.

WALTER DE LA MARE, *Behold, This Dreamer*, 1939

Once, I was lying prone upon a bed, under a great marble slab which had a steel spike running through my body. Another time, a terrible figure chased me out of bed: I sped madly down the passage to my father's dressing-room where he should properly be shaving, burst the door open with a cry, and he was not there! But the worst of all, the more horrible because the more inexplicable, was one which recurred at intervals, perhaps half a dozen times in all. It was a great rolling sphere, of which I could note confusedly that it was in fact a congeries of spheres, fitted like the layers of an onion and each with its own independent revolutions. It grew under my view with immense rapidity: imagination saw no limit to its possible size. I was not afraid that it would roll upon me: it did not seem material enough for that. The horror was not in anything it might do to me, but only in the thing itself and what it was doing to itself: and yet neither at the moment or afterwards could I explain why it should not have been what it was or seemed to be, and why it should not have done its own doings. Nor was there anything about it that could be called hideous in form. I can only ask the reader to believe that the disgust and loathing of these moments were proportionate to the impossibility of analysing the apparition, whether asleep or awake.

G. G. COULTON, *Fourscore Years*, 1943

A night disturbed by a sort of nightmare that is becoming more frequent with me and I am inclined to believe is peculiar to myself. Dreams of unendurable boredom – of reading page after page of dullness, of being told endless, pointless jokes, of sitting through cinema films devoid of interest.

EVELYN WAUGH, *Diaries*, 21 March 1943

As soon as Yossarian, Nately and Dunbar put [Hungry Joe] to bed he began screaming in his sleep. In the morning he stepped from his tent looking haggard, fearful and guilt-ridden, an eaten shell of a human building rocking perilously on the brink of collapse.

The nightmares appeared to Hungry Joe with celestial punctuality every single night he spent in the squadron throughout the whole harrowing ordeal when he was not flying combat missions and was waiting once again for the orders sending him home that never came. Impressionable men in the squadron like Dobbs and Captain Flume were so deeply disturbed by Hungry Joe's shrieking nightmares that they would begin to have shrieking nightmares of their own, and the piercing obscenities they flung into the air every night from their separate places in the squadron rang against each other in the darkness romantically like the mating calls of songbirds with filthy minds. . . .

'Who dreams?' he answered, when Yossarian asked him what he dreamed about.

'Joe, why don't you go see Doc Daneeka?' Yossarian advised.

'Why should I go see Doc Daneeka? I'm not sick.'

'What about your nightmares?'

'I don't have nightmares,' Hungry Joe lied.

'Maybe he can do something about them.'

'There's nothing wrong with nightmares,' Hungry Joe answered. 'Everybody has nightmares.'

Yossarian thought he had him. 'Every night?' he asked.

'Why not every night?' Hungry Joe demanded.

And suddenly it all made sense. Why *not* every night, indeed? It made sense to cry out in pain every night.

JOSEPH HELLER, *Catch-22*, 1961

The Absurd

❦

Dreams are often most profound when they seem most crazy.

SIGMUND FREUD, *The Interpretation of Dreams*, 1900

Sometimes one dreams strange dreams, impossible and grotesque dreams; on waking you remember them distinctly and you are amazed at a strange fact. To begin with, you remember that your reason never deserted you all through the dream, you even remember that you acted with great cunning and logic during all that long, long time when you were surrounded by murderers who tried to deceive you, hid their intentions, treated you amicably, while they had their weapon in readiness and were only waiting for some signal; you remember how cleverly you cheated them in the end and hid from them; then you realize that they are perfectly well aware of your deception and are merely pretending not to know your hiding-place; but you have cheated and hoodwinked them again – you remember all that clearly. But why does your reason at the same time reconcile itself with such obvious absurdities and impossibilities with which, among other things, your dream was crowded? One of your murderers turned into a woman before your very eyes, and from a woman into a cunning and hideous little dwarf, and you accepted it at once as an accomplished fact, almost without the slightest hesitation, and at the very moment when your reason, on the other side, was strained to the utmost, and showed extraordinary power, cunning, shrewdness, and logic? Why, too, when awake and having completely recovered your sense of reality, you feel almost every time, and sometimes with extraordinary vividness, that you have left some unsolved mystery behind with your dream? You smile at the absurdity of your dream, and at the same time you feel that in the intermingling of those absurdities some idea lies hidden, but an idea that is real, something belonging to your true life, something that exists and has always existed in your heart; it is as though something new and prophetic, something you have been expecting, has been told you in your dream; your impression is very vivid: it may be joyful or agonizing, but what it is and what was said to you – all this you can neither understand nor remember.

FYODOR DOSTOEVSKY, *The Idiot*, 1869

I remember of dreaming on one occasion that I possessed ubiquity, twenty resemblances of myself appearing in as many different places, in the same room; and each being so thoroughly possessed by my own mind, that I could not ascertain which of them was myself, and which my double, etc. On this occasion, fancy so far travelled into the regions of absurdity, that I conceived myself riding upon my own back – one of the resemblances being mounted upon another, and both animated with the soul appertaining to myself, in such a manner that I knew not whether I was the *carrier* or the *carried*.

ROBERT MACNISH, *The Philosophy of Sleep*, 1830

I had agreed to go picknicking on Sunday with two friends, but quite unexpectedly slept past the hour when we were to meet. My friends, who knew how punctual I ordinarily am, were surprised, came to the house where I lived, waited outside awhile, then came upstairs and knocked on my door. I was very startled, jumped out of bed, and thought only of getting ready as soon as I could. When I emerged fully dressed from my room, my friends fell back in manifest alarm. 'What's that behind your head?' they cried. Since my awakening I had felt something preventing me from bending back my head, and I now groped for it with my hand. My friends, who had grown somewhat calmer, had just shouted 'Be careful, don't hurt yourself!' when my hand closed behind my head on the hilt of a sword. My friends came closer, examined me, led me back to the mirror in my room, and stripped me to the waist. A large, ancient knight's sword with a cross-shaped handle was buried to the hilt in my back, but the blade had been driven with such incredible precision between my skin and flesh that it had caused no injury. Nor was there a wound at the spot on my neck where the sword had penetrated; my friends assured me that there was an opening large enough to admit the blade, but dry and showing no trace of blood. And when my friends now stood on chairs and slowly, inch by inch, drew out the sword, I did not bleed, and the opening on my neck closed until no mark was left save a scarcely discernible slit. 'Here is your sword,' laughed my friends, and gave it to me. I hefted it in my two hands; it was a splendid weapon, Crusaders might have used it.

Who tolerates this gadding about of ancient knights in dreams, irresponsibly brandishing their swords, stabbing innocent sleepers who are saved from serious injury only because the weapons in all likelihood glance off living bodies, and also because there are faithful friends knocking at the door, prepared to come to their assistance?

FRANZ KAFKA, Diaries, 19 January 1915

One night, I had this terrifying dream. A huge corkscrew, which was the Earth, was spinning round, turning on its axis and twisting in its own spiral, just like the signs outside American barber's shops, and I could see myself, no bigger than a bug but not hanging on so well, slither and stumble over the helix and with my thoughts sent whirling down moving staircases made of *a priori* shapes. Suddenly, the fatal moment, there is a loud crack, my neck snaps, I fall flat on my face and I emerge in a splash of sparks before the Kaffir who had come to wake me. He says: 'Did you have an attack of the nasties, then? Come and look at this.' And he leads me to the pigeon-loft and gets me to peep through a hole in the wall. I put my eye to it. I see a terrifying sight: a huge corkscrew, which was the Earth, was spinning round, turning on its axis and twisting in its own spiral, just like the signs outside American barber's shops, and I could see myself, no bigger than a bug but not hanging on so well . . .

RENÉ DAUMAL, A Night of Serious Drinking, 1938

> Dreams are but interludes, which fancy makes,
> When monarch-reason sleeps, this mimic wakes:
> Compounds a medley of disjointed things,
> A mob of cobblers, and a court of kings:
> Light fumes are merry, grosser fumes are sad;
> Both are the reasonable soul run mad:
> And many monstrous forms in sleep we see,
> That neither were, nor are, nor e'er can be.
> Sometimes, forgotten things long cast behind
> Rush forward in the brain, and come to mind.
> The nurses legends are for truths receiv'd,
> And the man dreams but what the boy believ'd.
> Sometimes we but rehearse a former play,
> The night restores our actions done by day;
> As hounds in sleep will open for their prey.
> In short, the farce of dreams is of a piece,
> Chimera's all; and more absurd, or less:
> You, who believe in tales, abide alone,
> What e'er I get this voyage is my own.

JOHN DRYDEN, from 'The Cock and the Fox', 1700

Romeo. I dream'd a dream to-night.

Mercutio. And so did I.

Rom. Well, what was yours?

Mer. That dreamers often lie.

Rom. In bed asleep, while they do dream things true.

Mer. O! then, I see, Queen Mab hath been with you.

Benvolio. Queen Mab! What's she?

Mer. She is the fairies' midwife, and she comes
In shape no bigger than an agate-stone
On the fore-finger of an alderman,
Drawn with a team of little atomies
Over men's noses as they lie asleep:
Her waggon-spokes made of long spinners' legs;
The cover, of the wings of grasshoppers;
Her traces, of the smallest spider's web;
Her collars, of the moonshine's watery beams;
Her whip, of cricket's bone; the lash, of film;
Her waggoner, a small grey-coated gnat,
Not half so big as a round little worm
Prick'd from the lazy finger of a maid;
Her chariot is an empty hazel-nut,
Made by the joiner squirrel or old grub,
Time out o' mind the fairies' coach-makers.
And in this state she gallops night by night
Through lovers' brains, and then they dream of love;
O'er courtiers' knees, that dream on curtsies straight;
O'er lawyers' fingers, who straight dream on fees;
O'er ladies' lips, who straight on kisses dream;
Which oft the angry Mab with blisters plagues,
Because their breaths with sweetmeats tainted are.
Sometimes she gallops o'er a courtier's nose,
And then dreams he of smelling out a suit;
And sometimes comes she with a tithe-pig's tail,
Tickling a parson's nose as a' lies asleep,
Then he dreams of another benefice;
Sometimes she driveth o'er a soldier's neck,
And then dreams he of cutting foreign throats,
Of breaches, ambuscadoes, Spanish blades,
Of healths five fathom deep; and then anon
Drums in his ears, at which he starts and wakes;

And, being thus frighted, swears a prayer or two,
And sleeps again. This is that very Mab
That plats the manes of horses in the night;
And bakes the elf-locks in foul sluttish hairs,
Which once untangled much misfortune bodes;
This is the hag, when maids lie on their backs,
That presses them and learns them first to bear,
Making them women of good carriage:
This is she—

Rom.   Peace, peace! Mercutio, peace!
Thou talk'st of nothing.

Mer.   True, I talk of dreams,
Which are the children of an idle brain,
Begot of nothing but vain fantasy;
Which is as thin of substance as the air,
And more inconstant than the wind, who woos
Even now the frozen bosom of the north,
And, being anger'd, puffs away from thence,
Turning his face to the dew-dropping south.

WILLIAM SHAKESPEARE, *Romeo and Juliet*, c.1595

I was in hospital for an appendectomy. There was somebody there
with green eyes and a terrifying affection for me. He cut off the arm
of an old lady who was going to do me an injury. I explained to the
doctors about him, but they were inattentive, though, presently, I
realized that they were very concerned about his bad influence over
me. I decide to escape from the hospital, and do so, after looking in a
cupboard for something, I don't know what. I get to a station,
squeeze between the carriages of a train, down a corkscrew staircase
and out under the legs of some boys and girls. Now my companion
has turned up with his three brothers (there may have been only
two). One, a smooth-faced, fine-fingernailed blond, is more
reassuring. They tell me that they never leave anyone they like and
that they often choose the timid. The name of the frightening one is
Giga (in Icelandic *Gigur* is a crater), which I associate with the name
Marigold and have a vision of pursuit like a book illustration and, I
think, related to the long red-legged Scissor Man in *Schockheaded
Peter*. The scene changes to a derelict factory by moonlight. The
brothers are there, and my father. There is a great banging going on
which, they tell me, is caused by the ghost of an old aunt who lives in

a tin in the factory. Sure enough, the tin, which resembles my mess tin, comes bouncing along and stops at our feet, falling open. It is full of hard-boiled eggs. The brothers are very selfish and seize them, and only my father gives me half his.

w. h. aud_en, *A Certain World*, 1970

A dream, the other night, that the world had become dissatisfied with the inaccurate manner in which facts are reported, and had employed me, with a salary of a thousand dollars, to relate things of public importance exactly as they happen.

nathaniel hawthorne, *The American Notebooks*, c.1843

Dreamed of being in a large room at a party, busy eating; called to listen to a piece on piano, played by the family. The piano was twice as wide as usual, and at the side of it there was a square hole cut, just enough for a little girl-baby to sit in, who played on about seven keys, set across the other keys, all for herself. Then the grandmama played the great keys and the mama played on a deep soup-plate, with a knife handle, all very prettily; and I was standing leaning against a sort of kitchen dresser, with my knife and fork stuck out awkwardly at the musicians till I thought I had better put them down; so I did, on the dresser; and then the cook, behind me, began finding fault with my coat collar and asking leave to put it right and brush it, and as he was brushing he cried out at something, and I looked to see what he meant, and the lappet of my waistcoat was all stained with blood, and I thought I had been going about all the evening like that, and so I woke.

john ruskin, *Diaries*, 26 February 1868

Some time ago I saw Adam — an old man, half stupefied with age; he lived in a little lonely cottage, and complained to me that Eve was grown old, and did not use him kindly — she did not get his supper comfortably for him. He told me there were a great many of his descendants whom he had never seen, and particularly one William Taylor, of Norwich, who, he had heard, was a very clever fellow, and he wished to know if I knew him.

robert southey, 7 December 1804

On the fragment of a letter to Mr. Ellis there is mention of a dream he had about his younger niece, 'so vivid that I must tell it. She came to me with a penitential face, and told me that she had a great sin to confess; that Pepys's Diary was all a forgery, and that she had forged it. I was in the greatest dismay. "What! I have been quoting in reviews, and in my History, a forgery of yours as a book of the highest authority. How shall I ever hold my head up again?" I woke with the fright, poor Alice's supplicating voice still in my ears.'

G. O. TREVELYAN, *The Life and Letters of Lord Macaulay*, 1878

Again last night I dreamed the dream called Laundry.
In it, the sheets and towels of a life we were going to share,
The milk-stiff bibs, the shroud, each rag to be ever
Trampled or soiled, bled on or groped for blindly,
Came swooning out of an enormous willow hamper
Onto moon-marbly boards. We had just met. I watched
From outer darkness. I had dressed myself in clothes
Of a new fiber that never stains or wrinkles, never
Wears thin. The opera house sparkled with tiers
And tiers of eyes, like mine enlarged by belladonna,
Trained inward. There I saw the cloud-clot, gust by gust,
Form, and the lightning bite, and the roan mane unloosen.
Fingers were running in panic over the flute's nine gates.
Why did I flinch? I loved you. And in the downpour laughed
To have us wrung white, gnarled together, one
Topmost mordent of wisteria,
As the lean tree burst into grief.

JAMES MERRILL, 'The Mad Scene', 1966

Last night I had a dream which I record as a curiosity, so far as I know, in the literature of dreams. I was staying, with my sisters, in some suburb of London, and had heard that the Terrys were staying near us, so went to call, and found Mrs. Terry at home, who told us that Marion and Florence were at the theatre, 'the Walter House,' where they had a good engagement. 'In that case,' I said, 'I'll go on there at once, and see the performance – and may I take Polly with me?' 'Certainly,' said Mrs. Terry. And there was Polly, the child, seated in the room, and looking about nine or ten years old: and I was distinctly conscious of the fact, yet without any feeling of surprise at its incongruity, that I was going to take the *child* Polly with me to the theatre, to see the *grown-up* Polly act! Both pictures — Polly as a child, and Polly as a woman, are, I suppose, equally clear in my ordinary waking memory: and it seems that in sleep I had contrived to give the two pictures separate individualities.

LEWIS CARROLL, quoted in S. D. Collingwood, *The Life and Letters of Lewis Carroll*, 1899

I dreamt last night that I had to rush every few minutes to see Russian trains come into a tube station as I was expecting a friend from Russia, I think. Between two trains, I strolled off the platform on to a bridge over a canal, on which were ships whose immense and very ornate bowsprits came up as high as the bridge. Turning another way I saw a very muddy road, and in this road a little acrobat (one of a troupe) was performing. He was 8 or 9 years of age. The greasy road was a very difficult 'take-off' but he had to do a double somersault with such a take-off, and he did it, two complete revolutions with only a slight slip on his back on alighting. He then lay on his back in the mud to do another trick, and then I noticed that he was smoking a thick strong cigar, puffing away at it all the time. He was forced by his brutal persecutors to smoke this awful cigar all the time, and to keep puffing at it continuously. A tremendous refinement of cruelty. Even as I write my gorge rises at the memory of the cigar in his small mouth. He clenched his small hands to prepare for the spring from his back. He did this several times, and then I woke up.

ARNOLD BENNETT, *Journal*, 7 September 1913

Today, in my dream, I invented a new kind of vehicle for a park slope. You take a branch, it needn't be very strong, prop it up on the ground at a slight angle, hold one end in your hand, sit down on it side-saddle, then the whole branch naturally rushes down the slope, since you are sitting on the bough you are carried along at full speed, rocking comfortably on the elastic wood. It is also possible to use the branch to ride up again. The chief advantage, aside from the simplicity of the whole device, lies in the fact that the branch, thin and flexible as it is, can be lowered or raised as necessary and gets through anywhere, even where a person by himself would get through only with difficulty.

FRANZ KAFKA, *Diaries*, 21 July 1913

Some whimsical person died, and it appeared by his will that he had left me an estate of ten thousand pounds a-year, on condition that I should never again wear breeches, pantaloons, trousers, or any other modification of that masculine garb. So I was deliberating whether to adopt a Moorish or a Highland dress, though I feared the former might not be allowed, or to wear coat and waistcoat with the philibeg.

ROBERT SOUTHEY, 10 May 1832

I slept poorly, dreamt voluminously. Once, that I was lowered down over a Lover's Leap by block and tackle, to relative safety below. Indistinct figures stood nearby, deriding it as a craven form of descent. The act of a poltroon. Another time I caught my foot in a tangle of barbed wire, driving up the price of eggs.

PETER DE VRIES, *Consenting Adults*, 1981

It was my eighth dream that I thought my tongue was so long that I wound it round the back of my neck, and forward into my mouth on the other side.

Thorsteins Saga, c.AD 900

I had a dream at this time that I was caught by the Nazis. They took me to an enormous wall built of Pelasgian blocks. In this wall was a great wrought-iron gate of eighteenth-century workmanship. They unlocked this gate and thrust me through it, locked it behind me. I found myself in the Alps with a narrow pass before me, began to ascend the rough and desolate track. Plodding upwards, looking straight ahead of me or hardly looking at all, I was conscious suddenly of something on either side, looked to the right and the left. On the right and the left of my track, padding along in parallel silence were bears. Bears of every size and colour, going inexorably forward, but looking at me sideways. I had the feeling they were 'not quite right', steeled myself to go on, careful not to annoy them. Then ahead of me, higher up the pass, I saw a woman, with a stab of joy in my diaphragm hurried to overtake her. Overtook her; she looked straight out of Bond Street, tall and blonde, the height of elegance. She too had been caught by the Nazis, I walked along beside her and the bears walked on each side of us. But everything was all right now.

'Who are you?' I said at last. 'Oh,' she said suavely, 'I am the Czar's governess.'

LOUIS MacNEICE, *The Strings Are False*, 1965

'Come and look at him!' the brothers cried, and they each took one of Alice's hands, and led her up to where the King was sleeping.

'Isn't he a *lovely* sight?' said Tweedledum.

Alice couldn't say honestly that he was. He had a tall red night-cap on, with a tassel, and he was lying crumpled up into a sort of untidy heap, and snoring loud – 'fit to snore his head off!' as Tweedledum remarked.

'I'm afraid he'll catch cold with lying on the damp grass,' said Alice, who was a very thoughtful little girl.

'He's dreaming now,' said Tweedledee: 'and what do you think he's dreaming about?'

Alice said 'Nobody can guess that.'

'Why, about *you*!' Tweedledee exclaimed, clapping his hands triumphantly. 'And if he left off dreaming about you, where do you suppose you'd be?'

'Where I am now, of course,' said Alice.

'Not you!' Tweedledee retorted contemptuously. 'You'd be nowhere. Why, you're only a sort of thing in his dream!'

'If that there King was to wake,' added Tweedledum, 'you'd go out – bang! – just like a candle!'

'I shouldn't!' Alice exclaimed indignantly. 'Besides, if *I'm* only a sort of thing in his dream, what are *you*, I should like to know?'

'Ditto,' said Tweedledum.

'Ditto, ditto!' cried Tweedledee.

He shouted this so loud that Alice couldn't help saying 'Hush! You'll be waking him, I'm afraid, if you make so much noise.'

'Well, it's no use *your* talking about waking him,' said Tweedledum, 'when you're only one of the things in his dream. You know very well you're not real.'

'I *am* real!' said Alice, and began to cry.

LEWIS CARROLL, *Through the Looking-Glass*, 1872

In his soft, low, yet clear, wistful tones, he [Thomas Hardy] related his perennial dream.

'I am pursued, and I am rising like an angel up into heaven, out of the hands of my earthly pursuers,' with a small, deprecating laugh, 'I

am agitated and hampered, as I suppose an angel would not be, by —
a paucity of underlinen.'

VIOLET HUNT, *The Flurried Years*, 1928

I imagined that I was with a dentist who was about to extract a tooth
from a patient. Before applying the forceps he remarked to me (at the
same time setting fire to a perfumed cloth at the end of something like
a broomstick, in order to dissipate the unpleasant odour) that it was
the largest tooth he had ever seen. When extracted I found that it was
indeed enormous, in the shape of a cauldron, with walls an inch
thick. Taking from my pocket a tape measure (such as I carried in
waking life), I found the diameter to be not less than twenty-five
inches; the interior was like roughly-hewn rock, and there were
sea-weeds and lichen-like growths within. The size of the tooth
seemed to me large, but not extraordinarily so. It is well known that
pain in the teeth, or the dentist's manipulations, cause those organs
to seem of extravagant extent; in dreams this tendency rules
unchecked; thus a friend once dreamed that mice were playing about
in a cavity in her tooth.

HAVELOCK ELLIS, *The World of Dreams*, 1911

I had an absurd and charming dream which made me laugh, alone
though I was, when I awoke. I saw myself once more at the age of
nineteen, riding along a bad road in Virginia. This ride went on for
some time, and then, suddenly, my horse spoke to me: 'I have been
carrying you for three hours. I am tired. Now it's your turn.' I
thereupon dismounted, only to see my horse growing smaller
beneath my very eyes. Very soon he was no larger than a pony, and
this pony grew still smaller, till his size was no greater than that of a
big dog. Without further ado, I took my horse under my arm and
carried him home.

JULIAN GREEN, *Personal Record 1928–1939*, 19 October 1933

Singularly enough, I seldom if ever dreamed of Lolita as I
remembered her — as I saw her constantly and obsessively in my
conscious mind during my daymares and insomnia. More precisely:
she did haunt my sleep but she appeared there in strange and
ludicrous disguises as Valeria or Charlotte, or a cross between them.
That complex ghost would come to me, shedding shift after shift, in

an atmosphere of great melancholy and disgust, and would recline in dull invitation on some narrow board or hard settee, with flesh ajar like the rubber valve of a soccer ball's bladder. I would find myself, dentures fractured or hopelessly mislaid, in horrible *chambres garnies* where I would be entertained at tedious vivisecting parties that generally ended with Charlotte or Valeria weeping in my bleeding arms and being tenderly kissed by my brotherly lips in a dream disorder of auctioneered Viennese bric-à-brac, pity, impotence, and the brown wigs of tragic old women who had just been gassed.

VLADIMIR NABOKOV, *Lolita*, 1955

Nothing is more common, or usually more pleasant, than to dream of flying. It is one of the best specimens of the race; for besides being agreeable, it is made up of the dreams of ordinary life and those of surprising combination. Thus the dreamer sometimes thinks he is flying in unknown regions, sometimes skimming only a few inches above the ground, and wondering he never did it before. He will even dream that he is dreaming about it; and yet is so fully convinced of its feasibility, and so astonished at his never having hit upon so delightful a truism, that he is resolved to practise it the moment he wakes. 'One has only,' says he, 'to give a little spring with one's foot, so, and—oh! it's the easiest and most obvious thing in the world. I'll always skim hereafter.' We dreamt once that a woman set up some Flying Rooms, as a person does a tavern. We went to try them and nothing could be more satisfactory and commonplace on all sides. The landlady welcomed us with a courtesy, hoped for friends and favours, etc., and then showed us into a spacious room, not round, as might be expected, but long, and after the usual dining fashion. 'Perhaps, sir,' said she, 'you would like to try the room.' Upon which we made no more ado, but sprung up and made two or three genteel circuits, now taking the height of it, like a house-lark, and then cutting the angles, like a swallow. 'Very pretty flying, indeed,' said we, 'and very moderate.'

LEIGH HUNT, 'Of Dreams', 1820

Since he weighs nothing,
Even the stoutest dreamer
Can fly without wings.

W. H. AUDEN, from 'Thanksgiving for a Habitat', 1966

Every one knows the sense of flying in dreams; with me it requires a perpetual effort of self-propulsion, and is accompanied with a sort of apprehension, upon rising to any height above the ground, that I may not be able to sustain the effort, and may therefore fall. Last night this very common form of dream was curiously modified, for I thought I was sitting upon a low stool, and made it fly through the air by the application of a short stick to the ground, in the manner of *punting*. While thus employed I met an ugly spectacle – a living human head, which had been so born without any *body* belonging to it. Waking then, and dwelling upon this till I presently again fell dreaming, I thought I was in a castle where there were several such heads, well-born, and enjoying respect and all the comforts that could be given them. They were sustained by odours, and had all the pleasure of taste, but swallowed nothing; and they had power enough of motion to turn themselves as they liked.

ROBERT SOUTHEY, 26 November 1818

In my dream I was present at a party given in the rooms of the Royal Society in Burlington House. Lord Kelvin, Lord Rayleigh, Sir William Ramsay, my brother-in-law Sir Arthur Rucker, and many others whom I knew, were there. They were standing together in a little group, and my brother-in-law asked me to explain to them my method of flying. I could not explain how it was done, only that it seemed to me much easier to fly than to walk. At his suggestion I made some experimental flights – circling round the ceiling, rising and falling, and showing them also the gliding or floating movement near the ground. They all discussed it critically as though they were rather 'on the defensive' about the proceeding, looking upon it, I think, as a new and doubtful experiment, rather savouring of a conjuring trick. Then Lord Kelvin . . . said that he felt the power of human flight to be less surprising, less baffling than the others seemed to think it. 'The law of gravitation had probably been in this case temporarily suspended.' – 'Clearly this law does not for the moment affect you when you fly,' he said to me. The others who were present agreed to this, and said that this was probably the solution of the puzzle. An assistant was standing behind the group of men, and in order to show them that flying is not really difficult, I took his hand, and begging him to have confidence in me and to trust to my guidance, I succeeded in making him fly a few inches from the ground.

MARY ARNOLD-FORSTER, *Studies in Dreams*, 1921

I was in that most frequent of all dreamy states: self-suspended in the air, exercising that power of moving without wings which is always accompanied by a sense of insecurity, a constant tendency to rise, and as constant a danger of falling headlong. Perhaps in such dreams the stories of saints being elevated in their prayers may have originated; they have dreamed that they were so, and mistaken, or chosen to mistake the dream for reality.

Last night I was not only thus buoyant myself, but had before me a volume of the *Acta Sanctorum* buoyant in a like manner, open as on a desk. Alighting after this, I went into a church with an old man, who had witnessed the miracle; but I had some vague notion that I was about to be ordained there, but the miracle had rather disturbed me than inspired confidence. I knew that it had not depended in any degree on myself as relating to the book, and that it could not possibly give any additional authority to the book itself, and that I could not render the book buoyant, though I might raise myself into the same precarious situation.

ROBERT SOUTHEY, 6 July 1830

Last night I dreamt of you, and you were flying along in a nightdress with an Elizabethan ruff. You called to me: 'Come along! Come along!' and I flew with you clumsily, and you called out over your ruff: 'If you saw better you'd fly better' – which somehow seemed to explain the Universe to me! And then suddenly – Oh Lor! your left wing broke – you fell, round and round like a top – and I woke up!

HUGH WALPOLE, letter to Sylvia Lynd, 1938, quoted in Rupert Hart-Davis, *Hugh Walpole: A Biography*, 1952

It is beyond dispute that I can fly in dreams. You too. I add 'in dreams' because my efforts, like yours, have not succeeded—by a sound, a strangled sigh—in crossing the frontier that separates the two worlds, only one of which we designate, arbitrarily, as 'real'. I can cross a valley; pivot, to turn, on one or other of my flying arms; and swoop down, head first, feet raised to gain speed, then straighten my trunk to regain the horizontal for climbing or landing. And how I sport with the wind, in this entire universe! Entire, because it possesses its pale day-star, its nights less dark than earthly nights, its plants, its population of the loved dead, of the keenly staring unknown, its animal life especially. The most recent animal I encountered there dates from last week, for the full moon, which sends cats delirious, authorizes my brief visits to this boundless continent. A black feline, as big as a Great Dane, was waiting to fight with me and we fought gravely, not in frenzy but as if for sport, while meantime I noticed the shape of its eyes, more horizontal than those of cats, and the particular pink of its mouth, opened whenever it wished to frighten or bite me. A very real animal, in fact, whose contact and appearance inspired my dreaming double with no more than normal curiosity, the normal desire to vanquish a strange animal, and the confused ill-formulated conceit of bringing off a victory *up there*: '*They* will be pleased with it; I'll display it to *them* as if it had always been mine. . . .' But it was the same with the beautiful black feline as with that little tortoise with the bird's head, so friendly, that climbs in the trees and cheeps . . . you know. No, you don't know. The bird-tortoise remained on the far side of the gate with the great black feline, the intelligent sociable serpent, the dog that silently regards me and puts his hand in mine, the man who holds out an open notebook which I never have the time to read. . . .

Thanks, no doubt, to my perfect digestion, animals and people in my exclusive nocturnal empire are courteous and peaceable, even in combat. The flights that carry me over a familiar valley of dark fir-trees do not break my bones and I land, instead of falling, in the middle of the bed after one of those jolts as severe as any earthquake. Did the same flight haunt the dreams of a Maneyrol, a Barbot, a Simonet, of all those who seek the dream-remembered motorless soaring, the everlasting wing? . . . Flight exists for us only in dream, the complete being is he who sleeps and is newly born, for the new-born swims at birth like the sightless kitten and puppy. But its human condition holds it back and denies it one more element; two months later the 'little man' can no longer swim.

COLETTE, Journey for Myself, 1949

When you're lying awake with a dismal headache, and repose is taboo'd by anxiety,
I conceive you may use any language you choose to indulge in, without impropriety;
For your brain is on fire, the bedclothes conspire, of usual slumber to plunder you:
First your counterpane goes, and uncovers your toes, and your sheet slips demurely from under you;
Then the blanketing tickles, you feel like mixed pickles, so terribly sharp is the pricking,

And you're hot, and you're cross, and you tumble and toss till there's
　nothing 'twixt you and the ticking;

Then the bedclothes all creep to the ground in a heap, and you pick
　'em all up in a tangle;

Next your pillow resigns and politely declines to remain at its usual
　angle!

Well, you get some repose in the form of a doze, with hot eyeballs
　and head ever aching,

But your slumbering teems with such horrible dreams that you'd
　very much better be waking;

For you dream you are crossing the Channel, and tossing about in a
　steamer from Harwich –

Which is something between a large bathing machine and a very
　small second-class carriage –

And you're giving a treat (penny ice and cold meat) to a party of
　friends and relations –

They're a ravenous horde – and they all came on board at Sloane
　Square and South Kensington Stations.

And bound on that journey you find your attorney (who started that
　morning from Devon);

He's a bit undersized, and you don't feel surpris'd when he tells you
　he's only eleven.

Well, you're driving like mad with this singular lad (by the bye the
　ship's now a four-wheeler),

And you're playing round games, and he calls you bad names, when
　you tell him that 'ties pay the dealer';

But this you can't stand, so you throw up your hand, and you find
　you're as cold as an icicle,

In your shirt and your socks (the black silk with gold clocks),
　crossing Salisbury Plain on a bicycle:

And he and the crew are on bicycles too – which they've somehow or
　other invested in –

And he's telling the tars, all the particu*lars* of a company he's
　interested in –

It's a scheme of devices, to get at low prices, all goods from cough
　mixtures to cables

(Which tickled the sailors) by treating retailers, as though they were
　all vege*t*ables –

You get a good spadesman to plant a small tradesman (first take off
　his boots with a boot-tree),

And his legs will take root, and his fingers will shoot, and they'll
　blossom and bud like a fruit-tree –

From the greengrocer tree you get grapes and green-pea, cauliflower,
    pineapple, and cranberries,
While the pastry-cook plant, cherry-brandy will grant, apple puffs,
    and three-corners and banburys –
The shares are a penny, and ever so many are taken by Rothschild
    and Baring,
And just as a few are allotted to you, you awake with a shudder
    despairing –
You're a regular wreck, with a crick in your neck, and no wonder
    you snore for your head's on the floor,
And you've needles and pins from your soles to your shins, and your
    flesh is acreep, for your left leg's asleep,
And you've cramp in your toes, and a fly on your nose, and some fluff
    in your lung, and a feverish tongue,
And a thirst that's intense,
And a general sense that you haven't been sleeping in clover;
But the darkness has pass'd, and it's daylight at last, and the night
    has been long – ditto, ditto my song –
And thank goodness they're both of them over!

W. S. GILBERT, Iolanthe, 1882

Transformations and Frustrations

My dreams uncommonly illustrative of the non-existence of surprise in sleep – I dreamt that I was asleep in the cloister at Christ's Hospital and had awoken with a pain in my hand from some corrosion / boys and nurses daughters peeping at me / On their implying that I was not in the school, I answered yes I am / I am only twenty – I then recollected that I was thirty, and of course could not be in the school – and was perplexed – but not the least surprised that I could fall into such error / So I dreamt of Dorothy, William and Mary [Wordsworth] – and that Dorothy was altered in every feature, a fat, thick-limbed and rather red-haired – in short, no resemblance to her at all – and I said, if I did not *know* you to be Dorothy, I never should suppose it / Why, says she – I have not a feature the same / and yet I was not surprised –

I was followed up and down by a frightful pale woman who, I thought, wanted to kiss me, and had the property of giving a shameful disease by breathing in the face/

And again I dreamt that a figure of a woman of gigantic height, dim and indefinite and smokelike appeared – and that I was forced to run toward it – and then it changed to a stool – and then appeared again in another place – and again I went up in great fright – and it changed to some other common thing – yet I felt no surprise.

S. T. COLERIDGE, *Notebooks*, 3 October 1802

She thought she was in a large old chamber belonging to the abbey, more ancient and desolate, though in part furnished, than any she had yet seen. It was strongly barricadoed, yet no person appeared. While she stood musing and surveying the apartment, she heard a low voice call her, and looking towards the place from whence it came, she perceived by the dim light of a lamp, a figure stretched on a bed that lay on the floor. The voice called again, and, approaching the bed, she distinctly saw the features of a man who appeared to be dying. A ghastly paleness overspread his countenance, yet there was an expression of mildness and dignity in it, which strongly interested her.

While she looked on him, his features changed, and seemed convulsed in the agonies of death. The spectacle shocked her, and she

started back, but he suddenly stretched forth his hand, and seizing
hers, grasped it with violence; she struggled in terror to disengage
herself, and again looking on his face, saw a man, who appeared to
be about thirty, with the same features, but, in full health, and of a
most benign countenance. He smiled tenderly upon her, and moved
his lips as if to speak, when the floor of the chamber suddenly
opened, and he sunk from her view. The effort she made to save
herself from the falling, awoke her.

ANN RADCLIFFE, The Romance of the Forest, 1791

I was disturbed by the wildest dreams. I thought I saw Elizabeth, in
the bloom of health, walking in the streets of Ingolstadt. Delighted
and surprised, I embraced her; but as I imprinted the first kiss on her
lips, they became livid with the hue of death; her features appeared
to change, and I thought that I held the corpse of my dead mother in
my arms; a shroud enveloped her form, and I saw the grave-worms
crawling in the folds of the flannel. I started from my sleep with
horror; a cold dew covered my forehead, my teeth chattered, and
every limb became convulsed: when, by the dim and yellow light of
the moon, as it forced its way through the window shutters, I beheld
the wretch – the miserable monster whom I had created.

MARY SHELLEY, Frankenstein, 1818

. . . such *contradictory* vagaries never did I know in my slumbers.
Incoherencies of incoherence!—For example—I was married to the
best of men: I was *not* married: I was rejected with scorn, as a
presumptuous creature. I sought to hide myself in holes and corners.
I was dragged out of a subterraneous cavern, which the sea had made
when it once broke bounds, and seemed the dwelling of howling and
conflicting winds; and when I expected to be punished for my
audaciousness, and for repining at my lot, I was turned into an Angel
of light; stars of diamonds, like a glory, encompassing my head: A
dear little baby was put into my arms. Once it was Lucy's; another
time it was Emily's; and at another time Lady Clementina's!—I was
fond of it, beyond expression.

I again dreamed I was married: Sir Charles again was the man. He
did not love me. My grandmamma and aunt, on their knees, and
with tears, besought him to love their child; and pleaded to him my
Love of him of long standing, begun in gratitude; and that he was the

only man I ever loved. O how I wept in my dream! My face and bosom were wet with my real tears.

My sobs, and my distress and *theirs*, awakened me; but I dropt asleep, and fell into the very same reverie. He upbraided me with being the cause that he had not Lady Clementina. He said, and *so* sternly! I am sure he cannot look so sternly, that he thought me a much better creature than I proved to be: Yet methought, in my own heart, I was not altered. I fell down at his feet. I called it my misfortune, that he could not love me: I would not say it was his fault. It might, perhaps, be his misfortune too!—And then I said, Love and Hatred are not always in one's power. If you cannot love the poor creature who kneels before you, *that* shall be a cause sufficient with me for a divorce: I desire not to fasten myself on the man who cannot love me. Let me be divorced from you, Sir—You shall be at liberty to assign any cause for the separation, but *crime*. I will bind myself never, never to marry again; but you shall be free—And God bless you, and her you can love better than your poor Harriet. Fool! I weep as I write!—What a weak creature I am, since I have not been well!

SAMUEL RICHARDSON, *Sir Charles Grandison*, 1753–4

In the early stage of my malady, the splendours of my dreams were indeed chiefly architectural: and I beheld such pomp of cities and palaces as was never yet beheld by the waking eye, unless in the clouds. . . .

To my architecture succeeded dreams of lakes – and silvery expanses of water: – these haunted me so much, that I feared (though possibly it will appear ludicrous to a medical man) that some dropsical state or tendency of the brain might thus be making itself (to use a metaphysical word) *objective*; and the sentient organ *project* itself as its own object. – For two months I suffered greatly in my head. . . . Till now I had never felt a headache even, or any but the slightest pain, except rheumatic pains caused by my own folly. However, I got over this attack, though it must have been verging on something very dangerous.

The waters now changed their character, – from translucent lakes, shining like mirrors, they now became seas and oceans. And now came a tremendous change, which, unfolding itself slowly like a scroll, through many months, promised an abiding torment; and, in fact, it never left me until the winding up of my case. Hitherto the human face had mixed often in my dreams, but not despotically, nor

with any special power of tormenting. But now that which I have
called the tyranny of the human face began to unfold itself. Perhaps
some part of my London life might be answerable for this. Be that as
it may, now it was that upon the rocking waters of the ocean the
human face began to appear: the sea appeared paved with
innumerable faces, upturned to the heavens: faces, imploring,
wrathful, despairing, surged upwards by thousands, by myriads, by
generations, by centuries: – my agitation was infinite, – my mind
tossed – and surged with the ocean.

THOMAS DE QUINCEY, *Confessions of an English Opium-Eater*, 1822

His guiding purpose, though it was supernatural, was not
impossible. He wanted to dream a man; he wanted to dream him
down to the last detail and project him into the world of reality. . . .
Almost at once, he had a dream of a beating heart.

He dreamed it throbbing, warm, secret. It was the size of a closed
fist, a darkish red in the dimness of a human body still without a face
or sex. With anxious love he dreamed it for fourteen lucid nights.
Each night he perceived it more clearly. He did not touch it, but
limited himself to witnessing it, to observing it, to correcting it now
and then with a look. He felt it, he lived it from different distances
and from many angles. On the fourteenth night he touched the
pulmonary artery with a finger and then the whole heart, inside and
out. The examination satisfied him. For one night he deliberately did
not dream; after that he went back to the heart again, invoked the
name of a planet, and set out to envision another of the principal
organs. Before a year was over he came to the skeleton, the eyelids.
The countless strands of hair were perhaps the hardest task of all. He
dreamed a whole man, a young man, but the young man could not
stand up or speak, nor could he open his eyes. Night after night, the
man dreamed him asleep.

In the cosmogonies of the Gnostics, the demiurges mould a red
Adam who is unable to stand on his feet; as clumsy and crude and
elementary as that Adam of dust was the Adam of dreams wrought
by the nights of the magician. One evening the man was at the point
of destroying all his handiwork (it would have been better for him
had he done so), but in the end he restrained himself. Having
exhausted his prayers to the gods of the earth and river, he threw
himself down at the feet of the stone image that may have been a tiger
or a stallion, and asked for its blind aid. That same evening he
dreamed of the image. He dreamed it alive, quivering; it was no

unnatural cross between tiger and stallion but at one and the same time both these violent creatures and also a bull, a rose, a thunderstorm. This manifold god revealed to him that its earthly name was Fire, that there in the circular temple (and in others like it) sacrifices had once been made to it, that it had been worshipped, and that through its magic the phantom of the man's dreams would be wakened to life in such a way that – except for Fire itself and the dreamer – every being in the world would accept him as a man of flesh and blood. The god ordered that, once instructed in the rites, the disciple should be sent downstream to the other ruined temple, whose pyramids still survived, so that in that abandoned place some human voice might exalt him. In the dreamer's dream, the dreamed one awoke.

JORGE LUIS BORGES, 'The Circular Ruins', 1944

It is seldom that sleep, after such violent agitation, is either sound or refreshing. Lovel's was disturbed by a thousand baseless and confused visions. He was a bird—he was a fish—or he flew like the one, and swam like the other—qualities which would have been very essential to his safety a few hours before. Then Miss Wardour was a syren, or a bird of Paradise; her father a triton, or a sea-gull; and Oldbuck alternately a porpoise and a cormorant. These agreeable imaginations were varied by all the usual vagaries of a feverish dream; the air refused to bear the visionary, the water seemed to burn him—the rocks felt like down-pillows as he was dashed against them—whatever he undertook failed in some strange and unexpected manner—and whatever attracted his attention underwent, as he attempted to investigate it, some wild and wonderful metamorphosis, while his mind continued all the while in some degree conscious of the delusion, from which it in vain struggled to free itself by awaking . . . He was then, or imagined himself, broad awake in the Green Chamber, gazing upon the flickering and occasional flame which the unconsumed remnants of the faggots sent forth . . . Brighter sparkles of light flashed from the chimney with such intense brilliancy as to enlighten all the room. The tapestry waved wildly on the wall, till its dusky forms seemed to become animated. The hunters blew their horns—the stag seemed to fly, the boar to resist, and the hounds to assail the one and pursue the other; the cry of deer, mangled by throttling dogs, the shouts of men, and the clatter of horses' hoofs, seemed at once to surround him—while every group pursued, with all the fury of the chase, the employment in which the artist had represented them as engaged. Lovel looked on this strange scene devoid of wonder (which seldom intrudes itself upon the sleeping fancy), but with an anxious sensation of awful fear. At length an individual figure among the tissued huntsmen, as he gazed upon them more fixedly, seemed to leave the arras and to approach the bed of the slumberer. As he drew near his figure appeared to alter. His bugle-horn became a brazen-clasped volume; his hunting-cap changed to such a furred head-gear as graces the burgomasters of Rembrandt; his Flemish garb remained, but his features, no longer agitated with the fury of the chase, were changed to a state of awful and stern composure. . . . Aldobrand held up his finger, as if to impose silence upon the guest who had intruded on his apartment, and began deliberately to unclasp the venerable volume which occupied his left hand. When it was unfolded, he turned over the leaves hastily for a short space, and then, raising his left hand, pointed to a passage in the page which he thus displayed. Although the language was unknown to our dreamer, his eye and attention were both strongly caught by the line which the figure seemed thus to press upon his notice, the words of which appeared to blaze with a supernatural light, and remained riveted upon his memory. As the vision shut his volume, a strain of delightful music seemed to fill the apartment—Lovel started, and became completely awake.

SIR WALTER SCOTT, *The Antiquary*, 1816

I was converted into a mighty pillar of stone, which reared its head in the midst of a desert, where it stood for ages, till generation after generation melted away before it. Even in this state, though unconscious of possessing any organs of sense, or being else than a mass of lifeless stone, I saw every object around – the mountains growing bald with age, the forest trees drooping in decay. At last, I waxed old and began to crumble into dust, while the moss and ivy accumulated upon me and stamped me with the aspect of hoar antiquity.

ROBERT MACNISH, *The Philosophy of Sleep*, 1830

I dreamed I held a kind of casket in my hands, and inside it was something very precious. I was walking up a long room, like an art gallery or a lecture hall, full of dead pictures and statues. . . . There was a small crowd of people waiting at the end of the hall on a kind of platform. They were waiting for me to hand them the casket. I was incredibly happy that at last I could give them this precious object. But when I handed it over, I saw suddenly they were all businessmen, brokers, something like that. They did not open the box, but started handing me large sums of money. I began to cry. I shouted: 'Open the box, open the box,' but they couldn't hear me, or wouldn't listen. Suddenly I saw they were all characters in some film or play, and that I had written it, and was ashamed of it. It all turned into farce, flickering and grotesque, I was a character in my own play. I opened the box and forced them to look. But instead of the beautiful thing, which I thought would be there, there was a mass of fragments, and pieces. Not a whole thing, broken into fragments, but bits and pieces from everywhere, all over the world – I recognised a lump of red earth that I knew came from Africa, and then a bit of metal that came off a gun from Indo-China, and then everything was horrible, bits of flesh from people killed in the Korean War and a communist party badge off someone who died in a Soviet prison. This, looking at the mass of ugly fragments, was so painful that I couldn't look, and I shut the box. But the group of businessmen or money-people hadn't noticed. They took the box from me and opened it. I turned away so as not to see, but they were delighted. At last I looked and I saw that there was something in the box. It was a small green crocodile with a winking sardonic snout. I thought it was the image of a crocodile, made of jade, or emeralds, then I saw it was alive, for large frozen tears rolled down its cheeks and turned into diamonds. I laughed out aloud when I saw how I had cheated the businessmen and I woke up. . . . I saw myself in a shop window: a small, rather pale, dry, spiky woman, and there was a wry look on my face which I recognised as the grin on the snout of that malicious little green crocodile in the crystal casket of my dream.

DORIS LESSING, The Golden Notebook, 1962

He dreamed lavishly, plunged, stage by stage, down into his dreams. Once awake, he never referred to his nightly adventures, for he was not willing to share a world which a delicate and badly-disciplined childhood had prolonged; nor did he want to share the beloved memory of long days passed in bed during his abrupt development into a tall, lank youth.

He loved his dreams, encouraged them, and would not for anything in the world have disappointed the halting-places waiting for him. At the first stage, where he could still hear the horns of the automobiles passing on the avenue outside his bedroom window, he would encounter familiar faces whirling about, distorted ones capable of lengthening and contracting themselves. He passed them

by as he would have passed through any good-natured crowd,
bowing first to this one and then to that. Moving, convex, they came
up nearer and nearer to Alain, getting bigger as they came. Clear
against a background, they became clearer still as though they might
be receiving light from the sleeper himself. Armed with one huge eye,
they progressed in easy gyration. But an underground thrust jerked
them back from a distance the moment they had touched an invisible
wall. In the watery face of a round monster, in the eye of a fat moon,
or in the look of a wandering archangel bearded with beams of light,
Alain recognized the same expression, the same purpose that no one
of them had yet made clear and which the Alain of the dream noted
confidently, 'They will explain it to me tomorrow.'

At times they would disappear, wisp off into nothingness,
scattering themselves in shreds, faintly luminous. Then again they
did not seem to exist except as a hand, arm, forehead, very
thoughtful eyeball, nose of starry dust, some chins, and always that
immense bulging eye, which, just at the moment of explaining itself,
turned away and would show nothing more except its other, black
face. . . .

COLETTE, The Cat, 1933

A shallow lake, with many waterbirds,
especially egrets: I was showing Mother around,
An extraordinary vivid dream
of Betty & Douglas, and Don – his mother's estate
was on the grounds of a lunatic asylum.
He showed me around.

A policeman trundled a siren up the walk.
It was 6:05 p.m., Don was late home.
I askt if he ever saw
the inmates – 'No, they never leave their cells.'
Betty was downstairs, Don called down 'A drink'
while showering.

I can't go into the meaning of the dream
except to say a sense of total LOSS
afflicted me thereof:
an absolute disappearance of continuity & love
and children away at school, the weight of the cross,
and everything is what it seems.

JOHN BERRYMAN, 'Dream Song No. 101', 1968

The lime-tree fruited in our poultry yard;
Sometimes I dream and see it; still quite small,
I stand in nightclothes, barefoot; on the ground
My shadow stretches, shaped like a hunched bird
And cast by moonlight; then I'm tiptoe tall
To take one of the limes into my hand.

It's best the dream ends there: that now the fowls
Their draggled plumage turned to silvery mail,
Don't rouse to mock me as I slip on dung
While tugging at the fruit—I fall, it rolls
Out of my reach; the hens more coarsely rail—
I try to shout them down, can't find my tongue.

Salt on my lips I taste my silent tears;
The deep sobs rack me, choke me till I wake
To find the hand still clenched that held the cheat;
All day that hand will show four sickle scars
Upon the palm, and, as I wait day-break,
Perfume of lime clings like the sweaty sheet.

EDWARD LUCIE-SMITH, 'The Lime-Tree', 1961

Miss Julie. . . . . I have a dream which recurs from time to time, and I'm reminded of it now. I've climbed to the top of a pillar, and am sitting there, and I can see no way to descend. When I look down, I become dizzy, but I must come down – but I haven't the courage to jump. I can't stay up there, and I long to fall, but I don't fall. And yet I know I shall find no peace till I come down, no rest till I come down, down to the ground. And if I could get down, I should want to burrow my way deep into the earth. . . . Have you ever felt anything like that?

Jean. No. I dream that I'm lying under a high tree in a dark wood. I want to climb, up, up to the top, and look round over the bright landscape where the sun is shining – plunder the bird's nest up there where the golden eggs lie. And I climb and climb, but the trunk is so thick and slippery, and it's so far to the first branch. But I know that if I could only get to that first branch, I'd climb my way to the top as though up a ladder. I haven't reached it yet, but I shall reach it, even if it's only in a dream.

AUGUST STRINDBERG, *Miss Julie*, 1888

Slept well: only dreamed of climbing a mast and not being able to get into the top.

JOHN RUSKIN, Diaries, 20 September 1884

She dream'd of being alone on the sea-shore,
    Chain'd to a rock; she knew not how, but stir
She could not from the spot, and the loud roar
    Grew, and each wave rose roughly, threatening her;
And o'er her upper lip they seem'd to pour,
    Until she sobb'd for breath, and soon they were
Foaming o'er her lone head, so fierce and high —
Each broke to drown her, yet she could not die.

Anon — she was released, and then she stray'd
    O'er the sharp shingles with her bleeding feet,
And stumbled almost every step she made;
    And something roll'd before her in a sheet,
Which she must still pursue howe'er afraid;
    'Twas white and indistinct, nor stopp'd to meet
Her glance nor grasp, for still she gaz'd and grasp'd,
And ran, but it escaped her as she clasp'd.

The dream changed: — in a cave she stood, its walls
    Were hung with marble icicles; the work
Of ages on its water-fretted halls
    Where waves might wash, and seals might breed and lurk;
Her hair was dripping, and the very balls
    Of her black eyes seem'd turn'd to tears, and mirk
The sharp rocks look'd below each drop they caught,
Which froze to marble as it fell, — she thought.

And wet, and cold, and lifeless at her feet,
    Pale as the foam that froth'd on his dead brow,
Which she essay'd in vain to clear, (how sweet
    Were once her cares, how idle seem'd they now!)
Lay Juan, nor could aught renew the beat
    Of his quench'd heart; and the sea dirges low
Rang in her sad ears like a mermaid's song,
And that brief dream appear'd a life too long.

LORD BYRON, Don Juan, Canto IV, 1820

Religious

❧

That there should be divine dreams seems unreasonably doubted by Aristotle. That there are demonical dreams we have little reason to doubt. Why may there not be angelical? If there be guardian spirits, they may not be unactively about us in sleep, but may sometimes order our dreams, and many strange hints, instigations, or discoveries which are so amazing unto us, may arise from such foundations.

But the phantasms of sleep do commonly walk in the great road of natural and animal dreams; wherein the thoughts or actions of the day are acted over and echoed in the night. Who can therefore wonder that Chrysostome should dream of St. Paul who daily read his Epistles; or that Cardan whose head was so taken up about the stars should dream that his soul was in the moon! Pious persons whose thoughts are daily busied about heaven and the blessed state thereof, can hardly escape the nightly phantasm of it, which though sometimes taken for illuminations or divine dreams, yet rightly perpended may prove but animal visions and natural night scenes of their waking contemplations.

SIR THOMAS BROWNE, 'On Dreams', c.1650

I saw that I was lying on a bed. . . . Observing my bed, I saw I was lying on plaited string supports attached to its sides: my feet were resting on one such support, my calves on another, and my legs felt uncomfortable. I seemed to know that those supports were movable, and with a movement of my foot I pushed away the furthest of them at my feet – it seemed to me that it would be more comfortable so. But I pushed it away too far and wished to reach it again with my foot, and that movement caused the next support under my calves to slip away also, so that my legs hung in the air. I made a movement with my whole body to adjust myself, fully convinced that I could do so at once; but the movement caused the other supports under me to slip and to become entangled, and I saw that matters were going quite wrong: the whole of the lower part of my body slipped and hung down, though my feet did not reach the ground. I was holding on only by the upper part of my back, and not only did it become uncomfortable but I was even frightened. And then only did I ask myself about something that had not before occurred to me. I asked myself: Where am I and what am I lying on? and I began to look around, and first of all to look down in the direction in which my body was hanging and whither I felt I must soon fall. I looked down and did not believe my eyes. I was not only at a height comparable to the height of the highest towers or mountains, but at a height such as I could never have imagined.

. . . I thought of what would happen to me directly I fell from my last support. And I felt that from fear I was losing my last supports, and that my back was slowly slipping lower and lower. Another moment and I should drop off. And then it occurred to me that this cannot be real. It is a dream. Wake up! I try to arouse myself but cannot do so. What am I to do? What am I to do? I ask myself, and look upwards. Above, there is also an infinite space. I look into the immensity of sky and try to forget about the immensity below, and I really do forget it. The immensity below repels and frightens me; the immensity above attracts and strengthens me. I am still supported above the abyss by the last supports that I have not yet slipped from under me; I know that I am hanging, but I look only upwards and my fear passes. As happens in dreams, a voice says: 'Notice this, this is it!' And I look more and more into the infinite above me and feel that I am becoming calm. . . . I see that I no longer hang as if about to fall, but am firmly held. I ask myself how I am held: I feel about, look round, and see that under me, under the middle of my body, there is one support, and that when I look upwards I lie on it in the position of securest balance, and that it alone gave me support before. And then, as happens in dreams, I imagined the mechanism by means of which I was held; a very natural, intelligible, and sure means, though to one awake that mechanism has no sense. I was even surprised in my dream that I had not understood it sooner. It appeared that at my head there was a pillar, and the security of that slender pillar was undoubted though there was nothing to support it. From the pillar a loop hung very ingeniously and yet simply, and if one lay with the middle of one's body in that loop and looked up, there could be no question of falling. This was all clear to me, and I was glad and tranquil. And it seemed as if someone said to me: 'See that you remember.' And I awoke.

LEO TOLSTOY, A Confession, 1879

I dreamt I was a soul. A soul resembles a grey ball of cloud, which turns over instead of walking, like a pumpkin. All souls looked alike, but within each was an individual. As this soul I wafted in and out of sunsets, sat upon soft heaps in the sky, and danced the polka; but mostly the soul bowled along in a nightmare of empty rooms; some large; some small, sometimes thirty or forty – I didn't count them – identical; a baffling honeycomb; and the poor soul despaired. But before I woke, I arrived. The rooms delivered me. I was precipitated into a vast, cavernous hall – heaven its ceiling – with steps, hundreds and hundreds of steep steps. It was extremely tiring, pushing through all the angels and the men – I don't recall any women – who were dead. At the very top was God. On the second step – the topmost step was narrow and would accommodate only a single pair of feet – and at God's right hand, stood Jesus; on God's left, or right as I mount the interminable steps, and I do reach the summit, at the other hand of God was my father, holding his sword.

God was kind. He made complimentary remarks.

I woke, at this excellent moment: I never dreamt beyond it.

ROSALIND BELBEN, *Dreaming of Dead People*, 1979

'Monday evening, July the 2nd, 1804. – Joanna tried to compose herself, after a hard contest with the devil, when at last she fell asleep; and whether awake or asleep,' continues Miss Townley, 'she does not know; but she remembers she was quite awake when she felt the hand of the Lord upon her, but in that heavenly and beautiful manner that she felt joy unspeakable and full of glory. She felt herself lying, as it were, in heaven, in the hands of the Lord. . . . "In this happy manner," affirms Joanna, "I fell asleep; and in my sleep I was surprised with seeing a most beautiful and heavenly figure, that arose from the bed, and his head almost reached the tester of the bed; but his face was towards me, which appeared with beauty and majesty, but pale as death. His hair was a flaxen colour, all in disorder around his face. His face was covered with a strong perspiration; and his locks were wet like the dew of the night, as though they had been taken out of a river. The collar of his shirt appeared unbuttoned, and the skin of his bosom appeared white as the driven snow. Such was the beauty of the heavenly figure that appeared before me in a disordered state; but the robe he had on was like a surplice, down to his knees. He put one of his legs to me, that was perfectly like mine, no larger; but with purple spots at the top, as mine are with beating myself, which Townley, Underwood, and Taylor are witnesses of. Methought in my dream, he got himself into that perspiration by being pressed to sleep between Townley and me. I said to him, 'Are you my dear dying Saviour, that is come to destroy all the works of the devil?' He answered me, 'Yes!' I thought I called Underwood, and waked Townley, to look at him, which they did with wonder and amaze. I then thought I would go out of my bed, and fall down on my knees before him, to return him thanks for his mercy and goodness; but as soon as these thoughts entered my head, he disappeared, and a woman appeared in his stead, which gave me pain to see he was gone. But the woman told me many wonderful things that were coming upon the earth, and what was coming upon the devil: yet I grieved at the loss of my dear Redeemer, for I saw no beauty in the woman; and though the woman would reason strong with me, her reasons I did not like. In this confusion I awoke, and heard the bell tolling for the dead, and the drums beating at the same time, which I remarked to Townley.'"

> MISS TOWNLEY, letter to Revd T. P. Foley, in 'Letters and Communications of Joanna Southcott', 1804

Now one monk whom I solely mention of this group of holy men
Was known as Athanael; he was famous near and far.
At fasting bouts or prayer with him no other could compare with him;
At ground and lofty praying he could do the course in par.

One night while sleeping heavily (from fighting with the devil he
Had gone to bed exhausted while the sun was shining still),
He had a vision Freudian, and though he was annoyed he an-
Alyzed it in the well-known style of Doctors Jung and Brill.

He dreamed of Alexandria, of wicked Alexandria;
A crowd of men were cheering in a manner rather rude
At Thaïs, who was dancing there, and Athanael, glancing there,
Observed her do the shimmy in what artists call The Nude.

Said he, 'This dream fantastical disturbs my thoughts monastical;
Some unsuppressed desire, I fear, has found my monkish cell.
I blushed up to the hat o' me to view that girl's anatomy.
I'll go to Alexandria and save her soul from Hell.'

> NEWMAN LEVY, from 'Thaïs', 1923

Alas! my dreams are as good as Nebuchadnezzar's, and I can remember them no better. Last night all that I can recall to mind is that an old man, I know not why or wherefore, was to leap from a precipice as high as the summit of Skiddaw. It was some religious act, or voluntary one, for everybody regarded him with reverence; I went to behold him, not without some struggle of feelings. The old man appeared upon the precipice, his stature seeming larger than life; he was in a full green habit, not unlike a friar's; he lifted up his right hand to heaven and said something which we could not hear, and then leaped off. I saw him descending in an upright posture; it was in a situation where I could not see him when he came to the ground, and I hastened away, deafening myself that I might not hear the fall. Altogether the effect was very awful, but I cannot call back the circumstances which sanctified it.

ROBERT SOUTHEY, 7 December 1807

Bruno bishop of Toul [subsequently Pope Leo IX] saw in his dream a deformed old woman who haunted him with great persistency and treated him with great familiarity. She was hideously ugly, clothed in filthy rags, her hair dishevelled and altogether one could scarce recognise in her the human form. Disgusted with her general appearance Bruno tried to avoid her; but the more he shrunk from her the more she clung to him. Annoyed at this importunity, Bruno made the sign of the cross; whereupon she fell to the earth as dead and rose up again lovely as an angel.

GUIBERTUS, *Life of St. Leo IX*, c.1075

All the more now was [Anselm] confirmed in the love of God and the contempt of the world, of which one night he had a vision as of a torrent filled with obscene filth, and carrying in its flood the countless host of people of the world, while apart and aloof from its slime rose the sweet cloister, with its walls of silver, surrounded by silvery herbage, all delectable beyond conception.

H. O. TAYLOR, *The Mediaeval Mind*, 1911

In my dream I saw something disastrous.

The full moon had crashed on to Halifax.
Black Halifax boiled in phosphorus.
Halifax was an erupting crater.

The flames seemed to labour. Then a tolling glare
Heaved itself out and writhed upwards –
And it was a swan the size of a city!

Far too heavy for the air, it pounded towards me,
Low over Hathershelf.

And it was no swan.

It was an angel made of smoking snow.
Her long dress fluttered about her ankles,
Her bare feet just cleared the moor beneath her
Which glowed like the night-cloud over Sheffield.

Mother, I cried, O Mother, there is an angel –
Is it a blessing? Then my mother's answer
Turned that beauty suddenly to terror.
I watched for the angel to fade and be impossible.

But the huge beauty would not fade.
She was cast in burning metal. Her halo
Was an enigmatic square of satin
Rippling its fringed edges like a flounder.

I could make no sense of that strange head-dress.

Till this immense omen, with wings rigid,
Sank out of my sight, behind Stoodley,
Under the moor, and left my darkness empty.

When I next saw that strange square of satin
I reached out and touched it.

When next I stood where I stood in my dream
Those words of my mother,
Joined with earth and engraved in rock,
Were under my feet.

                              TED HUGHES, 'The Angel', 1979

About this time, the state and happiness of these poor people at
Bedford was thus, in a dream or vision, represented to me. I saw, as if
they were set on the sunny side of some high mountain, there

refreshing themselves with the pleasant beams of the sun, while I was shivering and shrinking in the cold, afflicted with frost, snow, and dark clouds. Methought, also, betwixt me and them, I saw a wall that did compass about this mountain; now, through this wall my soul did greatly desire to pass; concluding, that if I could, I would go even into the very midst of them, and there also comfort myself with the heat of their sun.

About this wall I thought myself, to go again and again, still prying as I went, to see if I could find some way or passage, by which I might enter therein; but none could I find for some time. At the last, I saw, as it were, a narrow gap, like a little doorway in the wall, through which I attempted to pass; but the passage being very strait and narrow, I made many efforts to get in, but all in vain, even until I was well-nigh quite beat out, by striving to get in; at last, with great striving, methought I at first did get in my head, and after that, by a sidling striving, my shoulders, and my whole body; then was I exceeding glad, and went and sat down in the midst of them, and so was comforted with the light and heat of their sun.

Now, this mountain and wall, etc., was thus made out to me—the mountain signified the church of the living God; the sun that shone thereon, the comfortable shining of his merciful face on them that were therein; the wall, I thought, was the Word, that did make separation between the Christians and the world; and the gap which was in this wall, I thought, was Jesus Christ, who is the way to God the Father. But forasmuch as the passage was wonderful narrow, even so narrow, that I could not, but with great difficulty, enter in thereat, it showed me that none could enter into life, but those that were in downright earnest, and unless also they left this wicked world behind them; for here was only room for body and soul, but not for body and soul, and sin.

JOHN BUNYAN, *Grace Abounding to the Chief of Sinners*, 1666

'I sometimes dream of devils. It's night, I'm in my room, and suddenly there are devils everywhere. In all the corners and under the table, and they open doors, and behind the doors there are crowds of them, and they all want to come in and seize me. And they are already coming near and taking hold of me. But suddenly I cross myself and they all draw back, they are afraid, only they don't go away, but stand near the door and in the corners, waiting. And then I'm suddenly overcome by a desire to begin cursing God in a loud voice, and I begin cursing him and they all rush at me again in a crowd, they're so pleased, and they're again about to lay hands on me, and I cross myself again and they draw back at once. It's great fun. Oh, it takes my breath away.'

FYODOR DOSTOEVSKY, The Brothers Karamazov, 1880

Christiana. What was the matter that you did laugh in your sleep to-night? I suppose you were in a Dream.

Mercy. So I was; and a sweet Dream it was; but are you sure I laughed?

Christiana. Yes, you laughed heartily; but prithee, Mercy, tell me thy dream.

Mercy. I was a-dreaming that I sat all alone in a solitary place, and was bemoaning of the hardness of my Heart.

Now I had not sat there long, but methought many were gathered about me, to see me, and to hear what it was that I said. So they hearkened, and I went on bemoaning the hardness of my heart. At this some of them laughed at me, some called me Fool, and some began to thrust me about. With that, methought I looked up, and saw one coming with wings towards me. So he came directly to me, and said, Mercy, what aileth thee? Now when he had heard me make my complaint, he said, Peace be to thee. He also wiped mine eyes with his Handkerchief, and clad me in Silver and Gold: he put a Chain about my Neck, and Earrings in mine Ears, and a beautiful Crown upon my Head. Then he took me by the Hand, and said, Mercy, come after me. So he went up, and I followed, till we came at a Golden Gate. Then he knocked; and when they within had opened, the man went in, and I followed him up to a Throne, upon which one sat, and he said to me, Welcome, Daughter. The place looked bright and twinkling like the Stars, or rather like the Sun, and I thought that I saw your Husband there. So I awoke from my Dream. But did I laugh?

Christiana. Laugh: ay, and well you might, to see yourself so well. For you must give me leave to tell you that I believe that it was a good Dream, and that as you have begun to find the first part true, so you shall find the second at last. God speaks once, yea twice, yet man perceiveth it not. In a Dream, in a Vision of the night, when deep sleep falleth upon men, in slumbering upon the bed. We need not, when abed, lie awake to talk with God. He can visit us while we sleep, and cause us then to hear his voice. Our heart ofttimes wakes when we sleep; and God can speak to that, either by Words, by Proverbs, by Signs and Similitudes, as well as if one was awake.

Mercy. Well I am glad of my Dream, for I hope ere long to see it fulfilled, to the making of me laugh again.

JOHN BUNYAN, The Pilgrim's Progress, 1678

A friend of mine dreamed that he was at the Zoological Gardens, and observed that, while the tigers were closely caged, the lions were allowed to roam at large. He enquired the reason for this, and was told that it was because the lions believed in the immortality of the soul, and in a future state of rewards and punishments. Thereafter he went about in a mood of no small trepidation lest the lions should change their theological opinions.

WILLIAM ARCHER, On Dreams, 1935

Last night I had met a Mr. Trevilian, a Somersetshire man. I dreamt that I was visiting him in his own county, and this reminding me of Glastonbury, I thought that we went to see the ruins. But the ruins which I saw in my dream were far nobler than Glastonbury, or probably than any existing pile. I thought that, descending a long flight of steps ... we entered a prodigious church, deserted and bearing marks of decay, though all its parts were still entire. I have the picture vividly before me, the arched windows, and meeting columns, the grass between the stones; the sound of my own footsteps is still fresh in my ears, and the feeling of delight and reverence which made me in the dream stand half-way down the steps and shed tears. Presently I was led to a part of the building which was called the Beatorio; the most extraordinary place I ever fancied. It was so called as being the burial-place of the monks, who were all presumed to be in bliss, and the whole floor was covered with statues, admirably executed in a fine white stone, of these men rising from the dead all in different attitudes, each as large as life, and each made to the living likeness of the man whom it represented. One side of this place was open to the cloisters, so that all was seen in a strong light. The other walls were in like manner covered with figures issuing out.

I thought a sort of *Auto* of the Last Judgment was to be acted in the church. A number of the most ill-looking men had been got together to play the damned, and express as much damnation as possible in their looks and gestures when they were set aside after sentence. The dream now began to confound things: these persons seemed to be really the damned; and I, who did not quite like such company, as they were becoming obstreperous, rose to make my escape. Some fellow half-damned, half-devil, was placed in the gateway to prevent me from going out; I forced my way by, and creating wings with the effort, fled away. A long flight brought me to the mountains, and I awoke, just at the fit time, when the whole dream was fairly brought to a conclusion.

ROBERT SOUTHEY, 1805

I dreamed that I was reconciled to the Church of Rome. This troubled me much; and I wondered exceedingly, how it should happen. Nor was I aggrieved with myself *only by* reason of the errors of that Church, but also upon account of the scandal, which from that my fall would be cast upon many eminent and learned men in the Church of England. So being troubled at my dream, I said with myself that I would go immediately, and, confessing my fault, would beg pardon of the Church of England. Going with this resolution, a certain priest met me, and would have stopped me. But moved with indignation, I went on my way. And while I wearied myself with these troublesome thoughts, I awoke.

WILLIAM LAUD, *Diary*, 8 March 1627

An odd dream of which I remember very little, to this effect: I was somehow or other a relation – a brother, I think – of Christ. I expected his second coming, not on theological grounds, but rather as a piece of family news, and thought it my duty to prepare people for it. So I found myself in a railway station haranguing the bookstall clerk on faith – making a formal, oratorical speech, though I have no recollection of any audience except the clerk. I said that faith was the great thing – it did not matter what you believed, as long as you believed *something*. I had an impression of being very unctuous and eloquent, but the clerk was obdurate and quite unimpressed.

I myself was not at all in an emotional condition. It seemed all quite a matter of course. Nor did I think of Christ's second advent as a catastrophic, world-shaking event. I seemed rather to expect him to arrive by the next train.

WILLIAM ARCHER, *On Dreams*, 21–22 December 1918

He dreamt that he was at Trinity College Chapel, about to celebrate the Communion. But on reaching the altar he found a book printed in an unknown language. He said, 'I began to read, but could not remember how the sense went, so I kept up some sort of muttering, and the choir sang responses at intervals, while I beckoned to everyone within reach to come to my assistance. At last a grave-looking man like a verger came, and on my pointing out the book to him he said, rather severely, "Your Grace is not aware that this is one of the days when the Mozarabic liturgy is used."'

A. C. BENSON, *The Life of Edward White Benson*, 1899

I dreamt a dream; till morning light
A bell rang in my head all night,
Tinkling and tinkling first, and then
Tolling; and tinkling; tolling again.
So brisk and gay, and then so slow!
O joy, and terror! mirth, and woe!
Ting, ting, there is no God; ting, ting –
Dong, there is no God; dong,
There is no God; dong, dong!

A. H. CLOUGH, from 'Dipsychus', 1869

Interpretations

�֍

Now, Reader, I have told my dream to thee;
See if thou canst interpret it to me,
Or to thyself, or neighbour; but take heed
Of misinterpreting; for that, instead
Of doing good, will but thyself abuse:
By misinterpreting, evil insues.

Take heed, also, that thou be not extreme,
In playing with the outside of my dream:
Nor let my figure or similitude
Put thee into a laughter or a feud;
Leave this for boys and fools; but as for thee,
Do thou the substance of my matter see.

Put by the curtains, look within my veil;
Turn up my metaphors, and do not fail
There, if thou seekest them, such things to find,
As will be helpful to an honest mind.

What of my dross thou findest there, be bold
To throw away, but yet preserve the gold.
What if my gold be wrapped up in ore?
None throws away the apple for the core.
But if thou shalt cast all away as vain,
I know not but 'twill make me dream again.

JOHN BUNYAN, Conclusion to *The Pilgrim's Progress*, 1678

And it came to pass after these things, that the butler of the king of Egypt and his baker had offended their lord the king of Egypt. And Pharaoh was wroth against two of his officers, against the chief of the butlers, and against the chief of the bakers. And he put them in ward in the house of the captain of the guard, into the prison, the place where Joseph was bound. And the captain of the guard charged Joseph with them, and he served them: and they continued a season in ward.

And they dreamed a dream both of them, each man his dream in one night, each man according to the interpretation of his dream, the butler and the baker of the king of Egypt, which were bound in the prison. And Joseph came in unto them in the morning, and looked upon them, and, behold, they were sad. And he asked Pharaoh's officers that were with him in the ward of his 'lord's house, saying, Wherefore look ye so sadly today? And they said unto him, We have dreamed a dream, and there is no interpreter of it. And Joseph said unto them, Do not interpretations belong to God? tell me then, I pray you. And the chief butler told his dream to Joseph, and said to him, In my dream, behold, a vine was before me; and in the vine were three branches: and it was as though it budded, and her blossoms shot forth; and the clusters thereof brought forth ripe grapes; and Pharaoh's cup was in my hand: and I took the grapes, and pressed them into Pharaoh's cup, and I gave the cup into Pharaoh's hand. And Joseph said unto him, This is the interpretation of it: The three branches are three days: yet within three days shall Pharaoh lift up thine head, and restore thee unto thy place: and thou shalt deliver Pharaoh's cup into his hand, after the former manner when thou wast his butler. . . . When the chief baker saw that the interpretation was good, he said unto Joseph, I also was in my dream, and, behold, I had three white baskets on my head: and in the uppermost basket there was of all manner of bakemeats for Pharaoh; and the birds did eat them out of the basket upon my head. And Joseph answered and said, This is the interpretation thereof: The three baskets are three days: yet within three days shall Pharaoh lift up thy head from off thee, and shall hang thee on a tree; and the birds shall eat thy flesh from off thee.

And it came to pass the third day, which was Pharaoh's birthday, that he made a feast unto all his servants: and he lifted up the head of the chief butler and of the chief baker among his servants. And he restored the chief butler again; and he gave the cup into Pharaoh's hand; but he hanged the chief baker: as Joseph had interpreted to them.

Genesis 40

I could not but take notice how his female friends were irrationally curious so strictly to examine his dreams, and in this low state to hope for the fantasms of health. He was now past the healthful dreams of the sun, moon, and stars in their clarity and proper courses. 'Twas too late to dream of flying, of limpid fountains, smooth waters, white vestments, and fruitful green trees, which are the visions of healthful sleeps, and at good distance from the grave.

And they were also too deeply dejected that he should dream of his dead friends, inconsequently divining, that he would not be long from them; for strange it was not that he should sometimes dream of the dead whose thoughts run always upon death; beside, to dream of the dead, so they appear not in dark habits, and take nothing away from us, in Hippocrates his sense was of good signification: for we live by the dead, and every thing is or must be so before it becomes our nourishment. And Cardan, who dream'd that he discoursed with his dead father in the moon, made thereof no mortal interpretation: and even to dream that we are dead, was no condemnable fantasm in old oneirocriticism, as having a signification of liberty, vacuity from cares, exemption and freedom from troubles, unknown unto the dead.

Some dreams I confess may admit of easy and feminine exposition: he who dreamed that he could not see his right shoulder, might easily fear to lose the sight of his right eye; he that before a journey dreamed that his feet were cut off, had a plain warning not to undertake his intended journey. But why to dream of lettuce should presage some ensuing disease, why to eat figs should signify foolish talk, why to eat eggs great trouble, and to dream of blindness should be so highly commended, according to the oneirocritical verses of Astrampsychus and Nicephorus, I shall leave unto your divination.

SIR THOMAS BROWNE, 'Letter to a Friend', *c*.1656

A patient had a fairly long dream, part of which was as follows: *Several members of his family were seated at a table of a particular shape . . .* etc. This table reminded the dreamer that he had seen one of the same sort when he was visiting a certain family. From that his thoughts ran on thus: in this family the relation between father and son was a peculiar one, and the patient presently added that his own relations with his father were, as a matter of fact, of the same nature. So the table was introduced into the dream to indicate this parallelism.

It happened that this dreamer had long been familiar with the demands of dream-interpretation; otherwise he might have taken exception to the idea of investigating so trivial a detail as the shape of the table. We do literally deny that anything in the dream is a matter of chance or of indifference, and it is precisely by enquiring into such trivial and (apparently) unmotivated details that we expect to arrive at our conclusion. You may perhaps still be surprised that the dream-work should happen to choose the table, in order to express the thought 'Our relationship is just like theirs.' But even this is explicable when you learn that the family in question was named '*Tischler*'. (*Tisch*=table.) In making his relations sit at this table, the dreamer's meaning was that they too were 'Tischler'.

SIGMUND FREUD, *Introductory Lectures on Psychoanalysis*, 1915–16

Nothing could be madder, more irresponsible, more dangerous than this guidance of men by dreams . . .

GEORGE SANTAYANA, *Soliloquies in England*: 'Imagination', 1922

What, my dear, is the reason, that tho' we know these dreams, these fleeting shadows of the night, to be no more than *dreams*, illusions of the working mind, fettered and debased as it is by the organs through which it conveys its confined powers to the grosser matter, body, then sleeping, inactive, as in the shades of death; yet that we cannot help being strongly impressed by them, and meditating interpretation of the flying vapours, when reason is broad awake, and tells us, that it is weakness to be disturbed at them?—But Superstition is, more or less, I believe, in every mind, a natural defect. Happily poised is that mind, which, on the one hand, is too strong to be affected by the slavish fears it brings with it; and, on the other, runs not into the contrary extreme, Scepticism, the parent of infidelity!

SAMUEL RICHARDSON, *Sir Charles Grandison*, 1753–4

I resolved to fix my dream-state and learn its secret. 'Why should I not,' I asked myself, 'at last force those mystic gates, armed with all my will-power, and dominate my sensations instead of being subject to them? Is it not possible to control this fascinating, dread chimera, to rule the spirits of the night which play with our reason? Sleep takes up a third of our lives. It consoles the sorrows of our days and the sorrow of their pleasures; but I have never felt any rest in sleep. For a few seconds I am numbed, then a new life begins, freed from the conditions of time and space, and doubtless similar to that state which awaits us after death. Who knows if there is not some link between these two existences and if it is not possible for the soul to unite them now?'

From that moment on I devoted myself to trying to find the

meaning of my dreams, and this anxiety influenced my waking thoughts. I seemed to understand that there was a bond between the external and internal worlds: that only inattention or spiritual confusion distorted the outward affinities between them,—and this explained the strangeness of certain pictures, which are like grimacing reflections of real objects on a surface of troubled water.

GÉRARD DE NERVAL, *Aurélia*, 1855

Bomb. If a fair maiden should dream of seeing a bombshell, she must look out for a brave artilleryman coming to ask her to be his bride. If she dreams she sees one of these articles explode, she will have great peace and comfort in her married life. . . .

Flying. For anyone to dream of flying implies that they are aspiring to something they will never be able to attain, and unless speedily abandoned, will end in their discomfiture and ruin.

Harp. For a young woman to dream that she plays on a harp means that in her married life she will have much joy and harmony; in her union she will have a very good, true and honourable pianomaker for a husband. . . .

Gorilla. For a young woman to dream that she is in love with, and embraced by a gorilla, means that she will have one of the handsomest and wisest men in the neighbourhood for a suitor, and will be envied by all the marriageable ladies in the district. . . .

Falling. Nothing can be more unfavourable than to dream of falling from any place, in all cases it implies a loss of situation and property. Young persons need never expect to be united to the object of their affections after such a dream.

Naked. To dream that you are in a state of nudity is a dream of bad omen, foretelling to a certainty, poverty, disgrace, and misfortune. . . . To persons in love it shows that they will never marry the present object of their affections, but the person they will get will be cross-tempered, unkind and extravagant, and will, in a great measure, be the means of bringing you to poverty.

from *Napoleon's Book of Fate, Captured at the Battle of Leipsic, with Interpretations of Dreams, c.*1860

I bawl for Maria, and her *Book of Dreams*.

It anchored her sleep, that insomniac's Bible,
a soiled orange booklet with a cyclop's eye

center, from the Dominican Republic.
Its coarse pages were black with the usual
symbols of prophecy, in excited Spanish;
an open palm upright, sectioned and numbered
like a butcher chart, delivered the future. ⸗
One night, in a fever, radiantly ill,
she say, 'Bring me the book, the end has come.'
She said: 'I dreamt of whales and a storm,'
but for that dream, the book had no answer.

A next night I dreamed of three old women
featureless as silkworms, stitching my fate,
and I scream at them to come out my house,
and I try beating them away with a broom,
but as they go out, so they crawl back again,
until I start screaming and crying, my flesh
raining with sweat, and she ravage the book
for the dream meaning, and there was nothing;
my nerves melt like a jellyfish – that was when I broke –
they found me round the Savannah, screaming.

DEREK WALCOTT, from 'The Schooner *Flight*', 1980

People have dreams of climbing down the front of a house, with
feelings sometimes of pleasure and sometimes of dread. When the
walls are quite smooth, the house means a man; when there are
ledges and balconies which can be caught hold of, a woman. Parents
appear in dreams as *emperor* and *empress*, *king* and *queen* or other
exalted personages; in this respect the dream attitude is highly
dutiful. Children and brothers and sisters are less tenderly treated,
being symbolized by *little animals* or *vermin*. Birth is almost
invariably represented by some reference to *water*: either we are
falling into water or clambering out of it, saving someone from it or
being saved by them, i.e. the relation between mother and child is
symbolized. For dying we have setting out upon a *journey* or
travelling by train, while the state of death is indicated by various
obscure and, as it were, timid allusions; *clothes* and *uniforms* stand
for nakedness. You see that here the dividing line between the
symbolic and the allusive kinds of representation tends to disappear.

In comparison with the poverty of this enumeration, it cannot fail
to strike us that objects and matters belonging to another range of
ideas are represented by a remarkably rich symbolism. I am speaking

of what pertains to the sexual life – the genitals, sexual processes and intercourse. An overwhelming majority of symbols in dreams are sexual symbols.

SIGMUND FREUD, Introductory Lectures on Psychoanalysis, 1915–16

Freud was some wrong about dreams, almost all;
besides his insights grand, he thought that dreams were a transcript
of childhood & the day before,
censored of course: *a* transcript:
even his lesser insight were misunderstood & became a bore
except for the knowing & troubled by the Fall.

Grand Jewish ruler, custodian of the past,
our paedegogue to whip us into truth,
I sees your long story,
tyrannical & triumphant all-wise at last
you wholly failed to take into account youth
& had no interest in your glory.

I tell you, Sir, you have enlightened but
you have misled us: a dream is a panorama
of the whole mental life,
I took one once to forty-three structures, that
accounted in each for each word: I did not yell 'mama'
nor did I take it out on my wife.

JOHN BERRYMAN, 'Dream Song No. 327', 1968

Dreams of examinations: With some individuals the meaning of such dreams would be: 'You are not prepared to face the problem before you.' With others it would mean: 'You have passed examinations before, and you will pass the present test also.' One individual's symbols are never the same as another's. What we must consider chiefly in the dream is the residue of mood and its coherence with the whole style of life.

ALFRED ADLER, quoted in The Individual Psychology of Alfred Adler
(H. L. and R. R. Ansbacher, eds.), 1956

Now, everybody, I suppose, is aware that in recent years the silly business of divination by dreams has ceased to be a joke and has become a very serious science. It is called 'Psycho-analysis'; and is compounded, I would say, by mingling one grain of sense with a hundred of pure nonsense. From the simplest and most obvious dreams, the psycho-analyst deduces the most incongruous and extravagant results. A black savage tells him that he has dreamed of being chased by lions, or, maybe, by crocodiles; and the psycho man knows at once that the black is suffering from the Oedipus complex. That is, he is madly in love with his own mother, and is, therefore, afraid of the vengeance of his father. Everybody knows, of course, that 'lion' and 'crocodile' are symbols of 'father'. And I understand that there are educated people who believe this stuff.

It is all nonsense, to be sure; and so much the greater nonsense inasmuch as the true interpretation of many dreams – not by any means of all dreams – moves, it may be said, in the opposite direction to the method of psycho-analysis. The psycho-analyst infers the monstrous and abnormal from a trifle; it is often safe to reverse the process. If a man dreams that he has committed a sin before which the sun hid his face, it is often safe to conjecture that, in sheer forgetfulness, he wore a red tie, or brown boots with evening dress.

ARTHUR MACHEN, *The Children of the Pool*, 1936

I dislike the cult of dreams. They should be secret things, and people who are always telling you of what they have dreamt irritate me. Nor do I like hearing psychological discussions between those who do not really know what they are talking about. There is something soft and messy about such people.

SARAH FERGUSON, *A Guard Within*, 1973

When Alexander going to besiege Tyre dreamt of a satyr, it was no hard exposition for a Grecian to say, Tyre will be thine. He that dreamed that he saw his father washed by Jupiter and anointed by the sun, had cause to fear that he might be crucified, whereby his body would be washed by the rain and drop by the heat of the sun. The dream of Vespasian was of harder exposition, as also that of the Emperor Mauritius concerning his successor Phocas. And a man might have been hard put to it to interpret the language of Esculapius, when to a consumptive person he held forth his fingers, implying thereby that his cure lay in dates, from the homonomy of the Greek which signifies dates and fingers.

We owe unto dreams that Galen was a physician, Dion an historian, and that the world hath seen some notable pieces of

Cardan, yet he that should order his affairs by dreams, or make the night a rule unto the day, might be ridiculously deluded. Wherein Cicero is much to be pitied; who having excellently discoursed of the vanity of dreams, was yet undone by the flattery of his own, which urged him to apply himself unto Augustus.

SIR THOMAS BROWNE, 'On Dreams', c.1650

When I wrench myself away from the thicket of dreams, the dark forest of sleep, and retrieve myself, I slowly make myself whole again. For my dreams no longer interest me. To hell with Freud.

Everything we are, I grant, has this reverse dream side, this foundation or this messy pile of rubble underlying it. Some ironic soul might wonder what kind of dreams Kant, Descartes, Hegel, those monsters of reason, had. The total mental repression that their philosophic systems represent was bound to have a chaotic, painful, tormented reverse side. How do we deny the half of existence that lies in shadow, if that is where dreams are located? There is a time in our lives when we decide to be nothing but our dreams, and Surrealism is an age of adolescence insofar as it seeks its sustenance in dreams. There is a maturity, a classicism—that may come at any time in life—when we make a deliberate choice in favor of our reason, our rigor, our human stature. But so what? It is as childish to live on dreams as it is to live on syllogisms. One obviously lives on what one can, and it takes a long time to learn to live on realities, on things, on objects, as natural beings do. Man is a being who lives at a far remove from himself, someone has said. Yes, man is a being of utopias, of distant horizons, of 'lyrical projects'. Man must learn to be a creature who lives on what lies close at hand, a shepherd of the immediate.

My dreams give me only a hopelessly muddled version of something crystal clear that I possess. When I dream, I am the confused exegete of myself, the amanuensis whose handwriting is indecipherable, the pedantic bore who insists on noting everything down to the last trivial detail, thus making a mess of the whole business. Dreams offer a gratuitous and obscure commentary on my life, a life that has no secrets yet has a shadow.

On this point I agree with Sartre, who denies that dreams have any meaning and maintains that they are incapable of producing a single coherent image, for the moment that I form a coherent image 'I am already awake'. My dreams don't interest me, just as my past is of virtually no interest to me anymore. In dreams I make Surrealist poems out of the prose of life. André Breton lives in me and comes out at night to devour me bit by bit. To hell with Breton. I know that I consist of sewage, slime, putrefaction, but at this point I find it boring to search for corroboration of that fact, and I am no longer fascinated by my own faeces, that infantile fascination that lingers on in the poet, the neurotic, and the psychoanalyst. Only people with no imagination have to resort to their dream life. It is quite apparent that nothing ever happened to Breton or Freud. It is as primitive today to interpret dreams as a revelation of the past as it was in Joseph's day to interpret them as a revelation of the future. The feeble lantern of dreaming does not cast one iota of light on the future, and all that it projects on the past are vague shadows, blurred outlines, and ambiguous versions of what was once perfectly clear. To dream of my dead mother or of furnaces that I was entrusted with turning on and off as a child, and of the thousands of stairs that I climbed, is merely to repeat, in tedious detail, like a bad film whose reels are mixed up, a life that I don't want to remember. It is surrealistic enough that one's mother lies dying while one climbs thousands of stairs running errands. What Surrealism can dreams add to a reality that is already so unreal?

FRANCISCO UMBRAL, *A Mortal Spring*, 1980

Learn from your dreams what you lack.

W. H. AUDEN, *The Sea and the Mirror*, 1945

I discovered there was an endless source of robust enjoyment in trifling with psychiatrists: cunningly leading them on; never letting them see that you know all the tricks of the trade; inventing for them elaborate dreams, pure classics in style (which make *them*, the dream-extortionists, dream and wake up shrieking); teasing them with fake 'primal scenes'; and never allowing them the slightest glimpse of one's real sexual predicament.

VLADIMIR NABOKOV, *Lolita*, 1955

Waking

※

He slept feverishly, glutted with dreams. Two or three times he thought he was awake, and he was aware of the room where he was sleeping; but watching a winged eye fluttering about, each time he was deceived by the expression of the surly walls of his bedroom. 'But, look here. I'm asleep! I'm asleep . . .'

'I'm asleep,' he answered again to the crunching on the gravel. 'Since I tell you that I'm asleep,' he cried to two lagging steps which brushed by his door . . . The feet withdrew and the sleeper in his dream rejoiced. But under repeated solicitations the dream had come to an end, and Alain opened his eyes.

COLETTE, *The Cat*, 1933

> Dreams – are well – but Waking's better,
> If One wake at Morn –
> If One wake at Midnight – better –
> Dreaming – of the Dawn –

EMILY DICKINSON, *c*.1862

Sometimes, too, as Eve was created from a rib of Adam, a woman would be born during my sleep from some strain in the position of my thighs. Conceived from the pleasure I was on the point of consummating, she it was, I imagined, who offered me that pleasure. My body, conscious that its own warmth was permeating hers, would strive to become one with her, and I would awake. The rest of humanity seemed very remote in comparison with this woman whose company I had left but a moment ago; my cheek was still warm from her kiss, my body ached beneath the weight of hers. If, as would sometimes happen, she had the features of some woman whom I had known in waking hours, I would abandon myself altogether to the sole quest of her, like people who set out on a journey to see with their eyes some city of their desire, and imagine that one can taste in reality what has charmed one's fancy. And then, gradually, the memory of her would dissolve and vanish, until I had forgotten the girl of my dream.

MARCEL PROUST, *Swann's Way*, 1913

He dreamed that he was going into an empty house with white walls and that he was upset by the burden of being the first human being to enter it. In the dream he remembered that he had dreamed the same thing the night before and on many nights over the past years and he knew that the image would be erased from his memory when he awakened because that recurrent dream had the quality of not being remembered except within the dream itself.

GABRIEL GARCÍA MÁRQUEZ, *One Hundred Years of Solitude*, 1967

What did I dream? I do not know –
    The fragments fly like chaff.
Yet, strange, my mind was tickled so
    I cannot help but laugh.

Pull the curtains close again,
    Tuck me grandly in;
Must a world of humour wane
    Because birds begin

Complaining in a fretful tone,
    Rousing me from sleep –
The finest entertainment known,
    And given rag-cheap?

ROBERT GRAVES, 'What Did I Dream?', 1920

Captain Flume slept like a log most nights and merely *dreamed* he was awake. So convincing were these dreams of lying awake that he awoke from them each morning in complete exhaustion and fell right back to sleep.

JOSEPH HELLER, *Catch-22*, 1961

The hope I dreamed of was a dream,
    Was but a dream; and now I wake,
Exceeding comfortless, and worn, and old,
    For dream's sake.

I hang my harp upon a tree,
    A weeping willow in a lake;
I hang my silenced harp there, wrung and snapt
    For a dream's sake.

Lie still, lie still, my breaking heart;
  My silent heart, lie still and break:
Life, and the world, and mine own self, are changed
  For a dream's sake.

CHRISTINA ROSSETTI, 'Mirage', 1860

I run down the streets
Of dim houses, low,
Narrow and of few
Windows, looking down
Corners to find her.

There she stands under
An unlit street-lamp,
Smiling with someone
Else over what had
Been our own old joke.

Then I wake, moaning.
Why, O why? All this
Need not have been a dream:
It is what I see
With my opened eye.

Why does sleep reveal
What the day has not
Hidden, as if it
Were a dark secret
My heart could not keep?

JOHN HOLLANDER, 'The Dream', 1979

Near the gate is the quarry to which our heavier slumbers repair in search of substances which coat the brain with so unbreakable a glaze that, to awaken the sleeper, his own will is obliged, even on a golden morning, to smite him with mighty blows, like a young Siegfried. Beyond this, again, are nightmares, of which the doctors foolishly assert that they tire us more than does insomnia, whereas on the contrary they enable the thinker to escape from the strain of thought – nightmares with their fantastic picture-books in which our relatives who are dead are shown meeting with serious accidents

which at the same time do not preclude their speedy recovery. . . .
Next to this picture-book is the revolving disc of awakening, by
virtue of which we submit for a moment to the tedium of having to
return presently to a house which was pulled down fifty years ago,
the image of which is gradually effaced by a number of others as
sleep recedes, until we arrive at the image which appears only when
the disc has ceased to revolve and which coincides with the one we
shall see with opened eyes.

MARCEL PROUST, The Guermantes Way, 1921

'Hold your tongue!' said the Queen, turning purple.

'I wo'n't!' said Alice.

'Off with her head!' the Queen shouted at the top of her voice.
Nobody moved.

'Who cares for *you*?' said Alice (she had grown to her full size by
this time). 'You're nothing but a pack of cards!'

At this the whole pack rose up into the air, and came flying down
upon her; she gave a little scream, half of fright and half of anger, and
tried to beat them off, and found herself lying on the bank, with her
head in the lap of her sister, who was gently brushing away some
dead leaves that had fluttered down from the trees upon her face.

'Wake up, Alice dear!' said her sister. 'Why, what a long sleep
you've had!'

'Oh, I've had such a curious dream!' said Alice. And she told her
sister, as well as she could remember them, all these strange
Adventures of hers that you have just been reading about; and, when
she had finished, her sister kissed her, and said 'It *was* a curious
dream, dear, certainly; but now run in to your tea: it's getting late.'
So Alice got up and ran off, thinking while she ran, as well she might,
what a wonderful dream it had been.

LEWIS CARROLL, *Alice's Adventures in Wonderland*, 1865

Caliban. Be not afeard; the isle is full of noises,
 Sounds and sweet airs that give delight and hurt not.
 Sometimes a thousand twangling instruments
 Will hum about mine ears; and sometimes voices
 That, if I then had waked after long sleep,
 Will make me sleep again; and then, in dreaming,

The clouds methought would open and show riches
Ready to drop upon me, that, when I waked,
I cried to dream again.

WILLIAM SHAKESPEARE, *The Tempest*, c.1611

Conclusion: A Few Reflections

We are getting to the end of dreams!

THOMAS HARDY

Mrs Carter thinks on the subject of dreams as everybody else does, that is to say according to her own experience. She has had no extraordinary ones, and therefore accounts them only the ordinary operations of the fancy. Mine are of a texture that will not suffer me to ascribe them to so inadequate a cause, or to any cause but the operation of an exterior agency. I have a mind, my dear (and to you I will venture to boast of it) as free from superstition as any man living, neither do I give heed to dreams in general as predictive, though particular dreams I believe to be so. Some very sensible persons, and I suppose Mrs Carter among them, will acknowledge that in old times God spoke by dreams, but affirm with much boldness that He has since ceased to do so. If you ask them, 'why?' they answer, because He has now revealed His will in the Scripture, and there is no longer any need that He should instruct or admonish us by dreams. . . .

As to my own peculiar experience in the dreaming way I have only this to observe. I have not believed that I shall perish because in dreams I have been told it, but because I have had hardly any but terrible dreams for thirteen years. I therefore have spent the greatest part of that time most unhappily. They have either tinged my mind with melancholy or filled it with terrors, and the effect has been unavoidable. If we swallow arsenic we must be poisoned, and he who dreams as I have done, must be troubled. So much for dreams.

WILLIAM COWPER, letter to Lady Hesketh, 1787

We dream – it is good we are dreaming –
It would hurt us – were we awake –
But since it is playing – kill us,
And we are playing – shriek –

What harm? Men die – externally –
It is a truth – of Blood –
But we – are dying in Drama –
And Drama – is never dead –

Cautious – we jar each other –
And either – open the eyes –
Lest the Phantasm – prove the Mistake –
And the livid Surprise

Cool us to Shafts of Granite –
With just an Age – and Name –
And perhaps a phrase in Egyptian –
It's prudenter – to dream –

EMILY DICKINSON, c.1862

The sleep-flower sways in the wheat its head,
Heavy with dreams, as that with bread:
The goodly grain and the sun-flushed sleeper
The reaper reaps, and Time the reaper.

I hang 'mid men my needless head,
And my fruit is dreams, as theirs is bread:
The goodly men and the sun-hazed sleeper
Time shall reap, but after the reaper
The world shall glean of me, me the sleeper.

Love, love! your flower of withered dream
In leavèd rhyme lies safe, I deem,
Sheltered and shut in a nook of rhyme,
From the reaper man, and his reaper Time.

Love! *I* fall into the claws of Time:
But lasts within a leavèd rhyme
All that the world of me esteems –
My withered dreams, my withered dreams.

FRANCIS THOMPSON, from 'The Poppy', 1893

The Elgonyi say, there are big dreams and little dreams.
The little dream is just personal ...
Sitting in a plane that is flying
too close to the ground. There are wires ...
on either side there's a wall.

The big dream feels significant.
The big dream is the kind the president has.
He wakes and tells it to the secretary,
together they tell it to the cabinet,
and before you know there is war.

LOUIS SIMPSON, 'Big Dream, Little Dream', 1976

Such then, as while they lie asleep have no illusions arising in their brains to trouble them, but those dreams or visions only as be joyous, pleasant, plain and evident, not painful, not terrible, nothing rough, malign, tortuous and crooked,—may boldly say that these fantasies and apparitions be no other than the reflections and rays of that light which rebound from the good proceedings in philosophy; whereas, contrarywise, the furious pricks of lust, timorous frights, unmanly and base flights, childish and excessive joys, dolorous sorrows, and doleful moans by reason of some piteous illusions, strange and absurd visions appearing in dreams, may be well compared unto the broken waves and billows of the sea beating upon the rocks and craggy banks of the shore; for that the soul having not as yet that settled perfection in itself which should keep it in good order, but holdeth on a course still according to good laws only and sage opinions, from which when it is farthest sequestered and most remote, to wit, in sleep, it suffereth itself to return again to the old wont and to be let loose and abandoned to the passions.

PLUTARCH, *Of Proceeding in Vertue*, c.AD 100

Charlemont. O my affrighted soul, what fearful dream
    Was this that waked me? Dreams are but the raised
    Impressions of premeditated things,
    By serious apprehension left upon
    Our minds, or else th'imaginary shapes
    Of objects proper to the complexion, or
    The dispositions of our bodies. These
    Can neither of them be the cause why I

Should dream thus, for my mind has not been moved
With any one conception of a thought
To such a purpose, nor my nature wont
To trouble me with fantasies of terror.
It must be something that my genius would
Inform me of. Now gracious heaven forbid!
O let my spirit be deprived of all
Foresight and knowledge ere it understand
That vision acted, or divine that act
To come. Why should I think so? Left I not
My worthy father i'the kind regard
Of a most loving uncle? – Soldier, saw'st
No apparition of a man?

Soldier. You dream, sir, I saw nothing.

Charlemont. Tush. These idle dreams
Are fabulous. Our boiling fantasies
Like troubled waters falsify the shapes
Of things retained in them, and make 'em seem
Confounded when they are distinguished. So
My actions, daily conversant with war,
The argument of blood and death, had left,
Perhaps, th'imaginary presence of
Some bloody accident upon my mind,
Which, mixed confusedly with other thoughts,
Whereof th'remembrance of my father might
Be one, presented all together, seem
Incorporate, as if his body were
The owner of that blood, the subject of
That death, when he's at Paris and that blood
Shed here. It may be thus. I would not leave
The war, for reputation's sake, upon
An idle apprehension, a vain dream.

                    CYRIL TOURNEUR, *The Atheist's Tragedy*, 1611

            All would be well
    Could we but give us wholly to the dreams,
    And get into their world that to the sense
    Is shadow, and not linger wretchedly
    Among substantial things; for it is dreams
    That lift us to the flowing, changing world

That the heart longs for. What is love itself,
Even though it be the lightest of light love,
But dreams that hurry from beyond the world
To make low laughter more than meat and drink,
Though it but set us sighing? Fellow-wanderer,
Could we but mix ourselves into a dream,
Not in its image on the mirror!

W. B. YEATS, from 'The Shadowy Waters', 1906

Oh! that my young life were a lasting dream!
My spirit not awakening, till the beam
Of an Eternity should bring the morrow.
Yes! tho' that long dream were of hopeless sorrow,
'Twere better than the cold reality
Of waking life to him whose heart shall be,
And hath been ever, on the chilly earth,
A chaos of deep passion, from his birth!
But should it be – that dream eternally
Continuing – as dreams have been to me
In my young boyhood – should it thus be given,
'Twere folly still to hope for higher Heaven!
For I have revell'd, when the sun was bright
I' the summer sky; in dreamy fields of light,
And left unheedingly my very heart
In climes of mine imagining – apart
From mine own home, with beings that have been
Of mine own thought – what more could I have seen?
'Twas once – and only once – and the wild hour
From my remembrance shall not pass – some power
Or spell had bound me – 'twas the chilly wind
Came o'er me in the night, and left behind
Its image on my spirit – or the moon
Shone on my slumbers in her lofty noon
Too coldly – or the stars – howe'er it was
That dream was as that night-wind – let it pass.
I have been happy, tho' but in a dream.
I have been happy – and I love the theme –
Dreams! in their vivid colouring of life,
As in that fleeting, shadowy, misty strife
Of semblance with reality, which brings

To the delirious eye more lovely things
Of Paradise and Love – and all our own!
Than young Hope in his sunniest hour hath known.

EDGAR ALLAN POE, 'Dreams', 1827

Dreams are the subtle Dower
That make us rich an Hour –
Then fling us poor
Out of the Purple Door
Into the Precinct raw
Possessed before –

EMILY DICKINSON, c.1876

I can never decide whether my dreams are the result of my thoughts, or my thoughts the result of my dreams. It is very queer. But my dreams make conclusions for me. They decide things finally. I dream a decision. Sleep seems to hammer out for me the logical conclusions of my vague days, and offer me them as dreams. It is a horrid feeling, not to be able to escape from one's own – what? – self-daemon – fate, or something. . . .

D. H. LAWRENCE, letter to Edward Garnett, 29 January 1912

One night I dreamed I was a butterfly, fluttering hither and thither, content with my lot. Suddenly I awoke and I was Chuang-tzu again. Who am I in reality? A butterfly dreaming that I am Chuang-tzu or Chuang-tzu imagining he was a butterfly?

CHUANG-TZU (3rd century BC), quoted in Raymond de Becker,
The Understanding of Dreams, 1968

I dreamed of myself in a dream, and told the dream, which was mine, as if it were another person's of whom I dreamed. Indeed, what is life when thinking of the past, but dreaming of a dream dreamt by another who seems sometimes to be oneself?

STOPFORD BROOKE, *Diary*, 8 June 1899

'It seems to me I am trying to tell you a dream – making a vain attempt, because no relation of a dream can convey the dream-sensation, that commingling of absurdity, surprise, and bewilderment in a tremor of struggling revolt, that notion of being captured by the incredible which is of the very essence of dreams. . . .'

He was silent for a while.

'. . . No, it is impossible; it is impossible to convey the life-sensation of any given epoch of one's existence – that which makes its truth, its meaning – its subtle and penetrating essence. It is impossible. We live as we dream – alone.'

JOSEPH CONRAD, *Heart of Darkness*, 1902

Dreams, dreams that mock us with their flitting shadows,
They come not from the temples of the gods,
They send them not, the powers of the air.
Each man makes his own dreams. The body lies
Quiet in sleep, what time the mind set free
Follows in darkness what it sought by day.
He who makes kingdoms quake for fear and sends
Unhappy cities ruining in fire,
Sees hurtling blows and broken fighting ranks
And death of kings and sodden battle fields.
The lawyer sees the judge, the crowded court,
The miser hides his coin, digs buried treasure,
The hunter shakes the forests with his hounds,
The sailor rescues from the sea his ship,
Or drowning, clings to it. Mistress to lover
Writes a love-letter: the adulteress
Yields in her sleep, and in his sleep the hound
Is hot upon the traces of the hare.
The wounds of the unhappy in the night
Do but prolong their pain.

PETRONIUS ARBITER, 'Somnia', *c*.AD 75

We can perfectly well have in a dream the impression that what is happening in it is real. It would be impossible only for reasons drawn from our waking experience, an experience which at that moment is hidden from us. With the result that this suppositious life seems to us real. . . . Albertine was present in my dream, and proposed to leave me once again, without my being moved by her resolve. This was because a warning ray of light had managed to filter into the darkness of my sleep, and what deprived Albertine's future actions, her threatened departure, of any importance for me was the knowledge that she was dead. But often, even more clearly, this memory that Albertine was dead was combined, without destroying it, with the sensation that she was alive. I chatted to her, and while I was speaking my grandmother moved to and fro at the back of the room. Part of her chin had crumbled away like a corroded statue, but I found nothing unusual in that. . . . No doubt, once I was awake, this idea of a dead woman who continued to live ought to have become as impossible for me to understand as it is to explain. But I had already formed it so many times in the course of those transient periods of madness which are our dreams, that I had become in time familiar with it; our memory of dreams may become lasting, if they repeat themselves often enough.

MARCEL PROUST, The Fugitive, 1925

Dreams are the touchstones of our characters. We are scarcely less afflicted when we remember some unworthiness in our conduct in a dream, than if it had been actual, and the intensity of our grief, which is our atonement, measures the degree by which this is separated from an actual unworthiness. For in dreams we but act a part which must have been learned and rehearsed in our waking hours, and no doubt could discover some waking consent thereto. If this meanness had not its foundation in us, why are we grieved at it? In dreams we see ourselves naked and acting out our real characters, even more clearly than we see others awake. But an unwavering and commanding virtue would compel even its most fantastic and faintest dreams to respect its ever-wakeful authority; as we are accustomed to say carelessly, we should never have *dreamed* of such a thing. Our truest life is when we are in dreams awake.

H. D. THOREAU, A Week on the Concord and Merrimack Rivers, 1849

Segismund. And now experience shows me that each man
    Dreams what he is until he is awakened.
    The king dreams he's a king and in this fiction
    Lives, rules, administers with royal pomp.
    Yet all the borrowed praises that he earns
    Are written in the wind, and he is changed
    (How sad a fate!) by death to dust and ashes.
    What man is there alive who'd seek to reign
    Since he must wake into the dream that's death.
    The rich man dreams his wealth which is his care

And woe. The poor man dreams his sufferings.
He dreams who thrives and prospers in life.
He dreams who toils and strives. He dreams who injures,
Offends, and insults. So that in this world
Everyone dreams the thing he is, though no one
Can understand it. I dream I am here,
Chained in these fetters. Yet I dreamed just now
I was in a more flattering, lofty station.
What is this life? A frenzy, an illusion,
A shadow, a delirium, a fiction.
The greatest good's but little, and this life
Is but a dream, and dreams are only dreams.

PEDRO CALDERÓN DE LA BARCA, *Life is a Dream, c.*1635

Acknowledgements

In addition to the formal acknowledgements which follow, I should like to thank the many people who were generous with their time, suggestions, and libraries, and alerted me to the existence of dreams I might otherwise have overlooked. I cannot list individually the names of all those who helped me, but it would be churlish not to mention Ib Bellew, Hugh Brogan, Albert and Lee Braunmuller, Angus Easson, John Freeman, John Haffenden, Robert Hewison, Eric Homberger, Albert Hutter, George Landow, Zachary Leader, Simon and Anne Lowy, Andrew Motion, Dinos Patrides, Neil Rhodes, Nigel Smith, Keith Walker, and Kathleen Wheeler. I am especially grateful to Stephen Barber and Mary Hoffman for helping to get the project off the ground; to Philippa Brewster for her constant encouragement; to Heather Glen and to Peter Merchant, who exhumed some of the most splendid dreams in this book; and to Judith Luna of OUP, who wielded the editorial knife so firmly and skilfully.

I am grateful to the following for permission to reproduce copyright material:

Alfred Adler: from *The Individual Psychology of Alfred Adler*, ed. H. L. & R. R. Ansbacher (Basic Books, 1956). Reprinted by permission of Sanford J. Greenburger Associates.

Aeschlyus: from *The Choephori*, trans. Philip Vellacott. Copyright © 1956, 1959 Philip Vellacott. Reprinted from *The Oresteian Trilogy* (Penguin Classics, 1956, rev. ed. 1959) by permission of Penguin Books Ltd.

James Agate: from *Ego 5* (1942). Reprinted by permission of Harrap Ltd.

Martin Amis: from *Success* (1978). Reprinted by permission of Jonathan Cape Ltd., and A. D. Peters & Co., Ltd.

William Archer: from *On Dreams* (Methuen, 1935). Reprinted by permission of Curtis Brown Ltd., London, on behalf of the Estate of William Archer.

Mary Arnold-Forster: from *Studies in Dreams* (1921). Reprinted by permission of George Allen & Unwin (Publishers) Ltd.

Artemidorus: from *The Interpretation of Dreams*, trans. Robert White (1975). Reprinted by permission of Noyes Press, (New Jersey).

W. H. Auden: from *A Certain World: A Commonplace Book*. Copyright © 1970 by W. H. Auden. A William Cole Book. Reprinted by permission of Faber & Faber Ltd., and Viking Penguin, Inc. Extract from 'Thanksgiving for a Habitat', copyright © 1963 by W. H. Auden, from *Collected Poems*, ed. Edward Mendelson. Reprinted by permission of Faber & Faber Ltd., and Random House, Inc. Originally appeared in *The New Yorker*.

Charles Baudelaire: 'Sorrow of the Moon', trans. Roy Campbell, copyright 1952, from *Poems: A Translation of Les Fleurs du Mal* (Harvill Press). Reprinted by permission of Hughes Massie Ltd.

Raymond de Becker: from Chuang-tzu quoted in Raymond de Becker, *The Understanding of Dreams*, trans. Michael Heron (London: Allen & Unwin/New York: Hawthorn, 1968). Reprinted by permission of George Allen & Unwin Ltd.

Rosalind Belben: from *Dreaming of Dead People* (Harvester, 1979). Reprinted by permission of the author.

John Berryman: 'Dream Song No. 101' and 'Dream Song No. 327' published in the United States in *The Dream Songs* (New York: Farrar, Straus & Giroux, Inc.), copyright © 1965, 1966, 1967, 1968, 1969 by John Berryman, and in the UK in *His Toy, His Dream, His Rest* (London: Faber & Faber Ltd.); 'I dreamt he drove me back to the asylum. . .' (Sonnet 79) from *Berryman's Sonnets*, copyright © 1952, 1967 by John Berryman. All reprinted by permission of Faber & Faber Ltd., and Farrar, Straus & Giroux, Inc.

Louise Bogan: 'The Dream' from *The Blue Estuaries*, copyright © 1938, 1966 by Louise Bogan. Reprinted by permission of Farrar, Straus & Giroux, Inc.

Edward Bond: from *Restoration* (1981). Reprinted by permission of Methuen, London.

Jorge Luis Borges: from 'The Circular Ruins' from *The Aleph and Other Stories 1933–1969*, edited and translated by Norman Thomas di Giovanni in collaboration with the author. English translations © 1968, 1969, 1970 by Emecé Editores, S.A., and Norman Thomas di Giovanni. Reprinted by permission of Jonathan Cape Ltd., and E. P. Dutton, a division of New American Library; 'The White Deer', 'The Dream of Pedro Henríques Ureña', published in the United States in *The Gold of the Tigers: Selected Later Poems* (Dutton, 1977) and in the UK in *Book of Sand* (Penguin, 1979), trans. Alastair Reid and Norman di Giovanni. Copyright © Emecé Editores, S.A., 1972, 1975. English translation © Alastair Reid, 1976, 1977, 1979. Reprinted by permission of Penguin Books Ltd., and E. P. Dutton.

Gerald Brenan: from *Personal Record 1920–1972* (1974). Copyright © 1974 by Lynda Jane Nicholson Price. Reprinted by permission of the author c/o Margaret Hanbury, 27 Walcot Sq., London SE11 4UB.

Pedro Calderón de la Barca: from *Life is a Dream*, Act II, trans. Roy Campbell, in *The Classic Theatre*, Vol. 3, ed. Eric Bentley (Doubleday, 1959). Copyright © 1959, renewed 1987 by Eric Bentley. Used by permission.

William Cavendish-Bentinck: from *Men, Women and Things*. Reprinted by permission of the late Duke of Portland.

J. M. Coetzee: from *Waiting for the Barbarians*, © 1980 J. M. Coetzee. Reprinted by permission of Secker & Warburg Ltd., and Viking Penguin, Inc.

Colette: from *Journey for Myself*, trans. David Le Vay (1971). Reprinted by permission of Peter Owen Ltd., London. From *The Cat* (*La Chatte*), trans. Morris Bentinck (1936)

G. C. Coulton: from *Fourscore Years* (1943). Reprinted by permission of Cambridge University Press.

René Daumal: from *A Night of Serious Drinking*, translated by David Coward and E. A. Lovatt. American translation © 1979 Shambhala Publications, Inc. Reprinted by permission of Routledge & Kegan Paul Ltd., and Shambhala Publications, Boston, Mass.

Walter de la Mare: 'Dark Château' from *Complete Poems* (Faber, 1969); extracts from *Behold, This Dreamer* (Faber, 1939). Reprinted by permission of the Literary Trustees of Walter de la Mare and the Society of Authors as their representative.

Peter de Vries: from *Consenting Adults: Or, The Duchess Will Be Furious*, © 1980 by Peter de Vries. Reprinted by permission of A. P. Watt Ltd., and Little, Brown and Company.

Emily Dickinson: reprinted from *The Complete Poems of Emily Dickinson* ed. Thomas H. Johnson, copyright 1914, 1935, 1942 by Martha Dickinson

Bianchi, © renewed 1963 by Mary L. Hampson, by permission of Little, Brown and Co., and by permission of the publishers and the Trustees of Amherst College from *The Poems of Emily Dickinson*, ed. Thomas H. Johnson, Cambridge, Mass.; The Belknap Press of Harvard University Press, copyright 1951, © 1955, 1979 by the President and Fellows of Harvard College.

Fyodor Dostoevsky: from *The Idiot*, Part 3, trans. David Magarshack (Penguin Classics, 1955), copyright © 1955 David Magarshack; from *The Brothers Karamazov*, Book XI, trans. David Magarshack (Penguin Classics, 1958), copyright © 1958 David Magarshack. Reprinted by permission of Penguin Books Ltd. From *Crime and Punishment*, trans. Constance Garnett. Reprinted by permission of William Heinemann Ltd.

Daphne du Maurier: from *Rebecca*. Copyright Daphne du Maurier Browning, 1938. Reprinted by permission of Curtis Brown Ltd. on behalf of Daphne du Maurier, and Doubleday & Company, Inc.

J. W. Dunne: from *An Experiment with Time*. Reprinted by permission of A. P. Watt Ltd., for the Estate of the late J. W. Dunne and Macmillan London Ltd.

Mircea Eliade: from *No Souvenirs (Fragments d'un Journal)*. Copyright © Editions Gallimard 1973. Trans. F. H. Johnson, Jr., translation copyright © 1977 by Harper & Row, Publishers, Inc. Reprinted by permission of the publishers.

Havelock Ellis: from *The World of Dreams* (Constable, London, 1911). Reprinted by permission of Professor François Lafitte, Trustee of the Ellis Estate.

Ralph Ellison: from 'Prologue' from *The Invisible Man*. Copyright 1952 by Ralph Ellison. Reprinted by permission of Random House, Inc.

Gavin Ewart: 'Dreams'. Reprinted by permission of the author. First published in *Poetry Book Society Poetry Supplement*, 1980.

Ruth Fainlight: 'Sleep-Learning' from *To See the Matter Clearly* (Macmillan, 1968). Reprinted by permission of the author.

Sarah Ferguson: from *A Guard Within*, © 1973 by Sarah Ferguson. Reprinted by permission of Chatto & Windus and Pantheon Books, a Division of Random House, Inc.

Sigmund Freud: from *The Interpretation of Dreams*, translated from the German and edited by James Strachey, published in the United States by Basic Books, Inc., by arrangement with George Allen & Unwin Ltd., and the Hogarth Press. Reprinted by permission of George Allen & Unwin Ltd., and Basic Books, Inc. Extracts from *Complete Introductory Lectures on Psychoanalysis*, trans. James Strachey (W. W. Norton, 1966/Allen & Unwin, 1971). Reprinted by permission of George Allen & Unwin Ltd., and Liveright Publishing Corporation.

Carlos Fuentes: from *The Hydra Head*, trans. Margaret Sayers Peden, copyright © 1978 by Farrar, Straus & Giroux, Inc. Reprinted by permission of Farrar, Straus & Giroux, Inc., and Secker & Warburg Ltd.

William Gerhardie: from *Memoirs of a Polyglot*. Reprinted by permission of the copyright holder, Mrs Ann Amyes.

Robert Graves: 'A Dream of Frances Speedwell' and 'What Did I Dream' from *Collected Poems* (Cassell, 1975); from Apuleius, *The Golden Ass* (Penguin, 1960) and from Suetonius, *The Twelve Caesars* (Penguin, 1957), translated by Robert Graves. Reprinted by permission of A. P. Watt Ltd., on behalf of the Executors of the Estate of Robert Graves.

Julian Green: from *Personal Record 1928–1939*, trans. Jocelyn Godefroi, copyright Julian Green. Reprinted by permission of Editions du Seuil and

Georges Borchardt, Inc. From *Diary*, trans. Anne Green, copyright © Editions du Seuil. Reprinted by permission of Editions du Seuil.

Rupert Hart-Davis: from *Hugh Walpole: A Biography* (Macmillan 1952). Reprinted by permission of the author.

Seamus Heaney: 'Glanmore Sonnet X' from *Fieldwork*, copyright © 1976, 1979 by Seamus Heaney. Reprinted by permission of Faber & Faber Ltd., and Farrar, Straus & Giroux, Inc.

Joseph Heller: from *Something Happened* (1974), © 1966, 1974 by Scapegoat Productions, Inc. Reprinted by permission of Jonathan Cape Ltd., and Alfred A. Knopf, Inc.; from *Catch 22* (Cape/Simon & Schuster, 1961), copyright © 1957, 1961 by Joseph Heller. Reprinted by permission of A. M. Heath & Co., Ltd., for the author and Jonathan Cape Ltd., and Simon & Schuster, Inc.

John Hollander: extract from 'The Train'; 'The Dream', both from *Blue Wine and Other Poems* (1979). Reprinted by permission of Johns Hopkins University Press.

Homer: from *The Iliad*, Book 2, trans. Robert Fitzgerald, copyright © 1974 by Robert Fitzgerald. Reprinted by permission of Doubleday & Company Inc.; from *The Odyssey*, Book 19, trans. Robert Fitzgerald, copyright © 1961 by Robert Fitzgerald. Reprinted by permission of William Heinemann Ltd., and Doubleday & Company, Inc.

Ted Hughes: 'The Angel' from *Remains of Elmet,* copyright © 1979 by Ted Hughes. Reprinted by permission of Faber & Faber Ltd., and of Harper & Row, Inc.

James Joyce: from *Finnegans Wake*, copyright 1939 by James Joyce, copyright renewed 1967 by George Joyce and Lucia Joyce. Reprinted by permission of the Society of Authors as the literary representative of the Estate of James Joyce, and of Viking, Penguin, Inc.

C. G. Jung: from *The Collected Works of C. G. Jung*, trans. R. F. C. Hull, Bollingen Series XX, Vol. 8: *The Structure and Dynamics of the Psyche*, © 1960, 1969 by Princeton University. Reprinted by permission of Routledge & Kegan Paul Ltd., and Princeton University Press; from *Memories, Dreams and Reflections*, recorded and edited by Aniela Jaffe, trans. Richard and Clara Winston. Translation © 1961, 1962, 1963 by Random House, Inc. Reprinted by permission of Collins Publishers and Pantheon Books, a Division of Random House, Inc.

Franz Kafka: from *Diaries 1910–1913 and 1914–1923*, trans. Joseph Kresh, copyright © 1948, 1949 by Schocken Books, Inc. Reprinted by permission of Schocken Books, Inc., and Secker & Warburg Ltd.

Anna Kavan: 'The Visit' from *Julia and the Bazooka* (1970). Reprinted by permission of Peter Owen Ltd., London.

Yasunari Kawabata: from *House of the Sleeping Beauties* (1969), trans. Edward Seidensticker. Reprinted by permission of Kodansha International.

C. D. Kelchner: from *Dreams in Old Norse Literature and Their Affinities in Folklore* (Cambridge University Press, 1935, repr. Richard West, 1980).

Helen Keller: from *The World I Live In* (Hodder & Stoughton/Century, 1908). Copyright 1904, 1908 by the Century Company.

Francis Kilvert: from *Kilvert's Diary*, ed. William Plomer. Reprinted by permission of Mrs Sheila Hooper and Jonathan Cape Ltd.

Philip Larkin: from *Jill* (1946, new edn. 1975). Reprinted by permission of Faber & Faber Ltd. US rights © Overlook Press, NY.

Comte de Lautréamont: from *Maldoror*, trans. Paul Knight (Penguin Classics,

1978), copyright © 1978 Paul Knight. Reprinted by permission of Penguin Books Ltd.

D. H. Lawrence: from *The Collected Letters of D. H. Lawrence*, Vol. 1, ed. Harry T. Moore, copyright 1932 by the Estate of D. H. Lawrence, copyright 1933, 1948, 1953, 1954 and each year 1956–1962 by Angelo Ravagli and C. Montague Weekley, Executor of the Estate of ₑFrieda Lawrence Ravagli. Reprinted by permission of Laurence Pollinger Ltd., and of Viking, Penguin Inc.

Doris Lessing: from *The Golden Notebook*, copyright © 1962 by Doris Lessing. Reprinted by permission of Michael Joseph Ltd., and Simon & Schuster, Inc.

Newman Levy: extract from 'Thais' from *Opera Guyed*. Copyright 1923 by Alfred A. Knopf, Inc., and renewed 1959 by Newman Levy. Reprinted by permission of the publisher.

R. B. Lewis: from *Edith Wharton: A Biography*. © 1975 by Harper & Row, Publishers, Inc. Edith Wharton's diaries and personal letters copyright © 1975 by William R. Tyler. All rights reserved. Reprinted by permission of A. P. Watt Ltd., and Harper & Row, Inc.

Edward Lucie-Smith: from *A Tropical Childhood*, copyright © 1961. Reprinted by permission of Deborah Rogers Ltd.

Arthur Machen: from *The Children of the Pool* (Hutchinson, 1936), and from *The Great Return* (Faith Press). By permission.

Norman MacKenzie: from *Dreams and Dreaming* (Aldus Books, 1965).

Louis MacNeice: from *The Strings are False* (Faber, 1965). Reprinted by permission of David Higham Associates Ltd.

Nadezhda Mandelstam: from *Hope Abandoned*, trans. Max Hayward, © 1973, 1974 by Atheneum Publishers, Inc. Reprinted by permission of Atheneum Publishers, Inc., and Collins Publishers.

Katherine Mansfield: from *Journal of Katherine Mansfield*. Copyright 1927 by Alfred A. Knopf, Inc., and renewed 1955 by John Middleton Murry; from *The Letters of Katherine Mansfield*, ed. John Middleton Murry. Copyright 1929 by Alfred A. Knopf, Inc. and renewed 1957 by John Middleton Murry. Reprinted by permission of the publisher.

Gabriel García Márquez: from *One Hundred Years of Solitude*, trans. Gregory Rabassa, translation copyright © 1970 Harper & Row. Reprinted by permission of Harper & Row Publishers, Inc., and Jonathan Cape Ltd.

R. L. Mégroz: extracts from *The Dream World* (1939). Reprinted by permission of The Bodley Head Ltd.

James Merrill: 'The Mad Scene' from *Nights and Days*, © 1966 by James Merrill. Reprinted by permission of Atheneum Publishers, Inc. and Chatto & Windus.

Edwin Muir: from *An Autobiography*. Reprinted by permission of Gavin Muir and The Hogarth Press, Ltd.

Iris Murdoch: from *The Sacred and Profane Love Machine*, © 1974 by Iris Murdoch. Reprinted by permission of Chatto & Windus Ltd., and Viking Penguin, Inc.

Vladimir Nabokov: from *Lolita*, copyright © 1955 by Vladimir Nabokov. Reprinted by permission of Mrs V. Nabokov, George Weidenfeld & Nicolson Ltd., and G. P. Putnam's Sons.

Ogden Nash: 'My Dream' from 'My, My' from *Verses From 1929 On* (Little, Brown, 1959), copyright 1954 by Ogden Nash. First appeared in the *New Yorker*. Published in the UK in *Collected Verse* (Dent, 1961). Reprinted by permission of Little, Brown & Co., and Curtis Brown Ltd., London, on behalf of the Estate of Ogden Nash.

Gérard de Nerval: from *Gérard de Nerval: Selected Writings*, trans. Geoffrey Wagner, copyright © 1957 by Geoffrey Wagner. Reprinted by permission of the translator.

David Newsome: from *On The Edge of Paradise* (1980). Reprinted by permission of John Murray (Publishers) Ltd., and The University of Chicago Press.

Petronius: 'Dreams' ('Somnia') reprinted from *Medieval Latin Lyrics*, trans. Helen Waddell, by permission of W. W. Norton & Company, Inc., New York, 1977, all rights reserved, and by permission of Constable Publishers.

Plato: from *Phaedo* reprinted from *The Last Days of Socrates*, trans. Hugh Tredennick (Penguin Classics, 1954, revised edition 1959, 1969), copyright © 1954, 1959, 1969 Hugh Tredennick, by permission of Penguin Books Ltd.

Marcel Proust: extracts from *Remembrance of Things Past*, Vols. I, II & III, trans. C. K. Scott Moncrieff and Terence Kilmartin. Translation copyright © 1981 by Random House Inc., and Chatto & Windus Ltd. Reprinted by permission of the translator's Literary Estate, Terence Kilmartin, Chatto & Windus Ltd., and Random House, Inc.

Peter Redgrove: from *The Beekeepers* (1980). Reprinted by permission of Routledge & Kegan Paul Ltd.

Adrienne Rich: 'The Crib' and 'Her Waking' from 'Night-Pieces: For a Child' from *Poems Selected and New 1950–1974*. Copyright © 1975, 1973, 1971, 1969, 1966 by W. W. Norton & Company, Inc. Copyright © 1967, 1963, 1962, 1961, 1960, 1959, 1958, 1957, 1956, 1955, 1954, 1953, 1952, 1951 by Adrienne Rich. Reprinted by permission of the author and W. W. Norton & Company, Inc.

Salman Rushdie: from *Midnight's Children*, Book 3 (London: Cape/New York: Alfred Knopf, 1981). Reprinted by permission of Jonathan Cape Ltd., and London Management.

John Ruskin: from *The Diaries of John Ruskin*, selected and edited by Joan Evans and John Howard Whitehouse, 3 vols., 1956–1959. Reprinted by permission of Oxford University Press; from *Brantwood Diary of John Ruskin*, ed. Helen G. Viljoen (1971). Reprinted by permission of Yale University Press.

George Santayana: from 'Imagination' from *Soliloquies in England*. Reprinted by permission of Constable Publishers.

Anne Sexton: 'Dreaming the Breasts' from *The Book of Folly*. Copyright © 1972 by Anne Sexton. Reprinted by permission of the Author's Literary Estate, Chatto & Windus Ltd., and the Sterling Lord Agency, Inc.; 'Imitations of Drowning' from *Live or Die* (Houghton Mifflin Co., 1966). Copyright © 1966 by Anne Sexton. Reprinted by permission of the Sterling Lord Agency, Inc.

Penelope Shuttle: 'The Dream' from *The Orchard Upstairs* (OUP, 1980). Reprinted by permission of David Higham Associates Ltd.

Louis Simpson: 'I dreamed that in a city . . .' from *A Dream of Governors*, © 1956 by Louis Simpson. Reprinted by permission of Wesleyan University Press; 'Big Dream, Little Dream' from *Searching for the Ox*, © 1976 by Louis Simpson. Reprinted by permission of Laurence Pollinger Ltd., and William Morrow and Co.

Isaac Bashevis Singer: from *The Spinoza of Market Street*. Copyright © 1958, 1960, 1961 by Isaac Bashevis Singer. Reprinted by permission of Jonathan Cape Ltd., and Farrar, Straus & Giroux, Inc.

Stevie Smith: 'A Dream of Nourishment' from *The Collected Poems of Stevie Smith* (Penguin Modern Classics), © 1972 by Stevie Smith. Reprinted by permission of James MacGibbon and New Directions Publishing Corporation.

August Strindberg: from *Inferno*, trans. Mary Sandbach (1962). Reprinted by permission of Century Hutchinson Ltd; from *Miss Julie*, trans. Michael Meyer, in *Plays*, Vol. I (1975). Reprinted by permission of Secker & Warburg Ltd., and David Higham Associates Ltd: from *From An Occult Diary*, ed. Torsten Eklund, trans. Mary Sandbach. Copyright © 1963 by Albert Bonniers Forlag AB. English © 1965 Martin Secker & Warburg, Ltd. Reprinted by permission of Secker & Warburg Ltd., and Hill & Wang (a Division of Farrar, Straus & Giroux, Inc.).

Alexander Theroux: from *The Great Wheadle Tragedy*. Copyright © 1975 by Alexander Theroux. Reprinted by permission of David R. Godine, Publisher, Boston.

Paul Theroux: from *The Family Arsenal*, Chapter 2, © 1976 Paul Theroux (Hamish Hamilton, 1976; Penguin Books Ltd., 1977; Houghton Mifflin, New York, 1976). Reprinted by permission of the author and Gillon Aitken.

Leo Tolstoy: from *War and Peace*, trans. Louise and Aylmer Maude (1933); from *Anna Karenina*, trans. Louise and Aylmer Maude (1918), and from *A Confession*, trans. Aylmer Maude (1921). Reprinted by permission of Oxford University Press.

Ivan S. Turgenev: extract from 'A Lear of the Steppes' from *A Nest of Gentlefolk and Other Stories*, trans. Jessie Coulson, © OUP 1959. Reprinted by permission of Oxford University Press. From *Dream Tales* and 'The Insect' from *Prose Poems*, both trans. Constance Garnett. Reprinted by permission of William Heinemann Ltd.

Francisco Umbral: from *A Mortal Spring*, copyright © 1975 by Francisco Umbral, © 1975 by Ediciones Destino, English translation by Helen R. Lane © 1980 by Harcourt Brace Jovanovich, Inc. Reprinted by permission of the publisher.

John Updike: from *Couples*, Part 3 (1968). Copyright © 1968 by John Updike. Reprinted by permission of André Deutsch, and Alfred A. Knopf, Inc.

Virgil: extract from the *Aeneid*, Book VII, trans. Allen Mandelbaum (Bantam, 1971).

Derek Walcott: excerpt from 'Maria Concepcion and the Book of Dreams' from 'The Schooner *Flight*', from *The Star-Apple Kingdom*. Copyright © 1977, 1978, 1979 by Derek Walcott. Reprinted by permission of Jonathan Cape Ltd., and Farrar, Straus & Giroux, Inc.

Evelyn Waugh: from *Diaries*, ed. Michael Davie (Weidenfeld, 1976). Reprinted by permission of A. D. Peters & Co., Ltd.

Antonia White: from *The Hound and the Falcon* (Virago, 1980). Copyright © The Estate of Antonia White 1965. Reprinted by permission of Virago Press, Ltd.

Patrick White: from *The Twyborn Affair*, Part III, © 1979 by Patrick White; from *Voss*, © 1957, renewed 1985 by Patrick White. Reprinted by permission of Jonathan Cape Ltd., and Viking Penguin, Inc.

James Woodforde: from *The Diary of a Country Parson*, ed. John Beresford, 5 vols., 1921–1931. Reprinted by permission of Oxford University Press.

Virginia Woolf: from *The Diary of Virginia Woolf*, vol. 3, ed. Anne Olivier Bell, © 1980 by Quentin Bell and Angelica Garnett. Reprinted by permission of the Author's Literary Estate, The Hogarth Press Ltd., and Harcourt Brace Jovanovich, Inc.

W. B. Yeats: 'Men Improve with the Years', and extract from 'The Phases of the Moon'. Copyright 1919 by Macmillan Publishing Co., Inc. Renewed 1947 by Bertha Georgie Yeats; extract from 'The Shadowy Waters', all from *Collected*

Poems (New York: Macmillan, 1956/London: Macmillan, 1950). Reprinted by permission of Michael B. Yeats, Anne Yeats, Macmillan London Ltd., A. P. Watt Ltd., and Macmillan Publishing Co. Inc., New York.

While every effort has been made to secure permission, we may have failed in a few cases to trace the copyright holder. We apologize for any apparent negligence.

Index

✂